six to carry the casket and one to say the mass: reflections on life, identity, and moving forward

"A radiant, heartfelt mosaic of life's deepest intimacies and tiniest quirks. Hulseman's essays shimmer with truth and humor, inviting readers to stitch their own stories with meaning."

Ezra Bookman
Ritual designer, artist, and founder of Ritualist

"In the spirit of David Sedaris and Dorothy Zbornak, Bill Hulseman's witty debut offers a masterclass in learning to take pride in one's family, faith, and identity."

Terry Babcock-Lumish, PhD

"*Six to carry the casket...* speaks to our times. When so much of the contemporary essay narrows focus, finally, with Hulseman, we have an essayist brave enough to broaden, to broach the manifold issues of the day by a sweeping portrayal of where public and private, spiritual and secular, and international and domestic merge. Moreover, Hulseman manages this by intimate account. His prose rings with the relatable humor and warmth of a dear friend. Though he has left the world of professional education, he nevertheless remains our educator of the heart, and we would all do well to follow his lead."

Taylor Strickland
Author of *Dwell Time*

"*Six to carry the casket* is the story of how love wins, lessons gleaned from the past, and how to actively build a more just and loving future, especially for those whose survival and thriving have previously not been centered. This book gifted me with moments of joy and a grounding in hope."

Lauren Brownlee
Educator and Co-Leader of the Quaker Coalition for Uprooting Racism

"A beautiful set of reflections on what it takes to be known and a reminder that we are all worth knowing."

Shalini Vajjhala, PhD
Executive Director of PRE Collective

"You'll be transported to vivid moments: Marks & Spencer in Belfast during a bomb threat, a confounding sleepover with a neighbor, a ten-year-old announcing he's a pacifist, a smile during a sitcom that opens a door to understanding. Bill's writing is a cross between Frank Bruni and David Sedaris: honest commentary, vivid storytelling, and humor–a lot of humor. These thought-provoking, comforting, and inspiring pieces on humanity, individuals, and society did more than move me. It's as though the window I peer through to understand the world became a little less dusty (a film of dust I didn't even realize was there!)."

Alice Moody
Writing Instructor & Discussion Facilitator, Owner of Platinum Pen Consulting

"A tour de force, entertaining and timely journey of exploration, discovery and acceptance, of ourselves and of those we love most. Making sense of the world around us and the world beyond with the noble purpose of grounding ourselves in the here and now, this book helps find meaning in the gifts and obstacles the universe unapologetically and unrelentingly sends us slicing through the loud everyday noises of our busy world, staring us in the face for honest answers."

Adnan Kifayat
Former Secretary of State John F. Kerry's
Special Representative to Muslim Communities

"*Six to carry the casket and one to say the mass* masterfully distills wisdom from life's diverse experiences. Bill's compelling storytelling invites readers to remain attentive and embrace the abundant lessons life offers. With narratives that resonate deeply with your own life, he inspires you to explore your deepest curiosities, making the journey both personal and transformative."

Glenn Llopis
CEO at GLLG, Author, *Make Reinvention Your Superpower*
and Forbes Leadership Strategy Contributor

"*Six to carry the casket and one to say the mass* will resonate deeply with readers who appreciate stories about the ways we navigate life's joys and losses."

Books That Make You

[handwritten inscription]

Lori—
You've known me for
so long! I hope the read
is familiar. Thanks for
all you've given me, and
for your friendship with
Patti.

With love,
Bill

six to carry the casket and one to say the mass

reflections on life, identity,
and moving forward

bill hulseman

Peanut Butter Publishing
206-860-4900
info@peanutbutterpublishing.com
www.peanutbutterpublishing.com

And sometime it's enough
To lie down here on earth
Beside our long ancestral bones:

To walk across the cobble fields
Of our discarded skulls,
Each like a treasure, like a chrysalis,
Thinking: whatever left these husks
Flew off on bright wings.

from Rebecca Elson,
"Antidotes to Fear of Death"

———————

"Semantics is the problem with the world today."
Sheila Murphy Hulseman, 1935–2015

contents

Conclusion

INTRODUCTION

lists

places I want to visit
- India
- Japan
- Germany
- Brazil

places I don't want to visit
- North Korea
- Iran. Because, I mean, gay.
- Russia. #pussyriot #slavaukraini
- Mississippi. Goddam. Tennessee. Montana. The list keeps growing...

places I've lived
- (The Greater) Chicago(land Area), the center of the universe.
- Fairfield, Conn**ECT**icut. The Nutmeg State. And the most baffling drivers I've ever encountered.
- Cambridge, MA. Everything's better in Cambridge. And yes, I frequently parked my car near Harvard Yard, but people don't talk like that.
- Boston. And it's not funny. It's not even a good sentence to demonstrate a thick Boston accent. It is best demonstrated through impossible driving directions that include at least three references to Dunkies.

- New York, New York. It's a hell of a town. The Bronx is up, and the Battery's down. I talk about New York like a refugee longing for his homeland, but, I admit, I lived there for about seventy-three minutes.
- The District of Columbia. Where the summers are from the tropics, the winters are from the tundras, the locals know how to navigate an escalator, and the drivers are all from Connecticut.
- Tacoma. Grit City. The City of Destiny. I moved there, everyone died, I fell apart, I met my husband…holy shit! Grit *AND* destiny! Yeah, Tacoma's a cool place. No, it doesn't smell like that anymore.
- Seattle. Coffee, tattoos, men with long hair, you pay extra tax if you don't have a dog, and a flowerpot (and a place to buy pot flower) on every corner. I've started to blend in.

places I wish I'd lived
- 1920s CE Berlin
- 15th century CE Florence
- 5th century CE Teotihuacan
- 1950s Paris
- 1960s San Francisco
- Maui.

best bars in NYC
- Marie's Crisis.
- That one on Amsterdam near 109th. 190th? No, 109th. Yeah, that one.
- I actually can't remember the rest.

musicals I'd like to recast
- *Into the Woods*…with all the female roles by drag performers. Alaska as The Witch, Jinkx as Little Red Riding

Hood, Adam Lambert as Rapunzel's Prince. I've seriously thought seriously about this. Not a typo.

- *Chicago*, the movie. Remove Renee Zellewiger, replace with, well, anyone. Anyone who can actually dance and doesn't look like she's about to vomit all the time.

- *Les Miserables*, the movie. Russell Crowe…whoever thought it was a good idea to let Russell Crowe sing should be sacked. Whoever thought it was a good idea to let Russell Crowe sing *live* should be sacked, rehired, and sacked again. Really, the whole film should be sacked and replaced with "The Music of Les Mis with Anne Hathaway and Hugh Jackman" as a concert film. You know you'd rather pay money for *that*.

- *A Little Night Music*. Desirée *is* a drag queen or a trans woman. No ifs, ands, or buts, and the casting should match. With this, um, alteration, Frederick's unrequited love for her and inability to commit to seducing his still-virginal-wife, Anne, makes sense. It *also* explains Carl-Magnus' ongoing relationship with her and Charlotte's (his wife) tolerance of the relationship. Because, well, they're gay, or at the very least bisexual. Seriously, it's the missing piece of an otherwise perfect musical. OK, that's more of a rewrite than a recast, but it's the same general territory.

- While we're rewriting Sondheim, *Company*. Bobby is gay. Gay. That's why he's the single guy among a bunch of couples-friends. That's why he dates and dates and dates and just can't find the right woman. That's why his *Pygmalion* ballad has to piece together the traits of women in his life to describe his ideal match. Keep it set in the '70s, even the '80s, and I could believe even *Bobby* didn't know he was gay, which makes the final number, "Being Alive," such an emotionally impactful moment in the show and in every show-tune bar in America.

- *West Side Story*. The new one. Well, pretty much *all* of the old one, save Rita Moreno, of course. But in the new one…yeah, sorry, Ansel Elgort. Gotta go. Replace with any member of the cast of *Schmigadoon*.

Drag Race lip syncs I think about too much
- Rebecca Glasscock & Shannel, "Shackles"
- Raven & Nicole Paige Brooks, "My Lovin'"
- Jujubee & Sahara Davenport, "Black Velvet"
- Manila Luzon & Delta Work, "MacArthur Park"
- Dida Ritz & The Princess, "This Will Be"
- Latrice Royale & Dida Ritz, "I've Got to Use My Imagination"
- Jujubee & Raven, "Dancing on My Own"
- Detox & Lineysha Sparx, "Take Me Home"
- Alyssa Edwards & Roxxxy Andrews, "Whip My Hair"
- Trinity K. Bonet & April Carrion, "I'm Every Woman"
- Trinity K. Bonet & Milk, "Whatta Man"
- Joslyn Fox & Laganja Estranja, "Stupid Girls"
- Trinity K. Bonet & Adore Delano, "Vibeology"
- Kennedy Davenport & Katya, "Roar"
- Roxxy Andrews & Tatianna, "Shake It Off"
- Alyssa Edwards & Tatianna, "Shut Up and Drive"
- Chi Chi DeVayne & Thorgy Thor, "And I Am Telling You I'm Not Going"
- Peppermint & Cynthia Lee Fontaine, "Music"
- Sasha Velour & Shea Coulee, "So Emotional"
- BenDeLaCreme & Aja, "Anaconda"
- Shangela & BenDeLaCreme, "Jump"
- BenDeLaCreme & Shangela, "I Kissed a Girl"
- Naomi Smalls & Monet X. Change, "Come Rain or Come Shine"
- Aquaria, Eureka & Kameron Michaels, "Bang Bang"
- Kameron Michaels & Monet X. Change, "Good as Hell"

- Monet X. Change & Dusty Ray Bottoms, "Pound the Alarm"
- Brook Lynn Hytes & Yvie Oddly, "Sorry Not Sorry"
- Brook Lynn Hytes & Yvie Oddly, "Edge of Glory"
- Laganja Estranja & Trinity K. Bonet, "Physical"
- Crystal Methyd, "I'm Like a Bird"
- Denali & Kahmora Hall, "100% Pure Love"
- Anetra & Marcia Marcia Marcia, "Boss Bitch"

Madonna videos I don't watch enough
- "Love Profusion"
- "You'll See"
- "God Control"
- "Don't Tell Me"
- "Open Your Heart"
- Yep. The rest, I watch plenty. Plenty.

best episodes of *The Golden Girls*
- [ERROR] [IMPOSSIBLETORANK]

shows I used to watch and feel guilty about not watching anymore because they got canceled soon after I stopped watching
- *The Kids Are Alright*
- *Heroes*
- *Brothers & Sisters*
- *Rome*
- *Judging Amy*
- *Dead Like Me*
- *The New Normal*
- *Fresh Off the Boat*
- *black-ish*

pills I take
- This one to keep me alive
- This one to keep me happy

- This one to bolster the system
- This one to keep all things airborne from torturing me
- This one because I read somewhere men my age should take this
- This one because I saw my husband take it and thought I was neglecting my health
- This one to make my body think it's time to sleep
- This one to make my brain think it's time to sleep
- This one to loosen my muscles
- This one to really make me sleep

reasons I make lists
- Because, Virgo.
- Because, INFJ. Apparently, it's a thing, as one website puts it, "to rein in their dreamier, more chaotic inclinations." Good band name. *Please welcome to the stage the Chaotic Inclinations…*
- Because thinking keeps me up at night. Counting sheep is so last century. I count bullet points instead.
- Because they reinforce the delusion of order over chaos in my mind, world, and life.

voices

In 2019, I wrapped my career in education, moved to Seattle, and married. Needing time and space to rebuild from burnout, I gave myself one year to reflect, to heal, to adjust to a new home, a new city, and a new marriage, and to figure out what would be next. Then 2020 came. Seattle, my new home, was one of the first in the country to shut down in an attempt to stop the spread of the virus. Not working and stuck at home, all of my social interaction beyond my husband was funneled into Zoom calls. We found the silver lining (and kept ourselves from pulling out our hair) by treating quarantine as an extended honeymoon, a kind of wedding gift for two introverts and a rat terrier who relished time away from the world.

But then I watched from a distance as my colleagues in schools across the country struggled, both trying to navigate rapidly changing parameters and burdened with impossible expectations from districts, boards, and parents. I watched from a distance as friends struggled with the avalanche of loss and grief that buried us all. I watched from a distance as socio-political tribalism stoked hatred and fear of our neighbors, elevated latent prejudices, and weaponized extant ones. I watched from a distance as the murders of George Floyd, Breonna Taylor, and Ahmaud Arbery came to light, refueling in some a march toward justice and in others unthinkable regression from it.

In my previous career, when current events exploded I'd do my best to channel my questions and rage and despair into my work and make space for my students, my colleagues, and me to recognize what was happening and to prepare to respond. Professionally and socially isolated, I didn't know what to do with all those questions, all that rage. I wasn't the only one. Throughout 2020, social media was saturated with recommendations for books and articles to read, podcasts and personalities to follow, each post enthusiastically and legitimately endorsing a particular set as essential to navigating the world, to understanding the experiences of this or that group, to effect meaningful change. Cancelation has skyrocketed, but so has nuance. It's still saturated, but enthusiastic recommendations have evolved into urgent and often angry instruction as the voices grew frustrated by the lack of progress, by infighting, and by the decline of real engagement from White followers. Today, I have a better understanding of where I fit into the dialogue, but at the time, facing the avalanche of titles coming at me, I was overwhelmed—not just because of the daunting task of *reading* so much but at the diversity of frameworks, of worldviews, of definitions. I'll gladly admit that I overthink pretty much everything, but I found myself drowning in the competing semantics and structures underlying authors' thinking. I got caught up in my resolution to read as much as I could without clarifying what, exactly, I would do with all of this. Listening to and responding to all these voices will, or should, change me…but into what?

Thanks to an abundance of free time, I started reading a lot. Well, not always "reading," per se. When possible, I listen to audiobooks. And maybe not "a lot," but more than I had for a very long time. I used to resent people who talked about the pleasure they derived from reading because reading is incredibly difficult for me. I think it is for many people, but because it's such a fundamental skill, there's a certain amount of shame that comes with admitting it. Even as I write this, I wonder whether I've just put a dent into my credibility. Somehow, I made it through high school without anyone noticing this struggle, either because I actively disguised it or because nobody cared enough to notice.

Thinking this was just the way I was wired, I rolled with it assuming this was one more deficiency in my makeup, one more cross to bear, but it started to bother me after I started teaching. Weekly, my colleagues at each grade level met to talk about students—this one experienced success, that one is going through a rough patch, this one was behaving uncharacteristically. I saw the way my colleagues attended to students' needs. They brought their own human experience and their expertise as educators to shape a refined and revealing lens for their students, and when this lens revealed any hint of a pattern that might point to some unnoticed impediment, as a team we devised appropriate interventions with creative learning strategies or additional emotional support. Often I'd notice my distraction in these meetings as my own experiences as a student surfaced and I wondered why nobody noticed the things that I as a teacher would come to recognize as clear indicators of an unseen struggle.

Access to audiobooks would've been a game-changer for me as a student, and as an adult they've opened doors for me that had been shut many years ago. The experience of listening, instead of reading, has made me more aware of the experience of a text as a full-body encounter. It's not just a cerebral experience for me—all of my senses are engaged—and it's made me more aware of the diverse ways we access ideas and dialogues. It's also made the challenge of applying and being transformed by these ideas more pressing, more personal, more emotionally engaging, and more urgent.

Among all the texts I encountered in 2020, I found a group of voices who seem to be speaking to each other, even responding to each other, like I've just stumbled into my fantasy Sunday-morning talk show. I encountered them amid personal and global upheavals, and the dialogue between them and the insights I've gleaned have in some ways shattered and in other ways expanded my worldview. Theirs are not the *only* voices that inform me now—this book explores many that have impacted me at different junctures, and thousands more are hidden between the lines—but this imaginary round table gave me space and impetus to reconsider who I am, how I got here, and where I want to go.

In *The Evolution of Beauty: How Darwin's Forgotten Theory of Mate Choice Shapes the Animal World—and Us*, Richard O. Prum reclaims a significant thread of Darwin's theory that was actively shelved because it didn't resonate with social norms of the late 19th century and lays out the evidence to elevate the role of aesthetics in evolution. The ethical implications of this theory are potentially worldview-shattering—if we've misunderstood "natural law" all this time, then the foundation of Western ethics is in shambles (and I can't help but smile with that possibility). The questions that Prum poses reflect a pluralist outlook and anticipate the intellectual and social shift into the postmodern era.

Like *The Evolution of Beauty*, anthropologists David Graeber and David Wengrove systematically dismantle their field and everything we've ever been taught about the development of civilization. *The Dawn of Everything: A New History of Humanity* is a fascinating re-construction of human history that escapes the *paradise lost* paradigm that has dominated Western thought, sets aside any assumption of inevitability (the notion that history could only have happened as it has happened), and highlights the ongoing impact of human agency.

I read (well, listened to) Resmaa Menakem's *My Grandmother's Hands: Racialized Trauma and the Pathway to Mending our Hearts and Bodies* during the summer of 2020, after hearing Krista Tippett interview him for *On Being* in the wake of George Floyd's murder. Menakem examines racism through the lens of trauma and body-centered psychology and provides a critical resource for understanding, attending to, and healing the trauma that each of us inherits.

One book that I did actually read in paperback format was Ijeoma Oluo's *So You Want to Talk About Race*. Unlike many of the more academic titles that were highly recommended, Oluo makes plain the systemic injustice and institutional racism that characterize American culture through vignettes from her personal experience woven with supporting research. I think of the book like a candid conversation with a friend who is generous with her time and expertise and loving enough to tell me where I've fucked up, what I've inherited and how I've benefitted from a fucked-up system, and how I can listen, respond, and do better.

Ever read a book and think, *Damn, I wish I had written this*? Well, Priya Parker wrote the book that I wish I had written. *The Art of Gathering: How We Meet and Why It Matters* spins insights from ritual theory, sociology, and the field of conflict resolution into a practical and systematic guide for creating culture. Parker's approach applies to every size and type of gathering, from intimate dinner parties to enormous conventions, and I've been barking at everyone I know that this should be required reading, that this is the manual for developing a more intentional culture.

I stumbled into the poetry of Rebecca Elson through *The Marginalian*, Maria Popova's blog. Elson was an astronomer and poet whose unique intersection of passions and experiences helped her craft elegant and wise verses. In a period of immense, global grief compounded by the loss of my parents and sister just a few years before, I sat with "Antidotes to Fear of Death," a poem she wrote amidst her own struggle with non-Hodgkins lymphoma and published in *A Responsibility to Awe* a couple of years after she died. I found myself returning to these final stanzas with each new loss.

And sometime it's enough
To lie down here on earth
Beside our long ancestral bones:

To walk across the cobble fields
Of our discarded skulls,
Each like a treasure, like a chrysalis,
Thinking: whatever left these husks
Flew off on bright wings.

These folx have been asking big questions, bigger questions than we usually allow ourselves to ask. But…once I was able to ask these questions and started to hear some answers, I didn't know what to do with it all, how or where to apply it. Naturally, I started with reflection.

I love to reflect. Doesn't everyone?

[waits for affirmation]

Reflection gets a bad rap. Typically conflated with opinionizing or expressing feelings, reflection is a powerful and vastly underused tool for understanding ourselves, others, and the world around us and for determining the ways we want to grow and the world we want to build. Sitting at home with not many people to talk to and not much to do, I started to explore the ideas washing over me and reconsider my experiences—a kind of personal de- and reconstruction—and I returned to various forms of reflection that I'd learned and taught throughout my life. At different times, I was introduced to four particular approaches to reflection that I continue to apply: Ignatian Spirituality, the Patton method, Deweyan reflection, and storytelling.

Ignatian spirituality emerged out of Igancio de Loyola's recovery from a leg-shattering injury. In his confinement, he had two books to read—the Christian bible and an anthology of hagiographies or "lives of the saints"—and only one thing to do: think about his life. Reading about the lives of Jesus and the saints inspired in him a radical conversion, motivating him to leave his life as a soldier behind and start the Society of Jesus (the Jesuits) in 1540. What differentiates Ignatian spirituality from other forms of prayer, both in the 16th century and today, is that it doesn't begin with spiritual abstractions or lofty ideals—it begins with discernment, close examination of our experiences. Ignacio looked for evidence of God's presence and action in his brightest and darkest moments. I was introduced to this process in high school religion classes and retreats, and it continues to be a useful tool. The Examen, a contemplative practice that distills this process, applies to both the big, existential discernment that we all face (or should face) and to more mundane, more immediate experiences.

In one of my first courses in Divinity School, Kimberley Patton, my professor and advisor, introduced a method that I quickly adopted for both academic and personal reflection and later implemented into my teaching. She'd stopped assuming that her students understood the difference between reflection and opinion, even graduate students in an elite institution, so, each week, on whatever topic or text we were engaging, we each wrote a three-part essay: summary (a concise demonstration that we understood what we wrote about), analysis (picking one aspect of it to dive deep), and synthesis (connecting our analysis to another idea, text, practice, or even to a personal experience). It immediately gave me a new framework to process ideas and organize my increasingly scattered mind and interests.

While in an education leadership program, I was introduced to John Dewey's approach to reflection. An innovator whose vision for American education *still* hasn't been fully realized, Dewey looked to reflection as an essential process for learning, for building community, and for citizenship. As Carol Rodgers summarized, for Dewey reflection is a "complex, rigorous, intellectual, and emotional enterprise that takes time to do well." It's not opinionating—it's a meaning-making process that moves us from one experience to the next. It's not mushy—it's systematic, rigorous, and disciplined. It's not an isolated experience—it has to happen in interaction with others. It requires a disposition that values growth and is guided by whole-heartedness, directness, open-mindedness, and responsibility. Encountering Dewey's approach after eight years of teaching, I both felt vindicated for my insistence on the importance of reflection for learning and for building community and was more aware than ever of the serious deficit of authentic reflection in our world.

Unlike these other approaches, to which I was introduced through schooling at various junctures in life, I grew up with storytelling. My mother was an excellent storyteller—she valued family lore, from apocryphal stories about her ancestors leaving Ireland and the tales she heard of her parents' upbringing to her and her children's histories. Though she probably wouldn't use this language to describe it, for Mom, storytelling was an exercise in identity construction. When I started teaching, I quickly found storytelling as the most effective way to invite students to find personal connections to topics and ideas and to make meaning.

The essays that follow in this book emerged when, after personal and professional burnout, and trapped in quarantine with little else to distract me, I started to weave old practices of reflection with new voices. I excavated old relationships and experiences, in part to get a better perspective on what shaped me, and in part to discern how my life so far had prepared me for whatever would come next. Reflecting this way, I hoped, would help me to cultivate openness and maybe even hopefulness. My goal was never to be exhaustive or expert. Instead, I sought to deconstruct how the world shaped me, reconstruct a foundation for the person I want to become, and find the fuel I need to move forward.

I.
ORIGINS

---

origins

1932   Dad was born.

1935   Mom was born.

1956   They married.

1958   They had a child.

1959   And another.

1960   And another.

1961   And another.

1963   And another.

1964   And another.

1965   And another.

1968   And another.

1969   And another.

1976   And one more.

1986   I started playing piano.

1998   I graduated from college.

2001   I graduated from Divinity School.

2006   Their 50th Anniversary.

2020   I graduated from Teachers College.

2015   Mom died.

2016   My sister (#6) died.

2016   Dad died.

2019   I left education; I got married.

In the first section, I consider some of my most formative experiences and relationships, the moments and the people that shaped me. My intention isn't to entertain with family lore or to air dirty laundry but to offer what I've gleaned from reflection and meaning-making, and I hope the sheer sprawl of my family isn't a distraction. Here's what you need to know: I'm the youngest of ten siblings in a family deeply influenced by my mother's Irish-American culture, my father's company, and my parents' progressive Catholicism; I grew up in the suburbs of and am deeply attached to Chicago; I majored in religious studies as an undergrad and completed master's degrees in the comparative study of religion and private school leadership; I taught comparative religions and theology and led campus ministry and service programs; I served as an administrator in independent schools building accreditation and professional development programs and, finally, as a middle school principal; under the grief of losing a sibling and my parents and trying to keep up with the most challenging job I'd ever had, I burned out and took a self-imposed sabbatical to heal, rebuild, and figure out what's next; then the world shut down and I started writing.

borders

I was thirty when, for their fiftieth anniversary in 2006, my parents brought the family to Ireland. It's one of those things that a certain generation of descendants of Irish immigrants do. They'd hit a certain age or milestone and know it was time to make a pilgrimage to the homeland, to see the Ring of Kerry and all forty shades of green. They'd visit pubs to try *real* Guinness, learn (and later butcher) a few simple phrases in Gaelic, traipse through drafty, stone churches, look up their family names in local phone books, and knock on the doors of distant cousins, the descendants of the ones left behind, with a mix of curiosity and pity. They'd return with suitcases filled with thick, scratchy, cabled sweaters (which would appear all at once in that year's Christmas-card photo), Waterford crystal, Connemara marble crosses, Connemara marble rosaries, Connemara marble paper-weights, and stories about how friendly everyone was, how kind everyone was, how everyone suddenly looked like *them*.

If these ventures functioned as pilgrimages on one hand, on the other they were demonstrations of intergenerational success, proof that escaping the famine or the poverty or the oppression paid off, that the Irish landed at the feet of Lady Liberty and (eventually) thrived. After decades of "No Irish Need Apply" restrictions and anti-Catholic sentiments, one of their own ascended to the presidency of the United States, and his cousins (the rest of Irish-America) occupied the homes, clubs, and offices that once excluded them. They were doing so well they could bring their families via airplane (not the lower decks of a ship) to walk the paths of their ancestors and drop a little cash along the way, a kind of indirect compensation for being left behind and a direct incentive to keep Ireland cute, charming, and above all welcoming to their American cousins.

The centerpiece of our trip was a two-day sojourn through Cork. My parents hired a bus and driver to transport all thirty-three of us to meals in various parts of the county. No, this was not a gastro-tour—Ireland is not particularly known for its cuisine. The logistics of transporting and feeding the whole crew dominated our itinerary, and it never occurred to anyone to just let us split up and feed ourselves at appointed intervals. That, or my dad didn't trust that everyone would return at the appointed hour to stay on schedule and make it back to the hotel for cocktail hour. Either way, the experience felt less like a family vacation and more like the progress of a royal court, subjects trailing and appeasing their hosting monarchs as they visited and dined throughout their realm. Our driver had what is known as "the gift of the gab," and he was only too happy to have a mostly polite (and very trapped) audience in his care. His stories about Ireland and the local culture were colorful, even though most of their details were negated by a quick flip through my guidebook, and the only break we got from his jabber came when he realized he was lost and had driven us a solid forty minutes in the wrong direction.

We'd arrive at a town or a castle or a view, my father would announce, "You've got ten minutes," and we'd all scatter from the bus in search of bathrooms, souvenirs, pints of stout, and photos before filing back into the bus. Then we'd drive some more and arrive at lunch or dinner where service for thirty-three (plus a very chatty driver) would absorb two or three hours. Then we'd drive some more and arrive at a town or a castle or a view, my father would announce…well, you get the picture. Though most of our time was spent in the bus, admiring the blurry countryside, and sitting at long tables in small restaurants waiting for another round of poached salmon (and extra potatoes for the vegetarians) to emerge, we got to kiss the Blarney Stone (after a rapid sprint from the bus to meet Dad's twenty-minute allowance), drink a pint in an actual pub (which made the next leg of the journey and its ensuing sprint for bathrooms a wee bit uncomfortable), and experienced a bonafide celebrity sighting (after my niece asked, "Isn't that the coach from *Bend It Like Beckham?*" I walked past Jonathan Rhys Myers *twice*—to and from the men's room while waiting for my poached salmon and potatoes during an epic lunch in Kinsale).

For my mother, the high point of the trip was Cobh. She and my dad had visited Cobh a few years before, part of a day trip during a cruise through the British Isles. It was the place from which her grandparents had left Ireland. Her grandfather and two of his brothers sailed to the US—one stayed in Boston, where they landed, the other went on to Philadelphia, and her grandfather settled in Chicago. Because they couldn't read or write, they never saw or heard from each other again. Her grandmother worked as a maid in a grand home in Chicago— I like to imagine she's one of the kitchen or ladies' maids that lives in Julian Fellowes' imagination. They found each other, married, and raised two children. My mother's aunt worked for the A&P for 50 years, and when she retired, her bosses gave her a dozen roses and a sheet cake. "Very nice," my mother observed every time she told the story, "but how did those men think she was going to get a bouquet and a sheet cake home on the streetcar?" All I could think when I heard the story was, *What's a streetcar?* Her grandparents put her father through college and law school, a particular and deserved point of pride for any parents, but an especially poignant one for immigrants. He never practiced law, though, because on the day he passed the bar exam, an old classmate from elementary school, who by then was known to work for the mob, offered him "some work."

"Oh, I just did this as something to fall back on," he explained (in my mother's retelling), knowing that neither working for nor refusing to work for his old friend were options he could live with. "So Daddy never practiced a day of law in his life—he was so afraid of those gangsters." And I'd always marvel at this detail of the story—*gangsters?*

The stories weren't new—my nine siblings and I had heard them hundreds of times before—but they took on a new significance for my mom as the bus, by now nicknamed "The Handbasket to Hell" by a few of us, made its way into Cobh. For weeks, she'd built up our expectations about a moving and beautiful immigration museum dedicated to telling the story of why, when, and how people left. It was a sacred narrative for her, but the museum couldn't tell the story of how it all turned out—that was Mom's job. She primed us to see our grandparents and our ancestors in the exhibit, to feel a tangible connection to the experiences, especially the suffering (I mean, Irish-Catholic, right?) that paved a path to *our* lives. This would be our origin story, the final stone laid in the foundation on which our grandparents, parents, and we built our lives. This would inspire awe, admiration, respect, humility…

Then we arrived.

At least it was an hour off of the bus.

The "museum" of my mother's description was a series of posters recounting the history of Irish emigration to North America in the lobby of a shipping terminal. The posters led to a room of life-size dioramas, each depicting a phase in the journey to the "New World." The first featured a glimpse into the poverty that followed centuries of political, religious, and cultural oppression compounded by a blight on the potato crop. Children were in rags, parents were gaunt and distressed, and a hidden speaker issued the sounds of a crowded home. The next diorama depicted the journey itself—it recreated the lower decks of a ship filled with filthy passengers crowded into bed bunks and hunched over buckets. James Cameron's *Titanic* it was not. Instead of fiddles and festivity, we were treated to the sounds of people retching and moaning with crashing waves and the creaks of the ship in the background. It was charming. The final scene depicted the same figures scrubbed clean, dressed properly, and projecting an air of confidence and comfort. *This was the American dream fulfilled*, it suggested. *This was ridiculous*, my siblings and I agreed, more traumatized by the exhibit than inspired by the history Mom hoped we'd absorb. Then we scurried to the bathrooms and to grab a snack before my dad rounded us up for the next hour's journey to dinner, where we enjoyed poached salmon and potatoes and three hours of lovely conversation with the locals.

The "museum" reminded me of a memorial in Boston (where I lived at the time) that commemorates the Irish famine and ensuing immigration influx that delivered so many Irish to the city in the late 19th and early 20th centuries. The memorial is a small park with two sculptures. The first depicts a family; they are gaunt, clothed in rags, and melodramatically performing their suffering. A small boy is kneeling, about to topple over, the father is seated and hunched, his face collapsed into his hand, and the mother is on her knees, shaking her fist and screaming out to the sky. I wouldn't be surprised if the park planned to install a speaker so we could hear her wails of "Why, God, why?" A few feet away, the second sculpture rehabilitates the family. They're in clean clothes (though, inexplicably, only the father wears shoes), their bodies are strong and their hair kempt, and they seem to be moving forward, the mother casting a final glance over her shoulder at the misery they left behind. Among memorials in Boston, the Irish Famine Memorial is probably the worst. Unless *their* mothers dragged them into the tourist hub of Downtown Crossing to pay homage to their long-suffering ancestors, I doubt many descendants of Irish immigrants in Boston spend much time contemplating these statues.

For me, the first point of resonance between the "museum" and the Boston memorial was the caricatured and dramatic depiction of the people at the center of the story, but what really stuck with me was the common narrative that made it all so simple and straightforward: the Irish suffered; they came to America; it got better. However, neither provided sufficient context for understanding the complex relationship between Ireland and England, one that included through the centuries often brutal rule, cultural eradication, and religious persecution. Neither acknowledged the experiences of the folx who stayed, the ones who survived the poverty and starvation, of their descendants who won independence from the English crown, of their descendants who found themselves in a civil war that divided the island between "republicans" in the south and "loyalists" in the north. Neither does much to stoke sympathy for today's immigrants, despite obvious parallels of economic, cultural, and social barriers that still make integration into American society and equitable access to resources and political representation difficult. Though intended to spur connection to the Ireland left behind and pride in the impact of Irish-Americans, neither exhibit does much more than pat descendants of Irish immigrants on the back.

Our family's trip reinforced a feeling of connection to Ireland and Irish culture, but not the way my mom intended. In high school, I'd been part of the Ulster Project, which brought groups of teens from Northern Ireland to stay with American families for a month. Both groups (the visitors and the hosts) were evenly divided between boys and girls, Catholics and Protestants, and we spent almost every day together. Most of the month was touristy—trips into the city to see the sites, a day at Great America, a Cubs game—but at various intervals and for an overnight "lock in," we'd lean into the reason we were together and talk about difference. The Northern Irish kids would educate us about the very real social divisions between Catholics and Protestants and recount the experiences of threats and attacks, of family members and friends wounded or killed in conflicts at the hands of terrorists or at the hands of police. We were amazed and baffled by what we learned, but their stories helped us to see the inequalities in American society and in our daily lives that were driven not by the Catholic-Protestant divide but by racial animus and prejudice. The purpose of the Ulster Project was for our Northern Irish visitors to cultivate relationships with each other that they could bring home to heal their inherited hatred and to build a just and peaceful society, but the gift they gave us was both a window to the world and a mirror to see the actions and structures that perpetuated injustices in our own country, something (perhaps the only thing) of which this group of teenagers had been deprived.

At the end of the month and amid two days of very tearful farewells, several of our new friends made us promise to visit them, and, a year later, a handful of us traveled to their small town in Northern Ireland. They organized two weeks of adventures for us—touristy things, such as a day trip to Dublin (including a scintillating passport check by gruff and seriously outfitted border guards) and an adventure to the Giant's Causeway, and opportunities to better understand the history of the Troubles, those decades of conflict in Northern Ireland that originated in the 1960s, their legacy in ongoing conflicts, and the burgeoning hope for peace that would lead to the Good Friday Agreement six years later. We toured the Shankill Road neighborhood, the predominantly Protestant neighborhood that was the target of violent attacks for decades. Murals throughout the neighborhood memorialized people killed in the Troubles and depicted masked and armed loyalists to stoke pride and rage. Murals in other, predominantly Catholic neighborhoods did the same, except with virulent anti-loyalist and anti-British sentiment. In my experience, the primary function of a mural is to mark something from the past, to remember a legacy or to celebrate the contributions of a particular group, but when we visited in 1992, the Troubles were still raging. A year later, two members of the Provisional Irish Republican Army bombed a fish shop that we'd walked past on Shankill Road. The bomb killed ten people, including two children, and injured over fifty. Its number of casualties surpassed any other attack in the neighborhood, and it sparked a series of retaliatory attacks, including a mass shooting at a crowded pub during a Halloween party that killed eight and injured nineteen.

We got an education about life in a warzone in mundane moments, too. While shopping at Marks and Spencer in Belfast, where I discovered chocolate muesli and Cadbury Flakes, the store was evacuated because of a bomb threat. My American friends and I (there's no other way to say it) freaked the fuck out. I felt myself turn pale while I scanned the floor for exits or immediate threats, but our local friends kept shopping, feeling or picking up items while slowly moving toward the doors. Once outside, we saw the bomb squad arrive with a battalion of fire trucks and police cars. I asked (urged, really) if we should walk farther, at least to the end of the block, but one of the locals sat down on the sidewalk and popped a stick of gum into her mouth. "This happens all the time," one explained. "We'll be back in the shop in a few minutes." I looked around and absorbed details I hadn't even glimpsed before. The police, whose presence was visible throughout the city center, even before the bomb threat, wore camouflage and helmets and carried automatic rifles. A government building down the block had a sturdy barricade that reflected the evidence of frequent attacks over the years.

One afternoon, I sat and had a cup of tea with the father of the boy we hosted, whose dry and gruff exterior matched his wry and gravelly personality. He was not warm or gentle—there was no wink or subtle smile that followed a biting comment—but he was smart and sociable and eager to hear my impression of Northern Ireland. I hadn't really formed an opinion yet, and somehow we got to talking about religion. "I'm an atheist, you see," he explained, while talking about the Catholic-Protestant conflict that dominated the local culture, "because I live here. Who could believe in God after living *this* life?" Except for a few melodramatic friends who claimed the label to be interesting or oppositional, I'd never met an actual atheist. Or at least someone who publicly, earnestly and sincerely, identified as such. He didn't say it to be provocative, to convert me, or to challenge me in any way. He stated a fact, not an argument. He only wanted me to see and hear what I came to Northern Ireland to see and hear, the impact of centuries of violent oppression and religious conflict on generations that preceded us. *Who could believe...?* looped through my mind for months after our tea.

Mid-July, we learned, the time of our visit, was typically the time that Catholics in Northern Ireland went on holiday. They'd cross the border to camp in Donegal, or they'd plan a trip to the continent, or find whatever adventure would get them out of Northern Ireland. You see, July 12 marks the 1690 Battle of the Boyne, in which William of Orange defeated James II and ensured Protestant rule. Like the American Fourth of July observance, in the preceding days we saw decorations go up and heard plans of parties and parades, but when I donned an orange rugby shirt, my friend, Roisin, raised an eyebrow and warned me that it wasn't a good idea. This was a time for *Protestants* to wear orange and celebrate, and a Catholic wearing the color, even an oblivious American teenager, would invite outrage. I changed into neutral colors before we ventured out to watch one of our friends march in a parade, which we watched from a hill above the parade route. Even with vertical and horizontal distance from the crowd lining the street, I could see in Roisin's eyes that even this distance felt uncomfortable. One of us joked, "Should we shout *Erin go bragh*?" The Americans giggled, but our local friends, very seriously, cautioned us. "That's not a good idea." That night, bonfires would be set throughout Northern Ireland to celebrate King William's victory. In the past, those bonfires whipped up anti-Catholic feelings and inspired some to use the commemoration to intimidate and attack Catholic neighborhoods. When we returned from the parade and saw the look on Roisin's mother's face, a mix of anxiety and relief, I understood why they took a vacation in July.

One night, my friends hatched a plan to visit a local club. Though most venues were 18+, they knew which one was lenient with the rules (or that would welcome American passports, and dollars, at any age). We each had a drink, we danced a little, and then we were due at the pub. Well, not all of us. Roisin's father longed for the chance to take his son to the pub… but he had three daughters. My visit was the best chance he'd have to enact this rite of passage, so after the club, I was to be delivered to the pub where his other daughter's boyfriend and I would be his sons and he'd be our proud dad (for the night). When I arrived, he turned to greet me at the bar, revealing a pint of Guinness and a shot of whiskey. I was fifteen, tall, lanky, and had had exactly five alcoholic beverages in my life, the fifth just a few hours before. "Oh, you won't have to finish all of that," he said, referring to the beer. Throwing back the whiskey, however, wasn't optional. One shot of whiskey and five sips of Guinness later, an older man in a black suit, black bowler hat, and crisp white shirt tapped my shoulder and said, "So ye're the Yank, eh?" My dad-for-the-night saw the confusion on my face (my buzz made his accent all the more impossible to navigate), put an arm around my shoulder, and said, "I told yer man here…" My memory of the rest of the conversation is sketchy at best. Dad-for-the-night explained I was visiting; the old man had questions; he told stories; he told jokes. I understood little of what he was saying, so I laughed when it was time to laugh, looked serious when he seemed serious, and took a sip of my endless pint of Guinness when I wasn't sure what was going on.

Just shy of twenty-five, I returned to Northern Ireland in 2001 for Roisin's wedding. I was grateful to be able to walk a bit after a long trip, but my connecting flight from Heathrow to Belfast departed from the *very* last gate in the terminal, at the end of a long and increasingly sparse concourse. Someone explained later that the airlines kept flights to Northern Ireland at a distance from the main terminal in case of an IRA attack (this was three years *after* the Good Friday Agreement). Because my luggage went to Düsseldorf, I needed to find a suit for the wedding, so the groom took me into Belfast, to the same block where I'd once experienced my first bomb scare. The barricades were still up, but the only camouflaged, rifle-bearing police I could see guarded the entrance to that old government building. I stayed in a B&B whose host prepared a full, fried breakfast for me every day despite my request for just a cup of tea and some toast. Both Catholics and Protestants joined the wedding festivities—the morning ceremony in the stone church, the drinks, the food, the drinks, the dancing, the drinks. I ventured into Belfast and visited the two gay bars in town, The Kremlin and Parliament, and heard about a gay bashing that happened after a guy left one of the bars the week before. No one mentioned whether he was Catholic or Protestant. I visited Shankill Road—the murals were still vibrant and unsettling, but the mood was softer. During my first trip, I was an observer, a witness to a historical moment, but in 2001, I was just another tourist snapping pics of the murals that recounted a history everyone wanted to (but never would) forget.

By the time my parents brought the family to Cork in 2006, my visits to Northern Ireland had already dismantled the nostalgic portrait of Ireland that my parents, *The Quiet Man*, and Chicago's annual St. Patrick's Day parade had generated, so I wasn't keen to tap into their largely sentimental impetus to return to the homeland. I wasn't impressed by our resort, an old manor that had been restored and converted into a hotel and golf course to lure Americans, and about which the staff summoned dubious details from the history of the place. I wasn't charmed by the gift of the gab and the famous Irish hospitality that Americans expected. I didn't see a paradise lost or left behind in the rolling hills and forty shades of green. Instead, I noticed that most of the hotel's management were Irish, but most service staff were Polish, immigrants who landed in Cork from another corner of the European Union to find work and opportunity. I paid attention to the ways other Americans, including members of my own family, treated locals more as safe and charming exemplars from an idealized world, less as people with complex histories and aspirations.

In 2011, I went to an American friend's wedding in Donegal. I'd planned to fly to Derry (in Northern Ireland), rent a car, drive to Donegal (across the border, in the Republic) for a long weekend, and then return to Derry en route to the next stage of my trip. When I arrived at Derry's small airport, though, I learned that, despite my reservation, only vehicles with manual transmission were available. This was not, I thought, the moment to learn how to drive stick, so I asked the guys at the rental counter about how I might get to Donegal. "I can drive ya," one said. The other followed, "But you're in the middle of your shift." The first, without breaking eye contact with his colleague, drew out his timecard and punched it in the clock on the wall, saying, "Not anymore. Come with me." He was chatty and upbeat, likable without being overbearing, but because I was out of practice with the Northern Irish accent, I understood about a third of what he said. Thankfully, my ears were still plugged from the flight, giving me some cover while asking him to repeat what he'd just said, but as he slowed down the pace of his speech, it was clear that he appreciated my struggle with our language barrier.

As we neared the border between Counties Tyrone and Donegal, the border between the United Kingdom and the Republic of Ireland, I remembered crossing the border by train years before and the camouflaged and rifled border guards who walked through the car and inspected each of us and our passports. When I dug my passport out of my backpack, my new friend and driver gave me a puzzled look and said, "You won't be needing that." He didn't even have to slow down as we crossed the border and passed signs wishing us farewell from the UK and welcoming us to the Republic. Before he left me at the manor hotel that hosted wedding guests, he told me he'd return on Sunday at two p.m. to get me back to Derry for my flight to London. My friend's wedding was in a small, stone Presbyterian church, and the morning ceremony was followed by several rounds of Pimm's Cups, lunch, more drinks, more food, more drinks, more food, lots of dancing, and, well, more drinks. I made it back to my room in one piece, which is more than I can say for a few of the groomsmen who decided to go for a swim after the dancefloor closed. They made it through the woods around the hotel to a small lake and stripped their elegant kilts and coats to swim, but not all of the clothes returned. At dawn, one of the groomsmen returned to the hotel with only two hubcaps that had been discarded at the side of the road—he held one to cover his front, one to cover his ass. They were the only things, as the quickly spreading story recounted, he could find to return to the hotel with any semblance of dignity.

Thinking back to it, I don't remember whether the groom's family was Catholic or Protestant. It wasn't a question on anyone's tongue. As promised, the driver returned. He reminded me of my call to him at eleven p.m. the night before and teased me for my slurry explanation that I wasn't sure what, exactly, he'd said about a return trip. We chatted the whole way back to Derry, and I asked him only once to repeat himself, citing a mild hangover (which, I'd decided, would replace the buffer of airplane ears). I told him about the wedding—he had a good laugh about the groomsman's skinny-dipping fiasco and shared a few of his own past-wedding antics. I told him about my first trip to Northern Ireland and my memory of camouflaged police and our nerve-racking border crossing, and he replied with a list of the places in the US he hoped to visit. *The Grand Canyon? Really? Why does everyone want to see the Grand Canyon?* I told him all about the places I'd lived and encouraged him to make sure Chicago, Boston, and New York City were on his list. "What about Hawai'i?" he asked. "Oh, I've never been," I said. "It's too far."

dinner

It was an exciting Friday night: friends were coming for dinner. Back in the days of "normal," this wouldn't have been an extraordinary statement—hell, for my parents' generation, it was the standard for a Friday night—but, because my husband and I had had direct social contact with very few people since quarantine began early in 2020, I'd been deprived of one of my favorite things: entertaining.

Seems a funny thing for an introvert to say, eh? Indeed, throughout quarantine, introverts like me thrived in many ways—no crowds to navigate, no panicked reading of rooms, no straying from established plans—I mean, there were no plans to establish. Virtual platforms meant I could look twenty people in the eye in a meeting or happy hour without three hours of anxiety ahead of time or needing an hour of isolation when it wrapped up. I'm one of those "social introverts," and I thrive when I connect with other people. A costume party induces three days of pre-party anxiety and a solid week of post-party depression, but I could sit with a complete stranger for six hours if she has a story she wants to tell.

There's a curious phenomenon among some introverts: we love entertaining. (Note: I say neither "we love parties" nor "we love going to parties.") As soon as I lived on my own after college, I started throwing parties and quickly grasped the best part: getting everyone I want to see in one place and not needing to spend time with anybody. I'd greet people at the door, direct them to the bar or introduce them to that person over there who's also from wherever or who also knows whomever, and, once a new conversation bubbled, I'd "go check on something" or "check the door" (my cover for hiding in the bathroom for two minutes or stepping into my bedroom, closing my eyes, and counting to ten). Most of my guests were hungover the next day, but I'd spend the next three days, satisfied from a successful soirée, replaying conversations and recounting who left with whom while staring at a blank wall in an introvert's coma.

Every three or four months, I'd send an evite out to just about everyone I'd ever met and instruct them to "bring your significant (or not-so significant) other and a bottle of something for the bar." That guaranteed both a good crowd for the party and a well-stocked bar for the next three months. For days ahead of the party, I'd rearrange furniture, clean and vacuum furiously, and design the flow between conversation clusters, food, and drinks. Occasionally, I'd ask a few friends to come early for dinner to make sure that nobody made an awkward (for the guest *and* for the host) "first one to arrive" entrance.

For New Year's Eve, I devised themes to make sure folx dressed, if not "up," festively. For one, "A Very Madonna New Year's Eve," I promised prizes for the best outfits as voted-on by guests. I even dyed my hair black for my rip-off of the "Human Nature" video. For another, with the calendar turning to 2000, I asked guests to be inspired by various decades of the 20th century (and assigned decades by last name so everyone didn't show up in '60s garb). When my ex and I threw a Hitchcock-themed soirée, one couple dressed as *North by Northwest*—one in a suit and askew necktie, as Cary Grant running from the plane, and the other as the plane. Our last was our swankiest—a *Mad Men* theme inspired plenty of skinny ties and pencil skirts (and plenty, and I mean plenty, of martinis).

While others of my generation looked to Martha Stewart and the rapidly expanding DIY industry for guidance on party planning, I looked to my mother. As a kid, I wasn't impressed by my mother's capacity for feeding us (though, in retrospect, I should've been), but I revered her knack for entertaining. Three days ahead of the biggest gatherings like Christmas Eve or Easter, she'd extend the dining table and start thawing the main course. Two days ahead, the tablecloth was spread, the giant coffee percolator would land on the counter, and stacks of plates and piles of silverware would appear on the table. One day ahead, she'd delegate tasks: put out the plates, fold napkins, place silverware, set water and wine glasses. Days of steady preparation left the day-of for cooking (and grazing), enjoying the moment (drinking), and letting someone else do the dishes.

There wasn't anything unusual or extraordinary about my mom's table, but I loved its elegance, its functionality, its order. It lacked the cuteness we saw in friends' and neighbors' homes, but once the candles were lit, the table was perfection. Everyone sat, my Mom would improvise a blessing ("Well, let's think about all those people on the street tonight…"), and then the magic of the table overtook us. The placement of dishes and glasses, where utensils were placed, how dishes were passed—every object was placed intending clarity about when and how to use it. And once bodies were in seats, glasses were filled, and grace was uttered, we adhered to an unspoken but essential rule: no one left the table until everyone was finished with dinner. None of this was her innovation—the table manners with which we were raised came from the rules of etiquette, for which my mother was happy to serve as coach, manager, umpire, and league commissioner (*did I just make a baseball analogy?*). Ours was a crowded dugout (*what is happening to me?*), and all those rules just felt like a common-sense installation of order over chaos. Whatever their source, they all directed us toward one task: to focus on each other.

I've adopted Mom's approach, which was especially valuable in pandemic mode. When friends came over for a drink mid-quarantine, I designed a socially-distant yet intimate clatch with an assortment of napkins, plates, and small bowls filled with snacks near each end of the couch and a hospital-grade air filter in between. When a friend invited me to co-lead a virtual seder, though it only had places for me, my husband, and, adhering to tradition, the Prophet Elijah, I spent a solid two days creating the table and seder plate to ensure everything was at our finger-tips (and that everything looked good on camera). Even socially distanced, Mom's method kept us focused on each other.

When restrictions receded and we were vaccinated and ready to mingle, I could finally set the table for more than my husband and me (and Elijah). Plates under soup bowls, soup and dessert spoons in order of intended use, napkins folded, serving dishes placed at the outer edges of the table, wine and water glasses in place, and nothing in the middle. I even opted for short, stem-less glasses instead of my mom's tall crystal—there would be no barrier of any kind.

Some folx like to cook when their guests arrive, but I've never been much good with multitasking. Like a good OCD Virgo, I had the meal prep scheduled to be finished by the time our friends arrived. Proudly ahead of schedule, I set the cutting board on the counter, put Spotify on shuffle, grabbed the knife, started chopping celery, and found myself singing along with Paul McCartney, "When I get older, losing my hair…"

"When I'm Sixty-Four" was my mom's favorite song. That's a surprise to most folx who met her (she wouldn't have been confused for a Beatlemaniac), but she knew a good lyric when she heard one. Paul sang on, and I thought, *This would've been a moment to call her*. I would open with "Hey, your favorite song just came on," then tell her about the table and what I was mak-ing, talk about how work is going, catch up on family gossip, read into her silences and long pauses, get an update on their plans for heading to Arizona for the season, and hear the litany of who's sick, who's dying, and who's dead. I smiled, amused at this most Irish-Catholic habit of tallying local suffering before she could hang up, but as Paul and I sang, "Will you still need me, will you still feed me," I choked, unable to sing through the tears that suddenly came from the corner of my eye. *You know,* I muttered to myself-but-not-myself, *I think I finally understand why this is your favorite song.*

When I came out to her, Mom's soundest argument, one I hadn't anticipated, was the fact that she'd "never met a happy homosexual." Before she died, she never saw me in a truly happy, loving relationship. She never liked my ex (though she didn't tell me that till three months after we split), and she never met my husband (whom I think she'd *secretly* really like… she wasn't, let's call it, *effusive* that way). She never got to see me surrender to domestic bliss, table-setting and all. She never knew that her favorite song was the soundtrack in my head every time my husband bakes a loaf of bread.

I'm not surprised by how much I think about my mom while cooking—my kitchen is filled with so many triggers that I don't usually need Spotify to prompt a tumble down memory lane. For various birthdays or Christmases or housewarmings, she gave me a set of knives, a set of pots and pans, and a KitchenAid mixer (one of the reasons my husband married me). I added various things from her kitchen before and after she died, including measuring cups, serving plates, and salt-and-pepper shakers. Oh, and the Monsieur Crêpe I "borrowed" in 1997.

But hearing her favorite song made me look at the kitchen, really look at myself in the kitchen, differently. I've adopted her very solitary approach to cooking, something my husband has noted a few times. It gives me something to do with my hands and gets me out of my head. It helps me to turn down the volume on critical voices and to salve open wounds. I find myself making soda bread whenever I can't work through an idea or a dilemma. When I cook with others, however, I'm constantly attending to their needs or preferences and assuming that my cooking prowess will determine the future of our relationship. I doubt she carried the exact same kind of self-doubt and deference, but I think cooking gave Mom a similar oasis from a crowded life. By the time anyone else was rousing, she'd have breakfast made, lunches packed, a pot of tea brewed, and the day's crossword puzzle half finished. The first one to descend in the morning was greeted with a sigh of resignation, as if to say, *OK, here we go.*

It was an exciting Friday night: friends came over. We hugged, we talked, we drank, we listened, we ate, we talked, we breathed the same air, and nothing got in the way. But the table was more crowded than I planned. My mom was there. So were my dad and siblings, the team she trained so well in the rules of the table. So were the many friends and strangers who came to my parties, who stocked my bar and surpassed my hopes for making connections and getting creative with corny themes. So were my husband's family and our friends' families and friends and all the people we intersected together. And I'm so grateful that nothing got in the way.

Gershwin

My first piano lesson was shortly after my ninth birthday. Once a week for nine years, I'd sit at the Kawai in my teacher's studio at the music center to run scales and trudge through difficult passages of pieces I was learning. Around age thirteen, I briefly imagined my adult self as a professional musician, but when I asked her if I was on a trajectory to a music conservatory, Mrs. Neiweem said, gently but clearly, "No." Because she was so gentle, and so clear, it felt—not like a rejection—like a course correction, and I responded, "Oh. OK." Despite the fact that I'd never follow in the footsteps (or, rather, the glissés) of Daniel Barenboim and Arthur Rubenstein, she never stopped giving me more challenging pieces. She prepped me for recitals and helped me develop my stage presence like I was headed for The Cliburn, but I'd never be a virtuoso. Small successes, like making it through the final movement of the Pathétique cleanly, prompted an explosion of applause. My old sheet music is peppered with her affirmations of "Excellent!," "Great!," or, my favorite, "Wunderbar!"

I never got to be a great pianist. I struggled with reading music (reading the English language is hard enough for me...putting a Rachmaninoff prelude in front of me risks sparking a stroke) and had poor control of my fifth fingers (most folx call those "pinkies"). Despite these shortcomings, I got to be a decent amateur. I learned how to perform and how to not lose my shit in front of people. I learned how to lose myself in the music. I absorbed how music works, the structures and the physics that bounce and reverberate and echo or soothe or awaken or rattle the beating and the sighing and the violence of the human heart. When all I could hear was that the world hated me, I found octaves that propelled me out of it. When all I could see was failure and insufficiency, I found chords that refueled my pride. When loneliness was my companion, we found a home together inside the harmonies and passions captured on paper in a curious and beautiful series of lines and dots.

I started learning Gershwin's "Prelude II" during ninth grade, shortly after the word *faggot* was spit in my face for the first time. The adolescent body is cruel. It surprises you with spurts and bursts. Your brain does backflips, and your body is smeared with layers of awkwardness. No one tells you that your primary task (and pretty much the only thing you're able to do well) is to be a mess. You're still thinking like a child but appearing as an adult, and most teens don't get a course in how to be queer in the world, so every look at or from or near or toward or slightly by other bodies that stir and trigger un-honed instincts might be a glimpse of paradise or a path to brutal suffering. During free periods or lunch, instead of subjecting myself to the crowds in the student center or the treachery of the hallways, I stashed myself in the school's chapel and plunked away on its rickety upright. If others entered and asked what was up, I feigned a need to practice as cover for fear of the known.

At my saddest, at my happiest, at my most bored, I played Gershwin's prelude. The chords that kept the beat moving forward gave my left hand ebbing power, pulling and pushing steady and gentle waves that lapped over me and centered me. The melody is drawn out by the right hand, a slight shimmer that expands into a jazzy cascade whose notes *should* dissonate but float and land comfortably together. Some days, I could feel the melody start in my feet and crawl up through my spine, through my crown, and wrap around me. A few bars of music, and I was safe.

But then there's the bridge, which is published as Gershwin played it, with hands crossed. His right hand carried the melody down to the lower register while his left drove the rhythm with cool, almost lackadaisical intervals at the center of the keyboard. I tried, I tried, and I tried and tried and tried, and I could never learn to play it with my hands crossed. My brain just couldn't get the marks on the page and the soul of Gershwin into my hands. So for thirty years, at my saddest, at my happiest, I transferred the melody to my left hand and played it with a hint of shame that I couldn't *quite* do it right. Even in the safest of safe places, I was insufficient.

I stopped playing the piano for a long time, mostly because I didn't have room for a piano, but as the first winter of quarantine and the endless darkness of the northwest blanketed the region, I found myself craving time at a piano. In her estate, my mom left a little money for each of her children to be spent on something special, so I decided that her posthumous Christmas present to me would be a Clavinova. The first few weeks at the piano were painful, and the first hurdle was physical—getting my fingers back to a place of strength and precision, keeping my wrists and forearms from clenching, reacclimating to long stretches of sitting upright with no back support, triggering my muscles to remember basics like *How far from the keys do I sit? What do a fifth, an octave, a thirteenth, a C# minor chord feel like? How much 'forte' is too much 'forte'?* I stumbled through scales around the Circle of Fifths (C major, minor, minor harmonic, C minor melodic, G major, minor…D…A…E…B…) until my hands were jellied and exhausted, but I kept returning to the bench because, each day, I'd notice something different about the strength of my fingers, or the comfort of my posture, or the lovely feeling of sinking into the keys like a body into a just-right bed.

The second hurdle was reading music. Opening old pieces felt like unrolling ancient scrolls and finding fragments of a language that was simultaneously familiar and foreign. Getting my eyes to capture, brain to process, torso to lean into, arms to move with, and fingers to produce something that didn't frighten the neighbors (or spur my husband to reconsider his vows) hurt. My body hadn't responded with such an array of headaches, eye strains, and cognitive blubbering since that one time I gave up caffeine. (It didn't stick.) I spent hours reconstructing complex chords and slowly and evenly plodding through melodic lines, and at some point, like a long-neglected engine finally getting proper maintenance, and after a fair amount of sputtering and revving, something clicked. I found myself flying through old rep and even flipping the pages to pieces I'd never been brave enough to try. My newfound (or revived?) confidence convinced me: I could finally learn the bridge the right way.

I know. This doesn't sound like a revolutionary message or a particularly cinematic moment, but, for me, the piano was the place I always felt safest, most alive, most engaged, most interesting. No one tells you when you start playing an instrument that you might fall in love (or into a pattern of codependence) with a peculiar contraption of planks and strings. No one tells you that your fingers will always remember the piano you grew up on, the hairline cracks and razor-sharp edges your fingers learned to avoid, the spots on the most commonly played keys in the middle that your dad's fingers smoothed over decades before you were inceived, the way the room hummed when its lid was down and danced when it was fully open. No one tells you that your happy place isn't going to be a quiet spot on a beach or Grandma's kitchen, that it will be a bench in the corner of the room in the corner of the house where no one else ever went, or that you'll rely on the ability to sit down in the middle of a party or in earshot of people you want so badly to impress and traipse through Khachaturian's "Toccata" whose dissonance covers your slop and props up the idea that you're a man of many talents, especially when you're the most vicious inquisitor of your own worth. No one told me to hide behind the piano when the world was harsh.

It was mine, my mind palace, my refuge, the place where I was most *my* self. If I *couldn't* relearn the bridge, then confronting the ugly truth from so long ago that I was never good enough to play it *right*, would only confirm the fear that gnawed at me for so long: I am not, and never was, good enough.

And yeah, it unraveled. After a couple of days of intensively learning the bridge for each hand separately, I started putting them together...and it didn't go well. My hands cramped, my eyes blurred, my husband alternately chuckled and sighed from the next room when I'd make a funny sound or clunk through the same goddamned measure seventeen times. I couldn't remember what the piece was supposed to sound like, and, one particularly gray and rainy day (even by Seattle standards), I found myself weeping over the keyboard. It wasn't the passage or even the way I was playing it. The confrontation I'd been avoiding, as it turns out, wasn't with Gershwin, his prelude, or a persistent case of impostor syndrome. Relearning each note and interval and chord and dynamic unveiled versions of me the world told me to leave behind, versions of me who hid from the world, who hid from home at the keyboard, versions I couldn't bear to be because they were so unwanted, so unneeded, so unloved.

I didn't weep for grief—instead, it was relief. What started as an escape from the dulling monotony of quarantine became a reunion with my past selves. Maybe it's a product of finding myself in a place of true happiness for the first time, another piece to fall into place in an increasingly lovely puzzle. Maybe it's a vestige of the grief I thought I'd made peace with. Maybe it's the predictable outcome of the intersection of muscle memory and emotions. Arundhati Roy wrote that, after the pandemic, "nothing could be worse than a return to normality," so maybe this is my unconscious leading me forward, not back. For me, the real surprise was that I never let these old selves go and that, now, I wanted them back because I finally live a life where those discarded versions, those scared, isolated, insecure little boys, can be safe.

In thirty-something years of playing, I have never seen or even heard myself on the piano. This was a dramatic realization for me, but instead of whining about my parents' lack of interest in recording my recitals (or anything, really—ours was not a home with a video recorder and family movies), I wondered why, with a smartphone always within reach for over a decade, I never thought to record myself. Sure, most people don't like to watch or hear themselves. Haven't we all had the moment of hearing our voice on a recording and shuddering at the discrepancy between the sounds inside and outside? *Is that really what I sound like?* But no one took pictures of me as a kid. Even now, I'm not the one people take pics of to post on the socials with a funny or serious or calming or beautiful or ridiculous caption. Either manifesting a deep desire to know myself from all angles or as a persistent exercise in vanity, I'm the guy who takes so many goddamned selfies...and I've gotten pretty good at it (long arms and portrait mode are my best friends)...but never at a piano.

One morning, I was feeling pretty strong at the keys, and I thought, *I wonder...* I stacked a few books and positioned the phone to capture most of the keyboard and enough of my profile, and I hit the red button to record. *Is that what my hands look like? When did I get a double chin? Do I ever smile?* Listening to my left hand pull and push the rhythm gently, I couldn't stop obsessing over my appearance. *Am I really that gray? I need to stop telling people my hair is brown. I need to stop telling* myself *my hair is brown.* When the melody expands from a single line to fuller octaves, my hands looked so...easy, so at ease. They seemed to know what they're doing. That fifth finger didn't look so bad. And then the bridge... I'm hesitant, careful, particular. It's not as easy, as flowing as the start, but I didn't hit any clunkers. I hit every note right, with my hands crossed, my left hand pulsing in the middle and my right dancing in the lower register.

guide

"However we are, we don't know how to be
another way, that's the way we are!"

David Byrne, on *Here & Now*

During college, I spent summers working on tour boats in
Chicago. For the first summer, I was part of the crew. The
early shift would arrive very, very early to hose down and scrub
the two boats that would transport the tourists and local Chica-
go-geeks (and the people who love them too much to say no to a
ninety-minute cruise) for one of two routes along the city's river
and lakefront. The larger *Fort Dearborn* would meander up and
down the three branches of the always green (not just in March)
Chicago River for an introduction to the city's architectural heri-
tage, and the smaller *Marquette* would venture out through the
locks onto Lake Michigan for a historical tour. *You're right,* I'd
affirm for first-time visitors whose definition of "lake" exploded
upon encountering this longest and deepest of the Great Lakes,
you really can't see across it. The late crew took the ropes for later cruises, including the occasional evening booze cruise (they
were always boozy), and did the day-end scrub-down, garbage
haul, and sewage pump, which I typically avoided by offering to
drop the dress uniforms at the dry cleaner.

In the thirty minutes between tours, the two or three guys
working the boat (usually two, and it was always guys) would
gather the trash left behind (there was always trash, and a lot of

it, and most of it didn't originate on the boat), reset the plastic chairs with orderly and accommodating (and, if Captain Camilla was on duty, perfectly aligned) rows, refresh the water and iced tea dispensers, refill the cookie platters (and dutifully stash one away for each of us, especially if the peanut butter cookies were fresh), and get into place to welcome the next group. Captain Camilla would start her stopwatch the moment the last passenger disembarked and took pride in our ever-diminishing turnaround time over the course of the summer. During the heatwave of 1995, we'd take turns to sneak into the tour company's walk-in freezer, filled with beer kegs, take off our shirts, and cool down for five minutes before rushing back to greet the next sold-out tour. It was 105 degrees and 173 percent humidity, but they just kept coming.

Once folx boarded and got settled, the captain would take the mic to welcome people aboard and make the required safety announcement. Each captain would squeeze a big chunk of personality into their two-minute pitch, recycling jokes and cadences. I always liked Captain Skip's greeting the most. After introducing himself and the crew on board, his tone would shift to one of shared disdain, like a cue to start rolling our eyes. "I *have* to inform you that the Coast Guard *does* require that I *do* make this announcement." I don't know if all that extraneous language made people more aware of safety procedures, but it sure was endearing. Captain Skip was also the one friendliest to the crew. Unlike others who preferred solitude at the wheel, hanging out with Skip was welcome as long as you didn't talk too much. He'd give us turns at steering, and on slow days when tours were canceled, he'd let us practice more difficult turns and pivots. Bits and pieces of his life came out along the way: his seasonal moves between Florida and Chicago, his bouts with alcoholism and recovery, his old wife, his observations about locals and tourists, his new wife. He was direct when we messed up, but his temper never flared. The only mean streak in his personality that I witnessed was directed at the one docent who treated the captain and crew as her personal staff.

We called her Agent Orange. It wasn't a kind name, but then again, interactions with her weren't characterized by kindness. She was White and naturally fairly pale, but before the summer even started, thanks to a few months in Florida and/or on a tanning bed, her grandkids could've pulled the burnt sienna crayon out of the box to draw her. Her hair was roughly the same shade, maybe a hint blonder, and her lipstick was, you guessed it, orange. Bright orange. She'd elbow us out of the way at the bottom of the embarkation ramp to greet people and again at the end to make sure she could rake in the tips and sell a few copies of "her" book (she took all the photos, but, as one of my favorite docents, Phyllis, told us, she also plagiarized the content, including original research that Phyllis had integrated into her tour). At least twice every tour, Agent Orange would wave at whichever crew member was in her sight and snippily remind us to fetch her iced tea, which she never requested in the first place, and which really wasn't our job, even though most docents would refill their own thermoses before we left the dock. She frequently chastised whichever crew member was near for letting *this* man sit on a slightly bent chair or ignoring the piece of trash that *that* woman just dropped. Most days, we liked listening to the docents—we'd mimic the jokes they were about to drop or laugh about a new factoid that made its way into the monologue—but with Agent Orange aboard, we'd do our best to ignore her, partly because her jokes were all stereotypes but mostly because she was the one docent who just made shit up and buried it under her, um, "charm." But the worst part was that, at the end of Agent Orange's day, because she held the mic to her mouth like it was a breathing apparatus, the docent's mic was a nasty mess of orange lipstick and spit.

One hot, sunny, sold-out August afternoon, Agent Orange called in sick, and the backup docent was stuck in traffic coming from the South Side. We stood around in a circle—Captain Skip, the office manager, and three of us crew members—to figure out what to do with the 200 passengers who were on board, now two minutes to our scheduled departure. "Um, I could do it," I said. All summer, I'd been listening to the rotation of docents, each with a different frame or focus. Want to know how many miles of telephone cable are in the Sears Tower? Phyllis could rattle off any obscure detail about any skyscraper in the city. Want the saucier, more tongue-in-cheek gossip about the city's founders? Dan could tell a tale. Want to learn about the impact of good urban planning (and about the catastrophes that come with bad)? Jenny mingled politics, policy, and personalities into the phases of the city's development. And Agent Orange? Well, her tours sure were colorful. But, while most of them talked about the distinct phases of architecture in Chicago, few connected visual cues to aesthetic philosophies or invited folx to focus on the relationship between context and design.

Secretly, I'd been developing my own script all summer while riding up and down the river with other docents in my ear. They all taught me what to see, but I wanted visitors to know how to see and understand the city. I did my own reading about the city's history and major players (sometimes motivated by a desire to fact-check Agent Orange), and before or after work, I'd invite myself into the lobbies of the buildings that we'd cruise past on the *Fort Dearborn* so I could communicate what walking into the Lyric Opera or the Morton International felt like. Is this my big break? Years of piano recitals, community and high school theater performances, and hundreds—thousands—of hours immersed in my mother's lectures on the history of Chicago prepared me for this moment. Sure, it wasn't NPR calling, but, honestly, it doesn't take much to recharge my fantasy of hosting a talk show. A little bit of affirmation is all it takes to unleash my inner ham. Hand me a microphone? It's showtime. "Yeah, I could do it."

With Captain Skip's nod of approval, the office manager ran inside to get me a clean shirt, the engines revved, and I filled a thermos of iced tea. I got a round of applause when Skip explained this was my first tour. As we pulled away from the dock, I laid out the four big phases of architectural design in Chicago that we'd be talking about, told everyone I'd be talking about things on the right (I hated the way Agent Orange shifted from right to left or made the group turn around to see things she'd forgotten to talk about), and, as we passed under Columbus Drive and that gorgeous tableau that was the Tribune, Jewelers', Wrigley, and IBM buildings came into view, I felt a swell of pride and excitement, ready to make the tour mine. As we passed the Hyatt, I explained Mies van der Rohe's vision for a city within a city and added, "And that's where I had my senior prom." I made about twenty dollars in tips and got a lot of compliments from tourists who didn't know they'd been duped with an understudy's rookie performance, but the biggest affirmation came from Captain Skip, who patted me on the shoulder and said, "That was pretty good. You'll be better next time."

I spent the next three summers as a full-time docent. I shaped my own, distinct tour with a focus on the four major phases of Chicago's architectural styles and an emphasis on seeing—and evaluating—buildings in context. I gushed about modern and postmodern innovations that irked more traditional lenses, knowing that only enthusiasm and persistence could get the haters to love, or at least respect, brutalism. I mean, come on. You can do anything with concrete. I was determined to convince each group that the IBM building is one of the most beautiful and graceful buildings in the world. I practiced and practiced pronouncing the names everyone needed to remember—the Potawatomi, Jean Baptiste Point du Sable, Père Marquette and Louis Joliet, Mies van der Rohe, Fazlur Khan. Most folx coming aboard expected an informative and entertaining ninety minutes, but I wanted them to be able to tell their family and friends all about the meaning behind the Chicago flag, the impact of Louis Sullivan, Daniel Burnham, and Jane Addams, and why

New York wouldn't be New York without Chicago. *No*, I emphasized, *the nickname 'the Second City' does NOT mean 'second to New York.'* I wanted them to see what I saw: a city that benefited from good planning; a city whose buildings told a story about preparing for, welcoming, and pursuing what's next; a city whose story is a mosaic of insiders and outsiders, of the biggest of big money and the poorest of poor fools, of myths and realities about the American dream. With each tour, I floated down the river in awe of a city that asked all the questions the East Coast ignored and the West Coast refused to answer, of a city that sparked so many firsts and raced to avoid too many lasts, of a city whose segregated neighborhoods could be a model for pluralism, interdependence, and urban harmony.

Did that city ever exist? Are any of its remnants extant? I'm not so naive to ignore the darker history of the city, of the people who were pushed further back by its establishment and trampled by its expansion, of the communities marginalized and ghettoized and set up to fight each other along lines of race, religion, and national origin, of the legacy of city bosses and corrupt politics, of the big, bigger, and biggest mistakes of mayors and alderpeople, of the violence that persists and the city's failure (thanks in no small part to the increasingly conservative Supreme Court) to curb gun violence. But the job of the docent, the tour guide, the teacher, the journalist, the...well, any narrative-weaving role isn't merely to present what is—it's to plant seeds to recognize potential, to imagine something better, and to make it happen.

Some guides revel in this or that era of "glory days," but, with ninety minutes with a captive audience and a microphone, I wanted people to believe that the past might be beautiful, but how we shape the future, how we keep what serves us and delights us, how we shed what's weighing us down or pitting us against each other, how we steward the resources we've gathered and how we rectify the injustices of the past—that's what cities do, that's what shapes our world, and that's really what's most amazing.

how to put up a Christmas tree

1. Identify and prepare the ideal spot.

The best placement for a Christmas tree is in the center of everything but not in the way. You know, in full view for people walking by on the sidewalk but in an intimate corner of your home.

Ensure that any furniture adjacent to the spot won't inhibit the tree. If a side table is too big, sell it. Or burn it. Whichever is more dramatic. If your husband is storing gardening supplies on the lower shelf of the table, completely hidden from the rest of the room, let your obsessive need for giving every thing a place and occupying every place with its one thing override the more reasonable and simpler instinct to leave the seed packets and pots where they are.

Move any plants and be sure to take a photo of which plants are on which surfaces so you can ensure that all the plants will fit in their new location. Do not rely on your memory for this; you will not be able to get all the plants back to their correct spots again.

Vacuum the space and wipe down the baseboard and windowsills (you might not be able to do so again until January). Unless you're tired and/or a little stoned, in which case assess the spot with the question: is it *dirty* or just dusty? If it's just dusty, proceed to step two.

2. Pick a theme to inspire your tree.

The theme is Christmas. Don't overthink it.

3. Deliver the tree and its decorations.

If you're a suburban family in the 1960s with too many small children, consider placing the tree inside a playpen to avoid a toddler accidentally pulling down the tree while trying to stand. Take a few photos of the tree-in-the-playpen and tell the story about the tree-in-the-playpen for the next twenty years.

If you're a suburban family in the 1980s, make sure the father is committed to procuring a tree that is at least eight inches too tall despite the mother's emphatic reminder of the height of the room on his way to the tree lot. Because this will happen every year, hammer nails into the wood paneling on the walls adjacent to the ideal spot to secure a wire that will keep the too-tall tree from tipping. After the mother oversees the unpacking and unwrapping of ornaments, initiate a, well, not an argument but more of a standoff about whether the lights, the ornaments, or the garland should go on first. Pro tip: first the lights, then the ornaments, then the garland. Make sure a rickety, ten-foot ladder is on hand to place the highest ornaments and to nearly give the mother apoplexy every time the father reaches a little too far around the too-tall tree.

If you're an overly generous guy in your seventies and one of your best friends died a few months before, walk into the florist shop, point to a tree in the corner displaying various ornaments and ribbons for sale, purchase it all, and have it delivered— tree, lights, ornaments, ribbons, and anything else they would throw in—to your friend's widow who is still so heartbroken she doesn't have the energy to bring out all of her family's ornaments and the memories and pain that come with them. When your son asks why you did this, just smile.

If you're mostly retired and invite your unmarried children to spend Christmas with you in Arizona, have the guy who takes care of your house (and charges you too much money) put up a tree and decorate it with generic, all-matching ornaments and giant ribbons that no one likes. Make sure you comment frequently how much you like the tree, even though it makes your adult children sad while looking at a hotel-lobby-worthy tree while decades of ornaments are packed away in an attic at home.

If you're a postmodern, urban, gay couple, allow the handier of the two (we don't use the term "butch" anymore) to haul the bougie-ass artificial tree (that cost too much for a freaking tree that you'll use at most four weeks out of the year, but now that you own you can't imagine another tree) to the ideal spot in the corner of the room, where it will overlook the sidewalk and nestle into the space where you two and your dog spend the majority of each night lying next to and variably entwined with each other. Comment frequently about how much you like the tree and how easy it is to assemble. Allow the more neurotic of the two to slowly unpack and unwrap the ornaments you've gathered in the short time you've been together so that he can gently fold and store the paper towels and reuse them when the tree comes down after the Feast of the Epiphany in January—and *not* before. Be sure to take photos from several angles to encourage the delusion that, someday, you'll be a social media influencer because a famous drag queen will see your post and like it because she appreciates your aesthetic.

4. Decorate the tree.

Lights go on first. Start from the bottom, because if you start at the top, you'll be too generous with the strings and you won't be able to reach the plug, so you'll have to have an extension cord dangling from the lower branches or you'll have to systematically retrieve the lights, keep them from tangling on the floor and from stepping on them with your bare feet because that hurts like a motherfucker, and start over.

Ornaments go on second. Generic ornaments can be hung by anyone, but ornaments that are affiliated with you should be hung by you. For example, if you received the ornament as a gift, one of many that the childless friend of your mother would make—she *made* these—and give you each year along with a subscription to *Highlights*, you have the privilege and the responsibility to make sure its hook is on properly and to find the right branch for it. On the other hand, if you are living with someone who has a box of ornaments from his childhood, placing those ornaments yourself or attempting to art-direct your partner in his placement of them is a sign that your relationship should not last much longer. When your relationship finally ends and your possessions are divided and he moves to another city, be sure to get that box of ornaments to your ex. Otherwise, it will be a source of bitterness for years to come, and your folly may end up as a rant in his book.

Garland goes on last, if at all. Tinsel strands will haunt you for the rest of the year. Tinsel garland will look tacky because it clashes with *something* in the room. Ribbons are bougie. Strings of popcorn, cranberries, and other foodstuffs are nice in the abstract, but they only look right in a Hallmark ad or on the Hallmark Channel. Besides, they'll just make you hungry every time you look at the tree.

5. Bask in the glow.

It's best to decorate your tree in late afternoon so that you can immediately enjoy its warm lights in a darkened room. Accompany your basking with playlists of holiday music, but avoid artists like Wham!, Mariah Carey, and José Feliciano. You will hear them plenty in the coming weeks. Instead, focus on playlists that include music from *A Charlie Brown Christmas* and Ella Fitzgerald. If a recording of "Ave Maria" comes up, especially if it's by Harry Connick, Jr., or Beyoncé, immediately switch to a different playlist or throw the speaker out of the closest window, whichever is more dramatic.

Instrumental holiday jazz will enhance your emotional engagement with the tree and make you think about your featured solos in your college choir's holiday concerts, or about one particular song that was part of the show each year that always made you weep. It will also trigger memories of past Christmases with your parents, though they've been dead for many years, like the time your mother requested a roving quartet to sing "Silent Night" *in the original German.* And they did. Or the time you volunteered to bring a bûche de Noël for your eighth-grade French class holiday party, but you came down with chicken pox and your mom made the whole thing by herself (though you never said it had to be homemade) and delivered it to the school on the day of the party you were missing, and later that day, your French teacher stopped by with a piece of cake for you—the moment that sealed her spot as the favorite among your teachers, and how your mom told the story for the next thirty years about how she was so put out because you volunteered *her* to make a bûche de Noël. Or the Christmas Eve when your cousins didn't show up and nobody understood why, but for the next ten years your mom and aunt didn't talk to each other until suddenly they did again, the Christmas Eve where you saw your mom cry for the first time and inhaled Chardonnay with her breath when you kissed her on the cheek to say *good night.* Or about the time you were fourteen and so depressed and no one knew why or even that you were depressed and you burst into tears and went outside and sat behind a statue, and your older siblings eventually came outside to have a drink and didn't know you were there, and you heard them talking about you and mocking you and calling you a *scaredy cat,* and you feeling so hurt even though it was a comically vapid insult. Or that Christmas watching *It's a Wonderful Life* when your mom repeatedly informed everyone around, in varying form but in consistent detail, that Lionel Barrymore was in a wheelchair because he was "full of syphilis." Or the

Christmas Eve two days after your dad died when you looked out on a room full of siblings and niblings and offered a toast and then started giving away your dad's neckties so everyone could wear one to his funeral a few days later. Or your first Christmas Eve as a married couple in the audience of an irreverent drag show and your sudden desire to make it a tradition, and your delight that now you have someone you want to make traditions with. Or the next year, nine months into quarantine and when you found yourself warm and safe and happy in the glow of a beautiful, if bougie and overpriced, tree, husband on one side and rat terrier on the other.

Pro tip: If you do it right, even if a bûche de Noel and a rat terrier are not part of your story, all of your memories will come to the surface. Some are happy, some are not, but it's all good. Just let its branches shelter and hide the rough patches, and let the lights shine on the rest.

name

Juliet:
What's in a name? That which we call a rose
By any other name would smell as sweet;
So Romeo would, were he not Romeo call'd,
Retain that dear perfection which he owes
Without that title. Romeo, doff thy name,
And for that name which is no part of thee
Take all myself.

Romeo:
I take thee at thy word:
Call me but love, and I'll be new baptized;
Henceforth I never will be Romeo.
from William Shakespeare, Romeo and Juliet

"'Romeo! Romeo! Wherefore art thou Romeo?'
Translation: Desperate! Desperate! I am really desperate!
Are there any stalkers on my property?"

"I think you're fourteen, and you're an idiot. You took a
roofie from a priest. Look at your life. Look at your choices."
Sassy Gay Friend

Indeed, Juliet, what *is* in a name? Juliet dismisses its value—to
her, it's just an obstacle, an artificial hindrance to true love.
Kids say the darndest things, am I right? This lovely and oft'
quoted interaction from Shakespeare's famous tragedy points to

the naiveté of young love. Like most teenagers, Jules and RoRo (due in no small part to the limited development of their amygdalae and corresponding emotional maturity) have a hard time seeing beyond the edge of their, well, I'll just say "noses." They lacked awareness of, among other things, the trauma they inherited in their bones from generations of tribalism and enmity. And Jules, Jules, Jules...a name is so much more than a thin veneer that can be so easily doffed.

A name carries a story. Sometimes, it's a story worth telling. Sometimes, the story is a hoot, but, sometimes, it's more of a holler. Not like, *hollaaaaaa* but, like, *What the fuck?!* When I was born (legend has it), my parents named me David William Hulseman, but before the birth certificate could be completed, my grandmother objected. "You can't call him David Hulseman—people will think he's Jewish." This wasn't just a demonstration of irrational prejudice—it was an irrational prejudice rooted in experience. As a young couple searching for a home to shelter their rapidly expanding brood, my parents were denied entry to houses for sale in a particular town because the sellers or the realtors assumed our surname was Jewish. I wouldn't have described my parents as actively antisemitic, but this misidentification sure wasn't worn as a badge of honor.

As I approached the sacrament of Confirmation in the Catholic Church, I chose the name Maximilian, in honor of the Polish Franciscan priest Maximilian Kolbe, who was canonized as a martyr. Kolbe died in Auschwitz after he offered his life in place of a Jewish prisoner whose number had been called for execution. To young-me, Kolbe was the ultimate symbol of building bridges between Catholics and Jews, but then college-aged-me discovered that Kolbe was a pretty rabid antisemite who landed in the concentration camps *not* because of his concern for persecuted minorities but as part of a roundup of priests and nuns in retaliation for a church official's criticism of the Nazis.

When I started teaching about Judaism, I got the question from at least one student each year: "Wait, Mr. Hulseman...are you Jewish?" If not, they always reasoned, why would I know so much about Judaism? Because of the presence of both a chanukiah and a Christmas tree in the house, the woman who cleaned our home left a Christmas card for my now-ex and a Chanukah card for me. In the past few years, though no one has ever asked me to lead a celebration for Easter or any other observance in my own tradition, a friend who is Jewish has invited me to co-lead her Passover seder. What was a derogation for my parents is, for me, both a mark of pride and a reminder that there's still plenty of work to do to get people to understand and respect difference.

A name reveals and shapes relationships. Sometimes my mom called me "Double Digit" (I was #10 among my siblings). Occasionally, she'd sing a few bars from *Show Boat*, like it was my theme song. "Just my Bill, an ordinary guy..." I hadn't paid attention to the rest of the lyrics until I saw a revival of the musical when I was in college—it's less of a doting love song about someone named Bill and more of a list of his deficiencies. To my peers, I was Billy until high school, when I dropped the y in an effort to sound more grown up. Today, only three people can get away with calling me Billy—hearing it from anyone else is deeply, deeply triggering.

My housemates in college called me Dussel (itself a diminutive of Düsseldorf, because so many people mispronounced my last name as Husselman, which sounded, to them, like the name of the German city), and once I shocked an entire senior class when I clarified that my name was not, in fact, Kyle Husselman. A friend from grad school magnifies her Southern accent and adds a syllable or two to greet me as Bee-ill. As a teacher and administrator, students called me Mr. Hulseman (it took about three months to stop looking for my father when I heard it). People I've never met know me as dussel76 on Instagram. For me, each is a moniker that indicates a level of intimacy or facets of me—the professional self, the personal self, the childhood self I've tried and tried to leave behind—and a reminder that each person knows me in a different way.

A name facilitates the reconstruction of identity. When I was in college, a fledgling group formed on campus to advocate for queer students. Terminology for gender and sexual orientation was pretty primitive in the '90s—the majority of people on campus knew "straight," "gay," and "lesbian" and expected everyone to fall neatly into one of these categories. The group adopted the acronym SAYSO ("Students Accepting Your Sexual Orientation"), indicating that the cause provided an identity rooted in a particular value or disposition. I always found it curious and clever but also kinda clunky. It required explanation and reinforced the reality that, while some students accepted you, others didn't. When I was introduced to the idea of "internalized homophobia," that group's name was the example that jumped to the fore. We had adopted a name that dripped with pain. Queer in the '90s, right?

In recent years, the conventional initialism to denote non-heterosexual and non-cisgender people has evolved, shadowing the evolving understanding of how gender and sexual orientation intersect with other layers of identity. Some of this evolution is enshrined in the roster of queer organizations—GLSEN was the "Gay and Lesbian Student Educators Network," and GLAAD referred to "Gay and Lesbian Advocates and Defenders," but as "the community" expanded (the collection of folx who experience discrimination on the basis of gender identity and sexual orientation...which, for the record, are two very different facets of personhood) so did the scope of these organizations' work. The brand names survived, though their letters' referents changed. We went from Gay & Lesbian to GLB (when bisexuality was recognized as a legitimate category by the Gs and the Ls) to LGB (in a feminist nod to the displacement of women) to LGBT (with recognition that gender was far more diverse than the old categories of male and female) to 2SLGBTQIA+ (and various other initialisms that continue to chase after radical inclusivity and invite others who experience similar forms of marginalization into the fold). Those letters tell their own story, don't they? But even more profoundly, each tweak of the name opened another mirror in which people could see themselves (sometimes *finally*) as part of a group, as welcomed members of a community.

In recent years, we've seen the rapid shift from POC (People of Color), which identified non-White people who share the experience of racial discrimination, to BIPOC (Black, Indigenous, People of Color) in a deliberate recognition of the unique experiences of Black and Indigenous people that have recently (and *finally*) made it to the headlines that shape our national consciousness. While it provides a more nuanced description of the experiences people share, it's also an indicator of where someone is in the conversation. Hearing (mostly White) people stumble over the grammar for, integration of, and pronunciation of BIPOC is at once hilarious and depressing. Depressing? Yeah, because it usually indicates that they're more concerned with "saying the right thing" than reframing how they see the world.

In *The Book of Blessings,* Marcia Falk adapted a text by the Yiddish poet Zelda as a *kaddish,* a prayer recited in memory of the dead that is included in Jewish liturgies. The traditional Aramaic text of the *kaddish* celebrates the name of God—not unlike the theology behind Catholic funerals, the prayer invites us out of dwelling in grief and into wonder at life, at creation. Falk steps away from the ancient iteration in favor of a more modern, even postmodern recognition of the experiences that shape us, the layers of creation and living that form us. "Each of us has a name," the poem tells us—each of us has *many* names that point to people, places, things, events, relationships, the good stuff and the bad. Some names carry embarrassment or pain, others joy and nostalgia, but each gives us and others a starting point to recognize, to know, to nurture, and to delight in the experiences and relationships that shape us. So no, Juliet, don't ask Romeo to doff his name (any of his names). Embrace it, call him by it, because truly loving people requires recognition of their full, complex, and many-layered selves.

neighbors

Something there is that doesn't love a wall,
That sends the frozen-ground-swell under it,
And spills the upper boulders in the sun;
And makes gaps even two can pass abreast.
from Robert Frost, "Mending Wall"

I was almost ten years old when I declared that I was a pacifist. Nobody asked (who's interested in the ethical discernment of a child?); it was just an internal declaration. I didn't even say it out loud until a few years later when, during my first year in high school, a classmate asked if I played football. "No," I said, "I'm a pacifist."

A year before my bold declaration, I met the boy next door whose family was new to the neighborhood. My mom encouraged me to say *hello* and to invite him over, so a friend and I knocked on the door, invited him to hang out, and promptly fired a barrage of "get to know you" questions. I quickly learned that he was my first in a lot of categories: he went to public school (I only knew kids from Catholic schools); he didn't go to a church *or* a synagogue (to which my friend actually said, "So if you're not Catholic or Jewish, what *are* you?"); that he had two younger siblings (a brother and a sister) and an older brother away at college who had a different mom (blew my mind). He was tan and blond and played sports—he actually looked like he'd fit in with all the boys in our grade who made school a daily hell for us, but, unlike those boys, my new neighbor was laughing *with* us.

We'd see each other from our yards after school and drift toward one of our houses. His family mesmerized me—for one thing, the kids had private space. The boys shared a bedroom, and all three shared an exclusive playroom in the attic to which their parents might be invited but were never welcome to just show up. They were much more glamorous than I knew people could be, too. In the hallway leading from the front door, oversized photos from his parents' wedding looked like stills from a soap opera! Their mom, the bride, and her dozen bridesmaids wore broad-brimmed hats and long, shiny, flowy dresses, the height of mid-1970s wedding fashion. A wall in the den featured family photos: individual shots of the kids posing in matching outfits, the whole clan in a different set of matching outfits, and several photos of their older brother who, even my ten-year-old self could tell, was really, really, hot.

We'd sleep over at each other's houses from time to time. I woke up during a very warm summer night to find him lying in bed with me, above the blanket but alongside me. I spent the next few hours with my mind racing, wondering what to do, but I kept my eyes closed to prop up the illusion that I was deep-asleep. I wanted him there, but I didn't know why. I wanted to turn toward him, to touch him, to be touched by him, but I didn't know why. I wanted to fall asleep and wake up with him still there, but, after I finally and unwittingly did fall asleep, I woke to find him back in the other twin bed, lying on his side like he was gazing out the window. He didn't move when I sat up, when I got up to walk out to the bathroom, or when I walked back into the room. He only moved when my mom called us down to breakfast, and as we walked down the stairs, I convinced myself that I'd had a very odd dream.

But it happened again, a few weeks later at his house. I woke to find him under the blanket with me, his back to my front. A decade later I would've known to call it "spooning," but I wasn't concerned with what to call it. I was more concerned about who might see us, but I didn't know why. I was particularly concerned about his younger brother, who'd given me his bed for the sleepover and who might walk in at any moment, but I didn't know why. This time, I feigned slumber but kept myself awake, and as the room brightened he slowly came-to, stretched a bit, and slipped out from under my blanket and into his bed.

A few weeks after that, he proposed that we play "family" in the attic. "I'll be the dad," he instructed, "and you'll be the mom." I've never been particularly good at improv, but we went through the motions of some mom-like and dad-like behaviors until he said we should go to bed. So we flopped down on the floor. I was on my back, hands folded across my belly, pretending to sleep, but he sat up, leaned over me, and kissed me.

Through the school year, we played "family" frequently. It always started with parental role play, he always adopted a strange way of talking (his *dad voice* I'd guessed), and it always ended with us kissing and groping furiously for several minutes before we'd say "good night" and pretend to sleep. He slept at my house one night at the start of summer break, but this time I made the bold decision to slip into bed with him. In the dark, I sat up as quietly as I could, my face white-hot and my jaw clenched to keep my teeth from chattering, lifted the blanket covering his twin bed, and lay down behind him. We both lay on our sides, like we were just watching something through the window. We didn't touch. I kept a few millimeters' distance *just in case* (but I didn't know why), but I could feel the heat of my breath bounce off his neck and back into my mouth. I hoped he'd wake and want to resume our, um, character study, but he never did. My eyes closed, and when I opened them it was morning, and I was alone. I turned over to find him in my bed.

A few days later, we played running bases. It was a favorite game in my family's back yard—a runner would sprint between two makeshift bases, usually plastic plates, and hope to avoid getting tagged. The boy next door could run swiftly, spryly, and I could rarely catch him if I was guarding the base. This time, though, I did. He zigged thinking I'd zag, but I zigged and tagged him, tapping the small of his back. He kept sprinting toward the base, but when I breathily announced that I got him, he screamed back, "That was my shirt!" I felt the blood rise into my neck and face. I felt my mouth go dry. I felt the grass squirm under my shoes as my legs and arms stiffened. I engaged in a burst of back-and-forth accusations ("No you didn't!" "Yes I did!" "No you didn't!" "Yes I..."), meeting his steadily rising pitch and volume. When he shifted his argument to "You got my *shirt!*" I didn't know what to say. I wanted to say, *I know your back. I've seen your back. I touched your back. I groped it. I even caressed it while you kissed me.* I could only blurt out, "I know the difference between your shirt and your back." Without missing a beat and with all the venom he could muster, he hurled back, "You're a liar!" When I didn't respond, he said flatly, "I hate you."

I felt my body take two bold steps forward—right foot, then left. I felt my right arm lift and absorb the momentum of my gait. I watched it swing toward his face. I saw his eyes narrow and then flash. I felt my open palm slam into his left cheek. I stepped back silently. He stepped back and touched his face. Without a word, he turned and walked home. I never saw him again.

The feeling lingered, though—his cheek against my palm, his momentary, suddenly aware and indignant glare, his pain. And my pain, my shame—not (in retrospect, surprisingly) about our clandestine play—but about wanting to hurt him, about succumbing to an impulse that, I thought, I could've controlled. I never wanted to feel that again. I couldn't tell my parents or friends, but I didn't know why. I wasn't afraid of getting in trouble—my parents would've been more baffled than angered by my sudden turn from quirky-and-kind introvert to highly reactive brute. And I didn't really have friends to tell…or perhaps I didn't want anyone to ask how I knew the difference between his shirt and his back. I didn't want Jesus and the Virgin Mary to wonder why I knew what the boy next door's neck smelled like, so I *definitely* wasn't going to bring this up in the confessional. This was a sin I was going to have to carry, so I assigned my own penance: pacifism.

What started as penance became an internal shield against bullying and verbal violence (I repeated *I'm not a sissy, I'm a pacifist* like a mantra) and a smug differentiator (it's great to feel holier-than-thou in high school). Then I started learning about *actual* pacifists. Some reacted to an experience of violence, of being directly impacted by it. Some pursued religious or cultural ideals. Some politicked for peace to avert global calamity. *All noble motivations*, I thought. *Which one am I?* Sure, I started with impact (specifically, I started with the experience of morphing from the aggressor to the penitent pacifist), but my religious practice and cultural affinities gave me language to explore the ethical dimension of pacifism, everything from my vision of the world's potential to how I choose to treat my neighbors.

I don't mean to suggest that I always make *good* choices or that I *never* defer to violence. I haven't intentionally hit anyone since the boy next door, but I've often chosen to use words like spears. I've often lied or failed to tell the *whole* truth. I occasionally think cruelly about others and about myself, and I casually wish terrible things to happen to the people who've crossed me (I am a Virgo, after all). I still buy ethically questionable products and don't pay *that* much attention to the damage that my retirement portfolio or wardrobe are doing to the planet. It's only been about four decades, but I'm still learning.

In recent years, while I was listening to David Sedaris reading his story "I Like Guys" for the approximately eight-thousandth time, I recognized that my relationship with the boy next door also planted a seed that would be vital to me through adolescence and into adulthood. The story recounts his experience as a thirteen-year-old at a Greek summer camp. While his older sister took the opportunity to reinvent herself, Sedaris found himself isolated from other boys. He connects with a cabin mate "who tended to look away when talking to the other boys, shifting his eyes as though he were studying the weather conditions," Sedaris' evidence, collected by his un-honed gaydar, that his friend was different from other boys, too. One afternoon, they found themselves alone in the cabin.

> What started off as name-calling escalated into a series of mock angry slaps. We wrestled each other onto one of the lower bunks, both of us longing to be pinned. "You kids think you invented sex," my mother was fond of saying. But hadn't we? With no instruction manual or federally enforced training period, didn't we all come away feeling we'd discovered something unspeakably modern?

Listening to and reading the story so many times in the past, I'd always drawn on my own summer camp experience to bring the story to life. I didn't share his *particular* experience, but I understood his sense of isolation, the impact of his removal from trusted spaces and routines, and even his sister's desire to reinvent herself. This time, though, the boy next door came to mind. I started to see our relationship (can I call it a "friendship"?) as a profound and pivotal experience. We shared an invisible, unspoken need for intimacy, but we didn't know what to do with it. Despite the invisible and insidious structures that isolated us, that kept us all from knowing each other, that kept us all from knowing *I'm not the only one*, something—something two ingenuous kids couldn't articulate and nobody else seemed to notice—guided us beyond the lives we knew.

What started as my first crush and heartbreak inoculated

me and grew into a shield as I navigated the accusations, degradations, and condemnations that boys like me suffered. *You're unnatural. You're disgusting. You're going to hell.* The world provides endless instruction to boys and girls about how to channel those desires toward growing into men and women who want to be husbands and wives, but not every kid wants to be molded around those models. The ones who do can smell it on the rest, and something deep inside, something they inherited from generations of other boys and girls who wanted to be husbands and wives, whispered to them that *different* is bad. When I was the butt of their jokes (*You're unnatural*), of their name-calling (*You're disgusting*), of their intimidation (*You're going to hell*), they could only do so much damage. I was protected by…something, something I still can't articulate, something deep inside that bolstered me, that kept me looking beyond the pain I knew, that whispered in my heart, *You know who you are.*

religion

J esus Christ, you look like a fucking priest."

As we neared the end of our program in education leadership and members of our cohort were being hired left and right, a few classmates, puzzled by my lack of job offers (one needs an interview to get an offer), looked at my resumé. On one hand, they were generous and wanted to help; on the other, diagnosing my career woes was a lot more interesting than the group project we should've been working on. One, an experienced administrator who had seen thousands of resumés, gave my materials the quick review of a seasoned school leader who doesn't need more than a few seconds to know whether an applicant would merit an interview. Despite spending hours upon hours crafting my resumé and attending to the precision and variety of the language I used to describe my professional path, I failed to take the 30,000-foot view. I'm not sure I even took the thirty-foot view. Apparently, I looked like a fucking priest.

The emboldened names and titles throughout my resumé, my friends pointed out, distracted readers from the facts I *wanted* to convey. My undergrad major was religious studies, and I had minors in philosophy and Judaic studies. I have a master of theological studies degree from a Divinity School. My first professional title was "Campus Minister & Teacher of Religious Studies." The student programming I'd developed included retreats, liturgies, and service projects. I taught core religious studies courses in a Catholic school. My professional development included a fair amount of mission formation. I even coordinated a conference of campus ministers. *Oh*, I thought, *I look like a fucking priest.*

Instead of imagining me in a Roman collar, I wanted potential colleagues to see that my academic background was unique because of its interdisciplinary nature; that my master's studies focused on cultural construction and comparison; that the structure and content of the programs I'd built, all those retreats and liturgies, gave students space to develop skills for leadership, effective team building, and critical thinking and reflection; that my courses were innovative, engaging, and (unique among Catholic schools) driven by a commitment to religious pluralism; that attending to formation gave me and my colleagues a chance to add a meaningful dimension to our work and tools to identify clear connections between our personal values and our professional roles; that the conference I designed and hosted was hardly a pious assembly—it was a dynamic (and, dare I say, *fun*) networking event for a group of people whose professional development options were, at best, limited, and at worst, insultingly didactic. I wanted them to see that I was not only poised to lead a program or a division but to bring a fresh and unique perspective. To paraphrase the song, I wanted them to want me, but, judging by the lack of interviews on my calendar, all they saw was *religionreligionreligion*. And nobody wanted a fucking priest.

"What got you…interested in religion?"

I get the question frequently. It's a question that most people don't receive because most people didn't study, teach, or work in an environment infused with religion. There's often a slight pause before *interested*, indicating a search for the right word that will convey earnest curiosity (and shield the judgment simmering just beneath the question). It's not a neutral question (then again, is any question neutral?). When people ask history or political science majors about their chosen fields, they understand what one could do with such a foundation. They could teach history or poli sci; they might go to law school; they'd be dependably interesting guests to stoke conversation at brunches and cocktail parties. When people ask an astrophysicist or a celebrated sculptor how they got started, they ask with a real desire to get a glimpse into genius. However, when people ask, "What got you interested in religion?" they're assessing me.

Considering the damage done in the name of religion, the question and its barely-under-the-surface skepticism is fair... but frustrating. See, most people think about this in broad historical terms—they look to patterns of aggression motivated by or under the guise of religious fervor, or they draw on the endless conflicts between faith and reason, between spirituality and science, between tradition and progress, or they tap into the experience of marginalized groups for evidence of the evils of religion and the intellectual inferiority of religious people. This leads to heated (and typically poorly researched) retellings of the history of the Catholic Church or religiously motivated wars and why that proves the irrefutable corruption of institutional religious practice (anti-religion folx are big on *proof*) and accusations that I am "part of the problem" or unaware of my own internalized self-hatred. To me, these tacks constitute evidence of an empathy gap: they just can't believe that someone else's experience of religion—even this person standing before them with two degrees in the subject and years of personal and academic exploration under his belt—is valid.

I've always answered honestly, though my responses, according to my mood and the context, have swung across the spectrum from sharing my anthropological curiosity (at the purely intellectual end) to describing my own spiritual experiences (at the more personal, warm-and-fuzzy end). Sometimes, very rarely, my response is more complex (or just more complicated) than my inquisitors expect, throwing them off their guard and giving me a chance to jump to a different conversational track. Sometimes I respond by reflecting on my religion classes in high school, my favorites because they were the only truly interdisciplinary courses we had. Sometimes I geek out about the power of ritual to construct culture. Sometimes I tap into my own experiences of deep spiritual hunger and fulfillment. Sometimes I recount the conversations that I had with my parents about the primacy of one's conscience, even over the Church's teachings, that ignited a slightly rebellious spirit in my own practice and thinking. *See*, I whisper under my breath, *we're not all brainwashed fundamentalists who are out to save or suck out your soul.* Whatever tack I sail, though, I consistently crash into sweeping and unsubstantiated opinions, personal condemnations, and, for the remainder of our relationship's life, *that look* of subtle pity and condescension that says, "I can't believe you actually *believe* that crap."

But, in all those conversations, you know what *no one* has ever said to me? *Tell me more.* No one has ever asked for more details or for a recommendation for a book to learn more, for a community to visit, for a practice to try. No one has ever asked me what meaning I gleaned from my experiences, how it informs my worldview. No one has ever asked me what I believe, whether I conform to my church's teachings or how I diverge. I can intellectualize these encounters to recognize that they're symptomatic of a broader deficit in cultural or religious literacy and a lack of language to talk about spirituality. I can sympathize with these folx—I understand that their experience was different from my own. But no matter how I digest them, these encounters—especially with folx who proudly wave the flag of an open mind, a marginalized identity, or friendship—hurt. They hurt because they betray a fundamental lack of trust or respect, a refusal to acknowledge my whole personhood, or an inherent sense of superiority, and they affirm one of my greatest fears, that I don't deserve their respect, that I am not enough, that, despite wanting so badly to be known, to be respected, to be seen, I don't deserve the chance to tell them more.

OK, *once* someone said, *Tell me more.* He wanted to understand about my experiences, about how I understood the world, and I knew his question wasn't preamble to a pounce or condescension. It was rooted in love and a deep desire to find common ground. We got married three months later.

My family went to church every Sunday when I was a kid. My wife cannot believe this. She's like, "You went every Sunday?" "Yes." "What if you were out of town?" I was like, "They have them out of town." I don't know if you grew up going to church and now you don't, but it can be a weird existence. Because I like to make fun of it all day long, but then if someone like Bill Maher says, "Who would believe in a man up in the sky?" I'm like, "My mommy, so shut the fuck up! Stop calling my mommy dumb."

John Mulaney is a frequent visitor to our home (via Netflix, of course). By now, Mulaney's physical performances are burned into our memories, so my husband and I don't need to actually *watch* to be tickled by this gesture or that facial expression, and we can—and often do—recite his jokes and stories along with him. Mulaney and I come from similar worlds: we're both Irish Catholic Chicagoans who went to parish elementary schools and Jesuit high schools and colleges, and we're both close to (though on opposite sides of) the Gen X/Millennial divide. His stories about growing up, from school assemblies to being an altar boy, and glimpses into his family dynamic and humor feel very, very familiar to me. And for a few hours after he's on screen, my Chicago accent is just a little heavier than usual.

Mulaney's bits about church resonate especially loudly for me. Like him, I can even remember my father saying "God can't hear you" if I wasn't singing along with the cantor loudly enough, and, like Mulaney's now ex-wife, my husband listens to me talk about Catholic stuff with a mix of fascination and horror. But there's one bit where my experience diverges from his.

> If you grew up going to church and you have adult friends that didn't, they have a lot of questions. "Wait, so they forced you to go?" Yeah, I was five, I was forced to go everywhere. No kid is just going to church. Riding by on his Huffy, like, "Whoa! What's this place? A weird Byzantine temple with green carpeting where everyone has bad breath and I wear clothes that I hate on one of the mornings of my two days off? Let's do this."

I did. Well, not on a Huffy, on a Schwinn. On a warm summer day, about a month before I turned eleven, I was riding my bike past our church, just a few blocks from home. For no particular reason, I decided to go in. I'd been in this church a thousand times by then—my family was there every Sunday and every Holy Day of Obligation, and the student body of my school, attached to the parish, was there on Wednesdays for nine a.m. mass—but I'd never seen it empty. The huge, metal doors at the front of the church were unlocked, so, with great effort, I pulled one open and shuffled in.

It took a moment for my eyes to adjust to the darkness, but when they did I took in all the colors filling the space. When the lights were on in the sanctuary, I never really noticed them, but the afternoon sun streamed through the modern stained-glass windows and quilted the green carpeting, mahogany pews, and tan walls with messy, distorted, and fantastic patterns. I could see millions of dust particles swimming in the light. I knew it was dust, but to nearly eleven-year-old me, it gave the sanctuary an enchanting and lovely shimmer.

I walked up the aisle on the right side, under the west wall's windows, careful not to disrupt the bands of colors painting the space. At the top of the aisle, I turned left and noticed for the first time a gate in the substantial brass rail that separated the congregational pews from the altar. Later in life, I'd learn that the gate stayed open because of the liturgical reforms after Vatican II, and most churches removed the rails that delineated the spaces for the sacred and the profane, the saints and the sinners. This rail remained to keep people from falling off of the altar, five or six steps above the main floor. I slowly closed the gate, swinging first the heavy panel on the right to its close, then the one on the left, and I discerned two figures I'd never seen before, stylized portraits of…pelicans. *Pelicans?*

I drifted east, to the apse on the left side of the main altar, drawn to a small side chapel. It had a smaller altar to host the tabernacle, the holy of holies, where consecrated communion wafers were stored. Above it, a brilliant gold-leaf triptych depicted the Holy Family surrounded by children from around the world. We knew they were from around the world because they wore the traditional costumes associated with different cultures. I'd seen it before, but it suddenly reminded me of the It's a Small World ride at Disneyworld, which I'd visited earlier that year. I laughed, and then I marveled at the faint echoes of my laughter bouncing back toward me from the empty church.

I looked around, confirmed that I was alone, and cautiously climbed the one step up to the altar. There was a key in the small door of the tabernacle, so I turned it, opened the door, and found two ciboria, the hand-size brass bowls from which communion is distributed, filled with wafers. Without thinking, I reached in, ate a couple, and returned the ciboria to the tabernacle. I closed the door, turned the key, and left the church by the side door, where my parents entered and exited every day for seven a.m. mass.

When we returned for mass the next Sunday, I didn't feel any particular thrill, that buzz that comes with naughtiness, that titter that comes with secret knowledge. Instead, I started no-ticing more details throughout the space. Curious symbols and Greek letters were deliberately planted throughout the church. *That's got to mean something, right?* The one human and three animal faces on the ambo (the podium from which parishioners read passages of scripture and offered prayers of petition, where priests proclaimed the gospel and preached, and, after commu-nion, someone delivered the all-important announcements about upcoming events) stood out to me, shouted out to me. *Why is only one of you a person?* Behind the altar, twelve larger-than-life statues, representing Jesus' twelve apostles, were embedded in a giant screen that hid the pipe organ and choir's risers, but I'd never really paid attention to them or the dozens of angels that sprung from the angles of the screen. I started counting them until my eyes fell on the giant cross hanging over the altar. Jesus, naked, sinewy, and lean, didn't *hang* from the cross as much as he embodied it, his arms and legs perfectly outstretched. Above his head were four letters that one of my brothers told me meant "I'm Nailed Right In," a joke my mother typically pursed her lips or clucked her tongue at but never refuted. Suddenly, I ques-tioned whether my brother was telling me the truth.

I started to notice who sat where and to think about how their position opened or obstructed their views of the ambo and the altar. On weekdays, my parents sat in the apse, adjacent to the tabernacle, but on Sundays we'd always sat about a third of the way back in the nave, always on the left, giving us an opti-mal view of the ambo. We had a pretty good view of the altar, but the real privilege in our position was being able to see every-one going to and coming back from communion. We could see each person approach the priest from the center aisle, lift their hands to receive a wafer, hear the priest mutter "The body of Christ" and the person mumble "Amen." Our pew emptied, and I walked behind my mother toward the altar. When she received communion, she didn't say "Amen"; instead, she responded, with confidence and a hint of rebelliousness, "I believe." *Is she the only one who did that?*

When the boys in my grade were recruited to serve as altar boys (we didn't have altar girls yet), my mother was, perhaps unsurprisingly, enthusiastic. "What a privilege," she said after my first training session, "to be that close." *What a privilege?* I loved seeing my name on the altar-boy schedule, and my quick adaptation to the rituals and routines put me on the A-list for special altar-boy gigs. The money was in weddings (once, I got a crisp $100 bill in an envelope after a particularly lush ceremony), but we got pulled out of school for funerals. I jumped at any chance to skip PE or math, so whenever Deacon Roger, who coordinated altar boys, appeared at our classroom door, I'd start packing up my things and wonder, with a smile on my face, "Who's dead today?"

Most funerals were for old people, grand- and great-grandparents whose time had come. For some, the pews were packed, making the communion line last for close to twenty minutes, which is far too long for any group of Catholics to sing "On Eagle's Wings" on a loop. Others were quiet liturgies with a handful of offspring and the few friends who outlasted them. From the altar, I could tell who was popular and who was loved. For the popular ones, every local with an Irish surname and every major fundraiser within fifty miles would cram into the back rows under the guise of the old maxim that "Good Catholics sit in back," but really ensuring that they'd be seen by the entire congregation when they followed the casket out of the church. With that kind of an audience, priests would pull out their biggest guns to make their homilies smart, funny, and touching and praise the virtues that the deceased represented.

But people smiled at funerals for the ones who were loved. They cried, they wept, some mourners even wailed—but they smiled, as if their recently lost and much-favored friend or aunt or cousin had just reappeared and told *this* famous story or provided *that* trademark hug. During his homily, the priest would speak to the relationships impacted by this loss and point to specific moments in the dead's life that showed God's love at work. Some examples were familiar to everyone, and others stunning (if not surprising) revelations of kindness, generosity, and care. I'd find myself crying and smiling with them, coopting their grief, wondering if I'd ever be so well loved, or if I'd ever love so well, to have a funeral like that.

———————

Some people observe religious practice to connect to and perpetuate their culture. Some seek belonging and community. Some believe fiercely in a worldview and want to tell you all about it. Some, deep in their bones, feel at peace or in harmony with the ground under their feet. Some need a space to tremble at the thought of the limits of their existence. Some needed an escape, space and time to think, space and time that the rest of the world doesn't afford. For me, it was the things that made me *stop* thinking, the things that gave me a reason to step out of the echo chamber of my mind, to give into my senses, to just be. It gave me a space where I learned how to wonder, how to sit with ambiguity, how to be still, how to notice, how to feel joy *and* sadness and know that their mix is part of being alive.

———————

Late winter is a "slow season" for religion, but with the change of the calendar year, people around the world (or at least throughout the hemisphere) mark the darkest point in our lap around the sun and engage in some form of personal or collective renewal. As the days hint at lengthening, religious folx let out the steam and the frustration that builds amid the winter doldrums through holidays like Purim, Holi, and Mardi Gras, and as the spring equinox approaches, Ostara, Norooz, Pesach, and Easter remind us, fundamentally, that we're still alive, that life goes on.

I forget that, sometimes, that life goes on. *Don't we all?* But I know that it's a more frequent memory lapse these days, and that's because I don't go to church anymore. I haven't shed my religious identity or claimed the title of "post-" or "recovering Catholic," as some cheekily do. Just entering a church triggers a quake of emotions and pain. I was exhausted from navigating the line between being queer and being Catholic and dodging bullets from both directions. I couldn't, in good conscience, participate in a community that has made it very, very clear that my gay-ass self isn't fully welcome. However, I was also, and more so, sick of confronting anti-religious sentiment among people who advocate for diversity and pluralism *until it comes to religion.*

About a year after we married, my husband looked directly at me and asked, "Do you still pray?" I thought for a moment, surprised by his abrupt conversational turn, and said, without further explanation, "Yes." He nodded—not sure what to ask next. And I wasn't sure what to say. *Nobody has asked me about my prayer life since I was seventeen*, I thought. I don't go to church, but I meditate; I process; I laugh; I read; I listen; I think; I advocate; I sing; I reflect; I look; I serve; I notice. *Isn't that prayer?* Sometimes I just sit still and let the energy of the universe swirl and shimmer around me. *Isn't that religion?* I still strive to love so well that my funeral makes strangers weep. *Isn't that life?*

questions & answers

Dad died at eighty-four. Dodo, his mother, died at eighty-eight, and his father (Grampa, I guess? I don't actually ever remember addressing him directly) died at ninety. Based on their families' apparent longevity, I assumed Dad would easily make it to his nineties, but after a couple of strokes debilitated him, and my mom's cancer returned, he was dependent on twenty-four-hour, in-home care and an endless rotation of visits and help and support and meals and errands from my siblings. His condition didn't promise any quick resolution—I remember a doctor mentioning that he could sustain like this for many years. That terrified me more than anything—that he'd be trapped in a body for a decade or more that halted and confused his ability to process language, that diminished his once athletic frame to skin and bones transported by a walker and the hands of his caregivers at his waist, that made all but a few of his family and friends unrecognizable, that reduced a predictable but classy wardrobe of sport coats and slacks to sweatpants and loose pullovers that only magnified his frailty. Watching my father grieve and mourn after the death of my mother, his wife of almost sixty years, was heartbreaking, but when my sister died suddenly, one who like me lived out of town and was eager and proud to arrive for a long weekend or a week, to care for him and cook and bake and fill the kitchen and walk with him and give the local siblings a little break, his pain was overwhelming to me.

A few days before Christmas, Dad died, surrounded by my

siblings and extended family, but I didn't make it home in time. I got the message after landing in Denver for a layover and wept in a lonely corner of an airline lounge, swimming in regret. I didn't regret the chance to say goodbye—I'd done that before, when he was more lucid and death was only knocking on the door. Instead, I regretted not trusting an instinct to return home earlier, but I was tangled in my own busy-ness. As my family and I gathered and prepared for the funeral, I began to see the decline leading to that moment as an absurd and tragic coda for a man whose life spanned the century, whose sentimentality and compassion impacted the world around him, whose gifts for language and music were as much a draw for others as they were a protective shield for him, and who was respected by colleagues and friends as a leader in his industry though he hadn't even finished college. I wasn't surprised to hear many stories honoring his generosity or reveling in his humor, but I was suddenly aware of the incompleteness of my own knowledge of my father.

He was in his mid-forties when I was born, an old man by parenting standards, but my siblings knew him as a young father. As my parents expanded the family with child after child after child, they lived in homes I've only driven by, homes that frame the stories that defined my family's unique culture. I was a late addition to the family, what I think of as a "delightful surprise," and since my parents died, I've started to sift through photos on their birthdays to recall the stories attached to each image, the memories—happy and painful—from each encounter. Recalling what my parents shared or how my siblings described the settings captured in those images has become a bridge to connect the parents and world that only they and my siblings knew to the parents and world that only I knew.

Reconstructing the worlds of these images is itself a literal re-membering, putting people back together, trying to breathe life into them, and asking them to speak for themselves. I integrate the words and the events I can recall with the words others have shared, trying to move, inch by inch, closer to a full portrait. Sitting with these images, recalling what I can and what others have shared, has become a sacred process for me. Like other sacred and inspired images and texts, I find myself transformed by them—not because I find myself filling in my gaps of knowledge, but because I find myself becoming more comfortable in their absence, moving through the shadows they left, with the images that remain. What is important to me is not that the details of the stories flesh out, but that I listen to what the images and the people they glimpse have to say to me now.

No, I don't think my parents are speaking to me from old photographs. Instead, these old photos open the door to a kind of communion with them—what remains of them in my memory, heart, and actions ignites and casts light on my life today.

My dad grew up in a world that few knew. He was born on the south side of Chicago in the worst years of the Great Depression to a salesman who didn't like working for other people and a former Vaudevillian who was whisked away to the big city by her groom. The year he was born, his father started a business that by the 1950s had become a hugely successful manufacturer, a business that would be woven into the DNA of the entire family. As a young couple, my mother's middle-class Chicago roots were a contrast from the high society that my dad's parents mingled among, but it was a world they navigated well enough. Much of what I know about my father's childhood troubles me, mostly because he rarely talked about those darker forces. He skipped two elementary grades but took six years to finish high school because he kept running away from boarding schools; his mother was tender and soft while being ruled by a tyrannical husband whose emotional bullying impacted Dad until the day he died; he matriculated at multiple universities, but his father wouldn't let him finish a degree. Instead, we heard stories of an elegant and classy world, of playing polo in California and of starting to work in the factory of his father's company at eighteen. I don't have a clear idea in my head about my father as a child or of the world he was initially raised in, but something about my dad in a tuxedo seems right.

The image in my mind picks up around his late teen years and is a patchwork of old photos of him in slim suits, of stories and photos of glamorous parties at my grandparents' house, and of films from the era in which "semi-formal" meant black tie. Somewhere along the line, he planted the idea in my head that every gentleman should have a tux in his closet, because, well, you never know when you'll need one. And as an adult, I've always had a tux in my closet (and it's gotten plenty of wear... Don't you hate it when your parents are right?).

He didn't always wear a tux, of course—lounging around the house, we'd find him in his pressed wool slacks and a stiff, button-down shirt, typically covered by a thin wool V-neck. Whenever they left the house for dinner—to a restaurant, to the homes of friends or family, Dad always had a jacket on (and, until much later in life, typically a tie). "It's always better to be overdressed than underdressed," said my mom, explaining the logic behind the etiquette. "You can take the coat and tie off."

Sometimes I'd feel like the jacket was a bit much. When we traveled to Israel with a group from his parish after my first year of college, I questioned the need to wear his jacket every evening. And I mean *every* evening, whether we were heading to a large hotel lounge or a neighborhood restaurant or happy hour at a kibbutz. I don't think he understood the question—the rule was self-evident to him—but he did offer some justification. "Well, everyone looks better in a jacket."

For my dad, wearing a jacket was less about stuffy sartorial rules and more about demonstrating respect for the people he encountered. The well-mannered world that he lived in was dripping with privilege and elitism, but good etiquette, not bound by class or place (if Emily Post and my mother were to be believed) is about establishing and maintaining appropriate relationships and knowing-what-to-do-when-you-don't-know-what-to-do. When in doubt, my father taught me, wear a jacket.

Watching reruns of "The Dick Van Dyke Show" as a kid was a bit confusing. From the opening prat-fall sequence with the opening credits to the series' end, I was fairly convinced that Van Dyke's character, Rob Petrie, was based on my father (just as convinced as my siblings were that Dad was either/both a six-star general or/and a warlock). Physically, Dick Van Dyke and my father inhabited a type, and the character Rob Petrie's earnestness at home and at work still reminds me of my dad.

Look carefully, and there's a date-stamp on the frame of this photo, indicating that it was taken shortly after my parents moved into the house I grew up in. It's a remarkable photo for three reasons: first, it's a notably intimate picture—he wasn't fond of being captured in such a sincere state. Most pictures capture a dissatisfied grimace or a comically broad grin, reflecting his sense of humor but also suggesting a performative nature—he was playing a part. Here, though, he's unaware, uninterested in the camera's invasion into his bedroom. Second, he's alone. At this point, he was the father of seven (under nine years of age, which would over the course of the next dozen years become ten)...so, getting a picture alone itself is a feat.

But the most surprising aspect of this picture is its location: my parents' bedroom. There was something about the second floor, where we all slept; as much as our house had rotating doors from the steady flow of comers and goers, few guests made it to the second floor. Like the Petries, my mother always wore a long nightgown at night, and my father a two-piece pajama set (the rules of etiquette didn't stop at the bedroom door). My memory of the room was formed by playing Scrabble with Mom on the floor while watching *The Golden Girls* on the TV in the corner Dad is looking at. I can picture my mom napping on that bed while a five-year-old me tried to sneak down the stairs for a cookie—eyes closed and facing away from me, she muttered, "Back to bed." She was serious about naptime. In high school, I'd pop my head into the room to let them know I was home (before curfew, of course), and my mom would confirm with a few words. What occurs to me now is that I never thought of it as Dad's room—it was always Mom's. Except for a tall dresser with his stiffly pressed shirts, poorly hidden valuables and mementos, and tennis shorts, nothing in the room suggested that he lived there, too.

———————

Until he was a young adult, my dad took piano lessons, frequently coached on the piano bench by his mother to get the right feeling of a piece. When he was about eighteen, he had surgery to correct the imbalance that polio had left him from

childhood—he stood 6'4" on one foot and 6'2" on the other. At the time, the best method was taking two inches out of one leg, and while he healed in a wheelchair, he played an awful lot of piano. The loneliness and depression that can come with any surgery surely shrouded him, and as a young man, that separation from peers must've been awful. He didn't talk about it much. Recovery must've been a kind of spiritual crucible for him.

I followed in his footsteps (or in this case, in his arpeggi) and took lessons into early adulthood. Like my dad, I always had a few pieces ready to play. For me, it was Gershwin's second prelude or Khachaturian's "Toccata"; for my dad, it was Debussy's "Clair de Lune" or Sinding's "Rustle of Spring". It's an easy performance strategy—if there's a piano at a party, one can sit, play, and wow and dazzle the crowd. This fulfills two social functions: the pianist has contributed to the gathering, and the pianist has attracted sufficient attention to be able to predict conversations and small talk that follow. But it also fulfills an interior function: it gives the pianist a few moments to get lost in the music, escaping surrounding eyes and ears and budding topics for small talk. It's a phenomenon that any performer knows. While surrounded by dozens, hundreds, or even thousands of people, a solo can be the loneliest place in the universe, which is precisely what makes it a great party trick for introverts. My dad knew how to get the party going, play the part of the welcoming patriarch, and then find moments to disappear in plain sight.

This looks like one of those moments. It's a summer barbeque, a much-loved practice among my older siblings. Dad is standing adjacent to the grill, perhaps having just started its fire or put the first round of burgers on. Like a piano, the grill gave him a protective space, an aura of authority and distance. Perhaps there is a softball game happening on the other side of the fence and he's spied a fly ball, but I doubt it. I don't doubt that a game is afoot—but rather, that he's paying attention to it. Perhaps he's looking up at a cloud or a bird, or perhaps he's looking at nothing at all. Somehow he is unaware of a camera nearby, and even the milling of neighbors and family in the adjacent porch doesn't distract him from accessing that space that he first found at the piano, his mother sitting on the bench and teaching him the gentle touch needed for some pieces and the gusto for others.

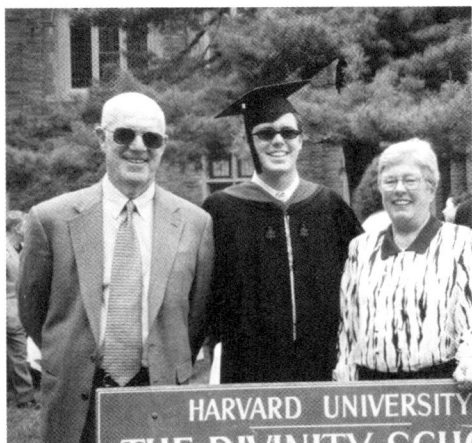

After three years of Divinity School, my mother was delighted to attend an ivy league graduation. The day began with the university-wide commencement ceremony, full of all the pomp and circumstance she expected, and continued with smaller ceremonies for each of the schools within the university. In our ceremony, we got to hear where our fellow graduates were headed—some to further graduate study, others to work, and still others, including me, were TBD—and for the PhDs and ThDs, we heard brief summaries of their dissertations. Mom must've taken notes, because after the ceremony, she walked through the titles with a mix of wonder and incredulity.

If my father had a reaction to the ceremony or to anything

about my program or life in general, I don't remember it. All I can remember is my fury, the disdain I held for him throughout that weekend. Their trip to Boston would be my father's first since I'd moved there three years previously, though Mom had visited a couple of times—once just to catch up (read: check on me) and once to help after a tonsillectomy. Unaware of newer techniques in surgery, she assumed that the stitches in my throat (which I didn't have because the scars were soldered) risked bursting and, living alone, I'd bleed to death in my sleep. She also clearly wanted to clean and reorganize my kitchen, a task she set to as soon as we returned from the hospital, knowing that I was too drugged up to notice (or argue).

As graduation and their visit approached, I made a series of plans, including a dinner at my place with my closest friends that would give my parents a glimpse into my sort-of adult life, and that would give my friends all the evidence they needed to see that the impressions of my parents that were part of my own schtick were spot-on. Upon arrival, though, Dad announced that we'd been invited by a business associate to dinner at the storied and exclusive (and historically restricted, aka, no Blacks, no Jews, no Catholics, etc.) Country Club in Brookline. My plans were trumped because they'd already committed to the evening, despite my reservations about the club's reputation and symbolism—not things that I wanted to mark my completion of Divinity School.

At the time, I hid behind a quickly assembled wall of self-righteousness, but reconstructing that time now, I recognize that I was hurt, that I was disappointed. What drove my tantrum was not the history of injustice embodied by the Country Club but my unmet desire for Dad to know me, to see me, to recognize that what I was doing was meaningful and impactful, and that I was worthy of his respect, but as our family didn't have much of a vocabulary for navigating feelings and negotiating conflict, I pouted. I snapped at him, I glared. I remember being perfectly unfriendly and unaccommodating to conversation with our hosts at dinner—the little bit of revenge I could muster—but the thing that bothered me the most was that Dad was unfazed. He didn't seem to notice my upset or aggravation, and he didn't bristle—or respond at all—to the game of passive aggression that I'd waged.

Does the photo betray any of that? Not really. We didn't have vocabulary for conflict, but we were masterful at disguising it. I wish I had listened to my gut and been more insistent, but I was raised to be deferential and accommodating, so family culture overrode my desires. I wish I regretted being a brat that weekend. I wish I didn't carry a grudge about it, but over the next decades it would be stoked and refueled frequently. After three years of teaching, Dad didn't know what I taught. After a decade of ignoring my invitations to visit me in Boston and see me perform, he didn't even remember I was still singing. Once, he even forgot I had a partner until we arrived for Thanksgiving. And worst of all, as many opportunities as I've had to let go of this grudge, holding on to it is so much more satisfying (did I mention we're Irish?).

Dad declined quickly in the last few years of his life, and his decline reshaped our family. A few months after turning eighty-two and a week before my parents' seasonal migration to Arizona, Dad had a stroke that debilitated his body, slowed his mind, and sapped his soul. The stroke hit hard his ability to communicate, his now-slow processing left him drifting while everyone around him bustled and moved forward, and it seemed to exacerbate Dad's already creeping dementia. He was never officially diagnosed, but his doctors referred to many of his new habits, weaknesses, and tics as Parkinsonisms—behaviors associated with Parkinson's Disease—and subsequent blood pressure episodes that puzzled his medical team would land him in the hospital for a few days to stabilize and then in a rehabilitation facility for a few more days. Each episode was a setback, leaving him more and more confused and, some days, despondent.

Some of the "locals," my siblings who lived nearby, were on call twenty-four seven to help care for Dad, and some of us "out of towners" would visit for a weekend or a week at a time, aiming to give the locals a break. As Dad declined and as Mom faced a return of cancer and submitted to its ravages almost a year after his stroke, this hamster wheel of caregivers rolled on. While the locals lived with his slow, daily decline, each visit startled me. This man who had been so tall, graceful, and gracious was reduced; whose speech had been poetic and lyrical was stymied; who was obsessive about punctuality and manners had lost all sense of time; who could sit down at any piano and meander through "Clair de Lune" from memory now looked toward his piano hopelessly. As my work schedule allowed, I was happy to be back in my parents' home for long weekends or for a week at a time, driving them to appointments, cooking and shopping for them, cleaning and organizing the kitchen, but the first day back was always the hardest. Each first-sight of the rapid decline in both my parents and then, after Mom died, in my father alone, tore at my heart, and I would spend the rest of my time searching for what was left of him.

There were bright moments. One of his kindest and more stalwart caregivers got Dad into a pattern of exploring the neighborhood. In a wheelchair and dressed in layers of baggy warmup pants and sweatshirts to keep him warm, even on muggy summer days (a far cry from his old leisure-wear of slacks and V-necks), his caregiver or I would push him around the neighborhood, typically following the crook of his finger that indicated which way he wanted to turn. Even in this state, he was in charge. We couldn't tell how much he remembered, but he remembered the way to Potbelly's, and about twice a week we'd do the cumbersome work of getting him dressed and into a car so that he could point the way to Potbelly's for a strawberry milkshake.

Back in the day, Dad was famous for ending a meal by lightly slapping the table with one hand, grunting a "Well…" and dropping his napkin on the table with the other hand as he stood—it didn't matter if anyone else was still eating. The only one who could halt this was Mom. She'd stretch out her post-dinner cup of tea to be able to relax at the table and finish a conversation, even (or especially) when Dad was done. Even in a wheelchair and without much language, he'd try to push back from the table and roll away. Mom figured out quickly how to keep him eating by trapping him between the wall and the table. It's a trick we all learned.

One late night, my sister and I were in the kitchen chatting over a glass of wine, and Dad came *running* through the kitchen like an extra in a Benny Hill sketch—no walker, no wheelchair, and, more importantly, no caregiver holding him up! His knees piked high, toward his chest, and as he passed us he gave us a gleaming look, one we'd seen hundreds of times before in his more mischievous moods. He made it to a chair in the kitchen, sat, crossed his legs, and folded his hands over his lap, as if he were preparing for a fireside chat, before the caregiver caught up with him, running into the kitchen yelling, "Robert! Robeeeert!" In each of these moments was a glimpse, a slight revelation that he was still there, or that there was enough left for me to reconstruct the man I used to know.

Holding on to those moments and retelling those stories to eke a laugh or two were necessary bolsters, because the hard parts were harder and more shattering than I could have imagined. My thirty-ninth birthday dinner at my brother's restaurant, a much-needed spot of joy shortly after Mom died, was cut short barely after entrees arrived because Dad was done (and there was no way to trap him at this table). During one of his hospitalizations, my sister and I accompanied him to a series of neurological tests that included strapping him to a large rack that tilted, not dissimilar from medieval torture devices. As he was being strapped and as the test seemed to send shocks into his hands and feet, my sister and I watched in horror as the few words he could muster were "Help" and "Get me off."

During another episode, I was alone with him in his hospital room when orderlies came to take him to physical therapy or for another test. He protested but couldn't articulate why—we found out soon enough. An orderly on each arm, as he was lifted from bed his hospital gown swung open, revealing a decimated body, skin hanging off bones, and shit poured out of him onto the bed.

In the middle of the night during one of my last visits home, I woke to the sound of a thud. While the caregiver was in the bathroom, thinking Dad was asleep, he got up out of bed and, perhaps making another run for the kitchen, he collapsed, broke a hip, and crumbled down against the wall. The caregiver, puzzlingly, just kept measuring his blood pressure and oxygen levels, and it was a few groggy minutes before I realized that I needed to call 911.

In each of the painful moments, we didn't know—or at least, I didn't—of how much he was aware. Did he know us, or were we just the closest ones who might respond to a plea? When my mother died, we really didn't know what Dad knew or how it was hitting him. Seeing her in a casket, laid out for her wake, he dissolved in tears. We planned to bring him home once the wake started and bring him back for the funeral a few hours later—the anticipated crowd would be too much for him, we thought—but he refused to leave. In fact, even in this debilitated state, even swimming in grief, he spotted old friends and colleagues from a distance. His caregiver and two of his children could barely keep up with him as he sprinted across the church with his walker. That was a story we told with amazement in the days and months that followed, but I shouldn't have been surprised. Earlier that day I was tasked with picking a suit and tie, and I ran several options by him. He knew exactly what he wanted.

———————

The summer after Dad died, my siblings and I cleaned out my parents' house. The out-of-towners arrived, and together we set out to identify things we wanted, things no one wanted, things someone should want. Once everything was sorted and laid out, we moved as a unit from room to room, claimed one item at a time according to numbers we'd drawn, and decided what to do with unclaimed items. By the end of the day, the house was empty, save clusters of boxes and furniture waiting to be picked up or shipped.

This wasn't the house we grew up in. It was a smaller place, but still full of furnishings and effects that ornamented my parents' life together. The Mason & Hamlin piano that my dad learned to play on and that I later learned to play on, still outfitted with ivory keys, sat in front of this bookcase until it was donated to a local school. One of the framed family portraits that used to line the front hall staircase, my husband's favorite (he thinks we look like the cast of *Dynasty*), leans against the cabinet. A few books and photo albums that hadn't been claimed remain on the shelves, as do binders filled with my dad's poetry.

Though he never strived to be a published poet, he wrote almost nightly after dinner. During warmer weather, he'd sit in a screened porch at the end of the house with a glass of wine and write, mostly inspired by scripture or by his fervent belief in angels and devotion to Mary, the mother of Jesus. Sometimes he wrote about the love that he and Mom shared—with broad abstractions and beautiful imagery, his poems became anniversary gifts that my mother framed and hung around the house. Mom kept her favorite on her dresser. After he retired, most of his poems were gifted to his weekly prayer group, a cluster of men in their seventies and eighties who gathered on Wednesday mornings for faith-sharing and reflection. Their friendship and their regular meetings were important components in his later life, especially as he struggled with being forced to retire, with watching the business he'd built over the course of more than half a century taken out of his hands and his legacy dismantled, and with the unchosen isolation of retirement.

Poetry provided one more buffer for Dad, one more layer of protection from social vulnerability. Instead of speaking openly and freely from the heart, he offered a poem to his prayer group. Instead of an impromptu toast on her birthday, he'd read a poem for my mother. After dinner at their house, whether you were a friend or a stranger, if you found yourself in my parents' library with a nightcap in one hand, you'd also find a copy of his most recent poem in the other with the solitary prompt, "Well, what do you think?" He was never actually open to criticism. In fact, he didn't really listen to feedback or engage in dialogue at all. That interaction always struck me as a glimpse into his inner tensions—a deep longing to connect, foiled by layers of pain and isolation and social convention—but to anyone else, it was the invitation by a mystic into his interior life.

"Answers"
Robert L. Hulseman

With gentle evening,
Clouded memories faded
Into a sunset
Of dreams.

In this quiet time,
This quiet place,
I loved
As I have never loved before.

A closeness of spirit
Bonded with my soul
With glimpses of tomorrow
Visions of what was to come.

Gone were the questions
Of a thousand yesterdays,
Selfishness and greed vanished
In the presence of Perfect Love.

six to carry the casket
and one to say the mass

My mother had a way with words.

At a party to celebrate her eightieth birthday, I was nominated (read: instructed) by my older sisters to give a toast. While some might've raised a glass to her accomplishments or to highlight peak moments from the previous seven decades, that, I thought, wasn't what she'd want to hear—nor was it the most accurate, most authentic way to portray her. So, instead of a walk down memory lane or a gush of superlatives, I decided to share some of her "greatest hits," the phrases that made their way into our memories, or at least into my memory, and since then, when I want to summon her memory or channel her wisdom, I don't return to photos. I return to her words.

Hers weren't zingers or one-liners aimed at anyone in particular. They were observational, almost footnotes that filled in missing links to conversations or ideas, or that efficiently and wittily wrapped them up. She was succinct, and, sometimes, she was too succinct, offering only an occasional *hmm* to let you know she was still listening.

Her phrasing was pithy. She made you think quickly to discern the hidden joke, which wasn't always clarified by her tone or gesture, and her deadpan was convincing. Most of her recurring phrases were useful. She kept an arsenal handy for lagging chatter or to cover awkward transitions. She knew how to keep a conversation moving, and she knew how to wrap things up. She could engage and detach in one fell swoop.

Inane arguments, whether at her dinner table or on the nightly news, would end not with her opinion but with a declaration that "Semantics is the problem with the world today." It wasn't a particularly revealing insight, but it did make you stop to wonder what *semantics* was.

She loved to spin classic proverbs with a turn that you didn't anticipate, always short of crass but often glancing toward coy. "Well, you know, people who live in glass houses...shouldn't take baths in the daytime." And when a conversation about large feet ensued (it comes up more than you'd think in a family of ten siblings), she'd tap the wisdom of her father and say, "You know what they say about men with large shoe sizes. They can kill a lot of ants in the summertime."

———————

Sometimes, she'd get political—but not too political. When given the opportunity to take a trip to the UK, she declared, "I'm not going to England until they let my people go." Her people were the Irish (well, some of her people...and it was a couple of generations back), who were apparently still being oppressed à la Cromwell by the English. My sister, Patty, and I quickly revised the lyrics of the old Spiritual and sang, "When Sheila was in Engl-land...let my...people...go..."

Eventually, my parents did visit England (just a few stops on a cruise, not a slash-and-burn campaign on behalf of the suffering Gaels). She loved to tell the story about subtly (read: passive-aggressively) wrangling with a tour guide over the proper honorifics for Thomas More. When the guide referred to "Sir" Thomas More, she pointedly corrected him, doing her part in the centuries-old Catholic-Protestant standoff, with a clipped, "*Saint*—Thomas More."

When my mom was eighteen, her mother gave her a subscription to *Good Housekeeping*, which she maintained for decades, but the magazine crossed a line. When an agent called to ask if she wanted to renew her subscription, she said, "No," (and here, in her retelling, she would shift her weight and her tone, assuming what I can only think of as her over-the-phone-power-pose), "I wouldn't." She described to the unwitting agent on the phone a recent cover of the magazine that featured Princess Diana ("Princess Charles. The Lady Diana," as she would, in other contexts, correct you). "Don't you people know we had a revolution? We don't have to pay attention to those people anymore." When she retold the story over dinner with Mrs. Crump, one of her closest friends and a fixture in family lore, my sister and I cringed while Mrs. Crump cheered her on.

She was a well-read woman and spoke with real authority, but once in a while I'd hope that she would cite her sources. She wouldn't travel to France because, "Well, they never paid their war debts," or to Japan "until they open up free trade for rice and computer chips."

I was—hmm...let's say "lucky"—to inspire in my mother two unique turns of phrase. At my Divinity School graduation, each of us was invited to submit a twenty-five-word message to be read while we walked to the daïs to receive our diplomas. Because I hadn't secured a job or a place in another graduate program just yet, as I walked to the stage, the Dean of Students read, "While pursuing his dream as a lounge singer with an NPR talk show, Bill will pursue paths in interreligious dialogue, Catholic education, and queer activism." Most folx laughed along with the juxtaposition of my dream job and three, seemingly unrelated trajectories, but I could hear *and feel* my mother's gasp—partial shock ("queer" was not in her vocabulary) and a little bit of delight (in the wit and economy of words that I learned from her), punctuated by a cluck of her tongue. Classic Sheila. Having heard a diverse range of academic foci and professional directions, one stuck out to her—when I found them after the ceremony, her initial response was, "Well, congratulations. That was lovely. Now, what the hell is," she slowed to enunciate a new term in her lexicon and to accentuate the absurdity she perceived, "*eco-fem-in-ist spirituality*?"

A few months later, as coverage of planes striking the Twin Towers spread, my mother called me and left a message on my voicemail. "Well, happy birthday...on this awful...awful day." (That was the entire message.) I forwarded the message to multiple friends who needed something to laugh at and can still do a perfect imitation. Dark, I know, but it's made people cackle.

Mom inherited her wit from her father. Actually, she cultivated it. She studied him, admired him, elevated him. Mom beamed when she spoke about her father, and a part of her withered when he died, about a year before I was born. As *she* told the story, he was the son of poor immigrants who worked the jobs and lived the life of the immigrant Irish in those days. They sent him to college, and he earned a JD, but when he picked up his license to practice law, an old classmate from elementary school was there to meet him. At the offer of some work for the old classmate, he declined, telling him that he never intended to practice law, that it was just something to keep in his back pocket. While my grandfather grew into a decent and honest man, the old classmate was a gangster. Fearing that world, Mom told us, he pursued other jobs that put to work his charm, his affable nature, his wit. Fearing that world might've morphed into regret, grief for a career that was lost before it began, but she never got that far in speculating about her father's choices. To my mom, it was a moment that revealed his integrity, and that was enough, but to me, it was a profoundly sad detail. Though I never met him, I could feel my grandfather's disappointment, I could feel his parents' confusion, I could feel the shame and disillusionment that swelled, a mixture that integrity is never quite able to absorb.

He was the one who coined the crack about "ants in the summertime."

He was also the one who, at a wake, when asked by a friend how my grandfather thought the deceased looked, said, "He looks dead."

He took her to every wake in town as a child.

He taught her to play golf.

He combed Vaseline through his hair every morning, giving it a dark and shiny texture, but after a stroke in his seventies, a nurse washed his hair and revealed a thick shock of white. After he died, my mom couldn't watch a movie with Spencer Tracy without a) reminding anyone around how much her father looked like Spencer Tracy, and b) quietly weeping. I always thought her mother looked like Barbara Stanwyck, but Mom was never interested in comparing *her* to celebrities.

We lived in an affluent suburb, but instead of reveling in the glories of suburban life, she told stories about the three-flat she grew up in with her parents, sisters, and cousins, where her father was the only man in the house (one aunt's husband left her during the War, another aunt died, and then so did her widower, leaving his second wife in the three-flat on Deming Place). She told a story (that I never really believed) about seeing a man get shot on her walk home from the beach with a friend. My disbelief was less about the facts of the story and more about the possibility that my mother grew up within blocks of imminent danger.

She talked about growing up in the city with pride and with the expertise of a London cabbie. Any directions requested would allow her to demonstrate her mastery of the grid of the city of Chicago. It was never enough to say "three lefts and a right." Any journey from point A to point B included a near-mathematical equation that taught you about the numerical system underlying the city's map. When I worked as an architectural tour guide, I geeked out about Daniel Burnham, the master planner who designed that city-grid masterpiece, and hoped my enthusiasm about Burnham's 1909 plan for Chicago would make her proud.

If a tutorial on urban planning wasn't enough, she'd frequently identify in which Catholic parishes the starting and ending points of the journey would be. If you were lucky (and I mean this sincerely), you'd pass by the church where her great uncle (a woodworker or carver or layer or something) did all the woodwork (he installed the floors or carved the sculptures or pews or something), all the scraps of which were integrated into an unusual little game table whose entire surface was patterned with tiny pieces of wood and whose corner pockets were hidden, but I figured out how to open them when I was about seven. The church on the near west side of Chicago and the game table in the corner of our living room were monuments to craft, to history, to stories that could be told.

She raved about working the reception desk at the Edgewater Beach Hotel, where all the ball players stayed while batting at Wrigley. If asked, she would tell you who the kind and courteous players were, evaluated according to how they treated hotel staff and whether they'd stop to sign admiring kids' collector cards. She also laughed at her own inadequacy for overbooking the hotel by ninety-eight rooms, a mistake that somehow (read: because her boss was a friend of her father) didn't cost her the job.

She told stories about treating boyfriends badly. "Teenage girls are the worst," she declared. "I know because I was one." One boy asked her to a dance months in advance, and she declined by telling him there was a funeral she needed to attend.

When I was in preschool or kindergarten, my grandmother had a stroke that paralyzed the left side of her body and required her to move out of her apartment and into full-time nursing care. I don't have the memories of "Grandma's House" that all the cookie commercials told me I was supposed to have. I do remember a long, shiny, linoleum-tiled hallway with rooms on both sides. I remember old people in robes and hospital gowns and pajamas, ambling up and down the hallway with a walker or cane. I remember a woman with a goiter on the right side of her neck that was as big as a grapefruit. I remember another woman who never said anything but who was very happy when I'd wander into her room and sit in the chair next to the pillow-end of her bed. I'd rearrange the few things that were on her bedside table (a frame, a book, a rosary, but I never touched the glass of water) and then I'd continue my rounds down the hallway, eventually making it back to Grandma's room, where I'd find Mom doing a crossword or needlepoint, maybe telling her mother a story or maybe sitting in silence. As long as she was in the nursing home, my mom and her sisters visited every day. One sister came for lunch, Mom arrived mid-afternoon with me in tow, and the other sister came for dinner.

It never occurred to me until after she was gone that one of Mom's deepest worries had been steeped in years of obliged devotion at her slowly-dying mother's bedside. When I asked her whether she was worried about dying, she confessed only to worrying about my father. She didn't want him to eat alone. Breakfasts, lunches, dinners...for the nearly sixty years they were married, the kitchen table was the thing that connected us. I grew up on a long butcher block table—five of us on one side, five on the other, sometimes a sixth if any guests or the milkman decided to stay, and a parent at each end. My dad came home for lunch every day (it wasn't until high school that I realized that most fathers brought their lunch to work, or had lunch with colleagues, or did "business lunches"), and in grade school we walked home for lunch every day. Dinner was a command performance, as was engaging in conversation. The standard "grace" was mumbled before Mom improvised. "Well, let's pray for all the people who are sleeping on the street tonight, because it's just so cold." Or she'd invite us to pray for someone's safe travels. Or she'd invite us to pray for someone who had no food. Or "the old ladies" that she drove home from the senior center on Wednesdays.

By the time I was in high school, she spent a good chunk of each Monday at a day shelter for women who were unhoused. A woman named Dolores quickly befriended her, and, after she made and served lunch, Mom and Dolores would play Scrabble. Dolores was the only person whom Mom permitted to play with unverifiable words, and while pre-dinner grace frequently featured Dolores's struggles, dinner conversation just as frequently included updates on her neologisms.

She arrived at the day shelter one Monday and learned that volunteers from the Junior League would be arriving soon with lunch for the clientele. With nothing to do while lunch was being served, Mom grabbed a newspaper and sat in the corner, waiting for lunch to finish so she could "visit with the ladies." One of the volunteers, whom Mom described variously as lovely, kind, sweet, perky, or persistent (depending on how much Chardonnay preceded the story), circled around to her several times with trays of food. When she came around with lemon bars, the volunteer leaned down to Mom and whispered, "Are you *sure* you won't have *just* a bite?"

In that moment, it dawned on Mom that this was her finest. Her daily ensemble typically included a wrap-around-skirt from a catalogue and a pair of plain, white Keds. She never dyed her hair and never put anything more than a comb into it. The only makeup she donned was a bright, coral-hued lipstick. When the Junior Leaguer made her way around the room, she assumed that Mom was a client, a woman who was unhoused, a woman with too much pride to take a free lunch, even from these lovely, kind, sweet, perky, and/or persistent volunteers. I'd bet she replayed the interaction in her head several times on the drive home, preparing to open dinner conversation with, "Well, I've finally done it. I'm a success."

After Grandma died, something happened between my mom and her sisters. One Christmas Eve, dinner was delayed because our cousins hadn't arrived. When she finally called her sister to find out where they were, she was told, "We were never invited," even though we'd done Thanksgiving at their house and Christmas Eve at ours for decades. When I found her to say good night, she was sitting on the couch in the living room with Mrs. Crump, crying. I leaned in to give her a kiss, but all I remember from the moment, my first really vivid Christmas memory, is the taste of Chardonnay.

I don't remember Mom *enjoying* holidays, but I remember her preparing for them. Three days before, the dining room table would be extended, the pads would be put out, and the tablecloth spread to ensure that any creases were gone by the time we sat down to dinner. Two days before, she'd set out stacks of plates, clusters of glasses. Everything was completed in stages so that by the time the hordes descended upon the house, final prep wasn't stressful and dinner service was a well-oiled machine. By the time I was in high school, I started to notice that my siblings were unexpectedly eager to be the first to clean up the kitchen, even while people were still eating. Perhaps Mom saw it as a well-trained and efficient staff, but I knew they just didn't want to be the one who had to refill her wine glass. "I'll have a little more of your wine," she'd say to whomever sat closest to the bottle. Sometimes she'd stumble through the phrase or just shake the glass while holding its stem, the universal symbol for "I'm soused."

One Christmas, we watched *It's a Wonderful Life*. When Mr. Potter came on screen, she gave us a brief lecture on Lionel Barrymore. "You know, when we were kids, we—just—worshipped him. And we all thought he was in that wheelchair because of polio. Well," she geared up, "it turns out, he was *FULL* of syphilis." Every time Barrymore rolled into view, someone got the nod for a refill, and we all got a different iteration of the Barrymore legacy. Some of the details would change, but one phrase was consistent. He was *FULL* of syphilis. And then when Jimmy Stewart started to berate Uncle Billy, Mom got up to exit, weeping, saying, "I—just—can't watch this."

———————

Dinner customs didn't change when there was only one bird (me) left in the nest. The butcher block table was gone by the time I was in high school, and except for the occasional sibling who was back for a short stint or just visiting for dinner, setting the table, clearing the table, and refilling my mom's wine glass were my exclusive ken. Dinners were less conversational—sure, with three people, there are fewer things to talk about, but the real shift was that conversations had become soliloquies, and soliloquies slipped into diatribes. There wasn't much I could say to steer the conversation, and there wasn't much I could say that would be remembered the next day. By the end of dinner most nights, Dad had finished two or three scotches ("Chivas Regal on the rocks with a twist and a little bit of water on the side" was the standard order I'd learned by the time I was seven), Mom had finished two or three vodkas-and-water-on-a-lot-of-ice, and they'd split one or two bottles of Chardonnay.

Once, when they came back from dinner at the home of friends, Mom was so drunk she tried to get into the house through the wrong door. The family room had an exterior door, a leftover from the room's original purpose (as a garage) that was adjacent to the kitchen door (our primary entrance). I was watching a movie and was startled when I heard a rap at the door. When I opened the very-much locked door, I was greeted with a look of shock and surprise that mirrored my own, a look that instantly made me think it was my fault she couldn't open the door, a look that humbled me and pushed my gaze away. I focused on the long necklace she wore, one she inherited from my dad's mother, a string of large, white coral beads. That's what had been rapping at the handle, *that's* what had startled me.

About a half-hour later, my dad returned to the family room where I was still, ostensibly, watching a movie. He told me without my asking that it was his job to take care of my mother. I said, "OK." Then he went to the fridge and took out a bottle of Chardonnay and poured himself a glass.

———————

My mom enrolled me in piano lessons in fourth grade. Apparently unlike most of my siblings before me, I stuck with the lessons—not because of some prodigious talent that was activated (because that definitely didn't exist) or because I particularly liked it (which I actually did), but because it was the first time I could claim some space of my own. If I practiced an hour a day, that meant that I had my thoughts and my feelings *to myself* for an hour. At school, I wasn't liked (or I was picked on, or

I was shunned, or I was targeted, as my mom would variously describe it, using codewords for "different," familiar to all mothers of queer children), and among my siblings, I was ornamental (you know, *there* but unheard, peripheral).

It never occurred to me that I should talk to someone, even when Mom arranged for Father Terry to talk to me, and by "talk to me," I mean, he came to the door of my classroom, asked the teacher if he could talk to me, and brought me out of school to the rectory next door. We went to his private office, and he asked, "How are you doing? I hear you're having a tough time." He was warm, and he was kind. I could smell the coffee on his breath and the cigarette-stink on his hands, and he opened a door that I didn't know how to navigate. I couldn't tell him that I felt different. I couldn't tell him that I felt lonely or that I didn't understand other boys. I didn't know how to play video games, because nobody showed me. I didn't know how to throw a football or any of the confounding and arbitrary rules of the game, because nobody showed me. And when my athletic incompetence became public knowledge during gym class, I didn't know why everybody laughed at me. I didn't know why Coach made me sprint out into the field in the first place. I didn't know I was supposed to go out about a hundred feet, turn around, and catch the football speared at me. I didn't know it was so funny that the coach was the first one to laugh. Then again, I also didn't know why I was the only one who could quote *Young Frankenstein* and *Murder by Death* by the time I was seven the way that other boys could rattle off baseball statistics and the names of basketball players. And I definitely didn't know that, a couple of years later, Father Terry would turn to my parents when he felt the pain of the conflict between his vocation and his sexual orientation, that he would turn to my parents for advice on how to break his vows and transition to life as a lay, openly gay man.

With enough time at the keyboard, I got to be pretty good. I struggled with reading music (I never got to be the "sit down at the piano and can play anything" guy that I secretly hoped I'd be), but I had a good teacher. Mrs. Neiweem spoke softly and directly. She sat not-too-close and not-too-far. She paid attention to things no one ever paid attention to. She praised me for being able to *express* when I played. Even her husband and duo piano partner, Mr. Neiweem, made a point to compliment seventh-grade me on the "gentle touch" I applied to the Rondo Alla Turca at a recital. It was the most important affirmation I'd ever heard. Between pieces or technical exercises, she told me stories about touring Italy as duo-pianists—Mr. and Mrs. Neiweem and a Kawai grand, driving up and down the Italian countryside, giving concerts here and there. It was, I thought, the most glamorous and magical life, a life I wanted to live (a life I still want to live). After mastering (read: making it through in one attempt) a particularly difficult passage in a Beethoven sonata, she exploded out of her chair, shouted, "Wunderbar!" and clapped her hands twice before she brought her pencil to the sheet music, where she scribbled "Wunderbar!" I'm not sure I've ever been prouder.

Mom kept track of my time at the piano, and she understood what it meant for me. Some time in my thirties, I found a form that she completed for my counselor at summer camp. To the question "When is your child happiest?" she wrote, "At the piano, alone." (She was half right.) At dinner, she'd note that I hadn't quite reached an hour "at the keys" that day. On summer days in high school, if I wasn't working or out with friends, I was at the piano, and, wherever she was in the house, Mom was listening. If she was in the next room, I'd hear her sighs at the end of tough passages and the cluck of her tongue at sloppy runs through a piece. Once, I rushed through a Chopin polonaise, and heard her, from the kitchen at the other end of the house, "That's not—*quite*—right!"

Occasionally, Mom would summon me if they had friends over for a drink (read: five drinks) to play for their guests. "No" was not in the vocabulary available to me at home, so I'd sit down and play. Sometimes politely and sometimes genuinely, their friends listened, rapt, marveling that a human could work eighty-eight keys with ten fingers. I learned to read my audience: if they wanted to keep chatting, I'd play something soft; if they'd run out of conversation, I'd play something showy; if they were sober, I'd get away with the second movement of the Pathétique and a Gershwin prelude; if they were wasted, I'd run through everything I could play from memory. They were usually wasted, so cocktail hour gave me plenty of time to practice.

A few weeks before she died, Mom decided she was finished with chemo. She was ready. So hospice care began, and in the fridge, in addition to the food that my siblings and I were making amidst our competitive caregiving, where there had once been a bottle or three of Chardonnay, there was now a stock of morphine and other specialties to "make her comfortable." A hospital bed arrived, and it quickly displaced the small couch in the den, where she slept at night and between visits from friends and relatives. Almost forty, I was sitting at the piano like a teenager, playing through whatever I could remember without sheet music, and Mom ambled by, headed toward a nap. I stopped playing and moved to stand up, and she chirped, "What are you doing?" I told her that I'd take a break so she could nap. She pursed her lips, shook her head, and kept moving. I understood my instructions: sit back down, but nothing too loud. I played Gershwin's second prelude (she always liked that one) and heard her sigh at the last note.

———

There are words that stick because they're frequently repeated, or because they evoke a happy moment, or a funny story, or a legacy. Those are words you want to repeat. Those are words I want to hear again. Then, there are words that stick, even if you only heard them once. Whether or not you want them to inhabit your mind, they stake a claim and tag a little footnote on every other memory that says, "Don't forget the time she said…"

Apparently, when I was in high school, a few of my siblings confronted Mom about her drinking. I'd heard rumblings of this or that sibling embarrassed by it or worried about her health. It's too bad they never asked me. I could've told them how much she drank each day, how much she drank when with my dad, how much she drank with friends, how much she drank when she went out to dinner, how much she drank at holidays, which was different—it always started later on holidays because she had too much cooking to do before she could make it through her dosage of vodkas-and-water-on-a-lot-of-ice before she could enjoy some Chardonnay. I could've told them what she thought about all of them, because once the second glass of Chardonnay was filled each night, the library was open, and she'd catalogue their offenses. I could've told them that I resented the fact that they got to jump up and exit the dinner conversation while I was pouring her "a little more of my wine," or that I resented their claim to suffering because of my mom's drinking because they got to go home, and the home they left me in was filled with too much Chardonnay. I could've told them that they were neglecting Dad, that he was the one who claimed responsibility to take care of her, that he was the one who opened the bottle every night, that he was the one who wandered to the other end of the house after dinner to write poetry and finish off any open bottles. I could've told them that he was the one who drove when they went out to dinner, that he drove home drunk, that he drove drunk with Mom in the car, that he drove drunk with Mom and me in the car. I could've told them that I watched them watch me get in the car and said nothing, that no one seemed to notice that Dad would never surrender the keys.

Once, a few weeks before I left for my junior year of college, Mom went on a tear about several of my siblings. I don't remember what prompted it or even much of what she said. I remember words like "thoughtless" and "ingrate" bouncing around, and I remember a coldness that overtook me, that started in my cheeks and slowly spread down to my stomach. I wanted to say something, but what? When my older siblings confronted Mom about her drinking—or really about anything—they were shunned. Shutting down a conversation and shutting out anyone who hinted at disloyalty were among her superpowers. If one of us irked her, we got that look and icy silence. When one sibling moved to the East Coast for a job, she took it personally and waged a decade-long cold war against him. After they confronted her about alcohol, my siblings were banished until the topic evaporated.

Despite a few years of therapy and occasional Al-Anon meetings, I never built the courage to address my parents' drinking. By the time it got bad, my siblings were out of the house, and I was, effectively, an only child, so where they might've felt empowered to speak up (because they had somewhere else to go), I was stifled. I coped the way many children of addicts cope: I repressed my own feelings and learned how to avoid the landmines. But this time, I'd finally reached my limit. I was done with repressing and appeasing. I was done waiting for my older siblings to protect me. I was done waiting for my father to do what he insisted years before was his job. I was done navigating the turbulence between the mother I admired and loved and woman I despised and feared. I remember looking at my fingers on the table, shaking ever so slightly, and the words coming out of my mouth slowly, cautiously, because I knew the wrong word, or the wrong look, or the wrong response, would draw her ire toward me like a dagger to the gut.

When I could finally speak, I told her I didn't want to listen to her talk about my siblings. My parents both gazed at me like I'd missed my cue, read the wrong line, but I continued and said, "When I come home from college, I don't want to have to hear this."

"Well, you don't have to come home."

———————

I loved going to church with my mom. When I complained that I didn't want to be an altar boy anymore, she slyly accepted it, but then talked about what a privilege it was to be on the altar, so close to the Eucharist. (I didn't quit.) Her brand of religion was practical, integrated, and just under the surface of every part of her life. There wasn't a line between church and not-church—like death, church was a part of life. And that meant that she was going to have *her* way with the words. She was always the first among a congregation to rise, the first to kneel, the first to sit. She was the pacer for the whole nave when it came to communal prayers, and just when you thought you understood her, just when you thought she was the model, compliant Catholic mother, she'd throw her own translation into the Lord's Prayer.

"Our Father, who is in heaven," she'd start, prompting the first wince from someone in earshot...*is that the right word?*

"Hallowed be your name." *Why is everyone else saying thy?*

"Your kingdom come, your will be done on earth as it is in heaven. Give us today our daily bread, and forgive our sins," *that's not right*, "as we forgive those who have sinned against us..." *What does trespass mean, anyway?*

"And lead us not into temptation, but deliver us..."

A speaker came to her Catholic, all-girls high school during her senior year and spoke so powerfully and so movingly about the religious life that "half the class was ready to join the convent." The Prioress met with each of the young women to discuss their newfound zeal, and she talked Mom (and most of the others) *out* of entering religious life. The moment reinforced something for her, though; it crystallized ideas like vocation and conscience, ideas that she'd actualize through parenthood and citizenship.

When young Catholics are introduced to the sacrament of the Eucharist, we're trained on the choreography of the event more than the theology behind it, since ontology and transubstantiation are a bit advanced for the seven-year-old brain. At mass one Sunday, a few weeks before my classmates and I were scheduled to celebrate our First Communion in a Mother's Day liturgy, Mom decided that I was ready ahead of schedule and instructed my father to take me back to the sacristy after mass. There, in the liturgical "green room" on a sunny Sunday morning, Father Sullivan gave me my First Communion as my dad rested his hand on my shoulder. When we found Mom back at the car, she looked at me, smiled, took a beat, and then abruptly turned to get herself into the passenger seat. The next Sunday, I joined the line of churchgoers moving up the center aisle, just ahead of my mom and dad (Dad, ever a gentleman, always stepped out of the pew to let my mother and anyone else in tow go ahead of him). I dutifully and in good form received the host (in my left, upward turned palm, my right hand beneath it, as high as my heart, said, "Amen") and turned left, but before I could scan the congregation to see if any of my classmates had seen me receive communion well ahead of schedule, I heard my mom receiving a host after me. When the priest held up the host and said, "The body of Christ," she responded, "I believe."

———————

Though we grew up in a neighborhood with numerous large families, a sprawling brood was still a conversation starter. When someone turned to her in disbelief to confirm, "Did you say you have...*ten* children?" (which people did, and frequently) she'd lean in and reply, with a half-cocked eyebrow, "They're from my husband's first marriage." Curiously, three sisters among the brood didn't seem to surprise folks, but *seven sons*—that was notable. "Well, God gave me seven sons for a reason. Six to carry the casket, and one to say the mass."

I was the seventh son, and by the time I was conscious in the world, it was clear that the first six were not headed to seminary. When I declared myself a religious studies major and took on a philosophy minor, she didn't object in the way that we're told parents are supposed to react to the news of majors that don't obviously and directly lead to a paycheck. Instead, I think she saw a prophecy coming to fruition, and when I'd send papers home for her to read, she'd write back or tell me on the phone, "Well, I don't understand all of it, but you write beautifully." After she died, I found a stack of essays that I'd sent to her while I was in college and Divinity School, and it was accompanied by a note from a friend of hers, a priest, with whom she'd shared my essays. He noted my writing and said something like "you must be so proud" or something else priests say to mothers. Obviously, he didn't understand her intention, that he was supposed to recruit me to holy orders.

After I accepted my first job, a position as a campus minister and religion teacher, she called me and, chuckling to herself, told me about a dream she had. "You were cutting letters out of all sorts of colors of construction paper and making a bulletin board." I laughed, understanding the joke between the words, that all that time devoted to highfalutin academics and ecofeminist spirituality had led to the world of chalk and stickers, and said (with the absurd confidence of someone who'd never taught before but always said to himself, "Yeah, I think I'd like to try teaching. How hard could that be?"), "Oh, that's not what teaching is going to look like for me." Three months later, as I was putting the finishing touches on an overly elaborate bulletin board for the Feasts of All Saints and All Souls, I fumed because she was right.

She always had not *good* but pointed timing. Her mother was buried on my sister Patty's thirteenth birthday, and our dog was put down on her fifteenth. The day before Patty's eighteenth wedding anniversary, Mom declared that she was done, and she died the next day. On the trip back to Chicago, I chuckled, thinking about the end of my sister's wedding reception in the back yard. Once the revelers cleared out, my brother, Joe, my dad, and I were the last three standing. We went to the family room where my dad opened a bottle of Chardonnay. I turned on the TV to find live coverage of the death of Princess Dia...or rather, the Lady Diana.

I didn't say the mass, but during my last visit before she died, we planned her funeral. While *The Sound of Music* was on TV, just before Maria arrived at the Von Trapp manse, she turned to me and said, "There's a song I want at my funeral..."

I fetched my laptop, started a new document titled with her initials, and started taking notes. She had already selected readings and a few pieces of music, and she dictated the words that would be on the prayer cards and in the programs that we'd distribute. She had some very definite ideas—no sad music, no white flowers, lots of color, even where the post-funeral reception would be—but when I asked about a eulogy, she rolled her eyes and said, "Anything that lasts more than five minutes is *verboten*." But who, I pressed, should deliver it? "Oh, you'll all have to figure that out."

I often joke that my mother prepared me for her death from the moment I was born. Whenever one of us gave her a gift, a permanent marker would appear out of the blue and she'd write our name or initials on the bottom. If anyone ever asked, she'd respond, "Well, I don't want these kids to be fighting over *stuff* when I die." I've inherited her penchant for remarking on a song or a reading, "Oh, I want that at my funeral." But that moment, sitting a few feet from each other while Maria and Georg slowly fell in love on the screen, was her final lesson. She approached death with confidence, not resignation. She wanted her funeral to communicate what was important to her and to be a space for the people who loved her to move forward, not to wallow. She knew the line that separated her ken and where her children needed to figure it out. And while I wasn't able to say the mass, planning her funeral together was a gift I never wanted but I'm so glad I received.

The next day, I was due to fly out and prepare for my first weeks as a middle school principal, I waited as long as I could to leave for the airport. She'd taken a nap after lunch but was in a deep sleep by the time I needed to leave. I thought about waiting for her to wake, but I also inherited from her a compulsion for punctuality. And I don't think I could've borne the guilt she would've cast had I missed my flight. So I wrote her a letter and included words that I'd written to her before.

"Thank you for giving me life, and thank you for giving me a wonderful life to live."

II.
TRADITION

---

tradition

Tradition," the first big number in *Fiddler on the Roof*, emerges from Tevye's introduction of Anatevka, the shtetl where the play is set. Instead of describing the village with geographic features or summoning its history, Tevye introduces the (heavily idealized and insanely reductive) roles at the heart of Jewish life, the context for the play's deeper story about cultural change that lurks between the verses of "Matchmaker" and "Sunrise, Sunset." The Papa, the master of the house, "must scramble for a living, feed a wife and children, say his daily prayers." The Mama "must know the way to make a proper home, a quiet home, a kosher home." The Son started Hebrew school and learns a trade while the Daughter shadows Mama, each waiting for the spouse that Papa picks. Encountering the modern world, Tevye's daughters stray increasingly far from the path he thought they were on, and, caught between the conquest of empires and two millennia of targeted persecution, the town and everything it signified crumbled.

Any mention of *Fiddler* typically gets a groan from most folx, even die-hard musical theater lovers, mostly because its songs are so easily parodied, its characters so often exaggerated and inflated to the point of caricature. That's too bad, because it's a show that peeks into change at the atomic level. Right off the bat, it introduces the types that had been constructed and reinforced for generations, and it goes on to show how well and how poorly those types navigated the reality of living. Characters are forced to make choices, and because it's a musical, each choice comes with all sorts of heightened drama. But those are the choices that shape the *rest* of the story, the history that could only be written after it was lived because the reality was too unpredictable and too painful. The sorrowful lilts of *Fiddler's* melodies are reminders of the grief that always, always comes with change.

A key piece of that story, perhaps one that's easily overlooked, is the part played by the daughters. They're comically introduced as beloved burdens on their poor parents, but as each marries and drifts a little further, Golde and Tevye don't just grieve the transition in each young woman's life. They grieve the death of the woman they imagined, the woman who would fulfill and perpetuate the structures that fulfilled and protected them for so long. That woman and the life she lived were gone. Tevye's daughters left not just because they fell in love and that worked well for the script—they left because they no longer wanted to uphold an increasingly decrepit structure.

The essays that follow in this section explore those moments when I, like Tevye's daughters, confronted the structures that confined me and embraced my own agency. If the first section considered the experiences and relationships that shaped me, these essays consider how I took the reins to shape myself. That growth began well before 2020, but the isolation of quarantine gave me time and space to unpack and unlearn, to deconstruct and rebuild, to process and project a path forward. Throughout 2020 and 2021, I found myself frequently returning to Arundhati Roy's essay "The Pandemic is a Portal," published early in the crisis. I returned to the essay not just because of the way she captured the scale of the catastrophe. I returned to the essay because she reframed the pandemic as, among all the chaos and grief, an opportunity and identified the one glimmer of hope that I so desperately needed.

Whatever it is, coronavirus has made the mighty kneel and brought the world to a halt like nothing else could. Our minds are still racing back and forth, longing for a return to "normality," trying to stitch our future to our past and refusing to acknowledge the rupture. But the rupture exists. And in the midst of this terrible despair, it offers us a chance to rethink the doomsday machine we have built for ourselves. Nothing could be worse than a return to normality.

For a world roiling in calamity and for me personally, nothing, *nothing* could be worse than a return to normality. Beyond providing a critical and optimistic lens to understand what's happened in the last couple of years, Roy recognized that our response to the crisis and our desperate search for "normal" was shock-driven, a collective knee-jerk response. The scale and duration of the pandemic overwhelmed any routine's power to steady the decks. Add to that the cultural reckoning in the wake of George Floyd's murder and a divisive and ultimately existentially threatening federal election. As a whole, we didn't know what to do beyond our initial, instinctive response to cling to the illusion of control, and we were hooked on the question, "What is the new normal?"

That was the wrong question. Semantically, it's the wrong question because it's passive. It assumes someone else will figure it out and assents to whatever will happen, as long as there's no disruption in relationships or standards of living. Nothing has to change, and we'll all have a good story to tell about how hard it was. Instead, Roy gave us the *right* question to ask: if, as she writes, "pandemics have forced humans to break with the past and imagine their world anew," what do we want to keep, what do we want to let go, and where do we want to go? Guided by my personal and professional experiences, my pursuit of these questions enabled me to confront one of my favorite phenomena in human culture: tradition.

As an educator, I came to believe that each school is a laboratory for creating culture, and tradition is a significant factor in *how* schools create it. Schools aren't the only spaces in which we create culture, but, in the US, it's a hot spot that is somehow simultaneously under intense scrutiny and severely lacking in resources. As a nation, we have not funneled the resources needed to achieve the kind of world our educational system imagines. Historically, independent schools, where I spent my career, generally seek to bridge that gap—they pop up in response to a lack of quality or accessible educational institutions, or they serve a population neglected by the people in control.

Of course, there's a dark side to independent schools. Often disguised by elaborate, coded, and much-loved traditions, many private schools popped up with less-than-noble motivations. Independent schools have always served as escape hatches for the privileged to retain privilege, both in the early days of the nation, in response to the expansion of mandatory, public schooling, and in response to integration ("White flight" schools). Even more progressive schools whose mission statements profess commitment to social justice and equity somehow miss a basic contradiction: even these schools were founded as escape hatches for the privileged to escape from the automatization of students in the service of industry, the dominant purpose of American education around which our standard curricula and school cultures are designed. Public schools play an essential role in preparing students to contribute to or be trampled by the economy; independent schools give the privileged a chance to ensure they're the tramplers, not the trampled.

American public education was initially rooted in the vision of John Dewey. He imagined a public education system that primarily served to shape citizens, to enable people with the skills necessary for them to participate in a democracy, but, in time, American education was restructured to serve the needs of the industries that dominate the national economy. Wrapped in the myth of the American dream, the attainment of an education—reflected first in a high school diploma, then a college degree, then a specialized master's degree—both promised an antidote to becoming the trampled and completed a necessary step on the road to financial security.

When I bounce this idea off people, that our education system serves industry instead of citizenship, I meet skepticism, typically bolstered by someone's own contrary and anecdotal experience. *Well, it wasn't like that for me; therefore, it can't be true.* In the face of such anecdotes, I pull out the evidence. Take the case of acquiring languages: rooted in European cultural norms, including the university system and the world of academia, the priority for learning a language wasn't to be able to engage in international business or to communicate directly with waitstaff while on vacation. It was about accessing the foundational texts, written in Greek or Latin, that inspired and informed Western culture or about engaging in ongoing intellectual dialogue that required fluency in French and German. Yes, the Eurocentrism of it is problematic, but that's a different book.

Which languages students could study drifted from these highfalutin aims and conformed to the needs of dominant industries (and the perceived threats of rising competitors in the global market). Public schools started emphasizing German in the early 20th century, in no small part a response to the initially economic and later socio-political threat of Germany. Throughout the Cold War, study of Russian was promoted. Spanish became dominant both to reflect the growing population of Spanish speakers in the US *and*, echoing the Monroe Doctrine, to prepare to communicate with/manage a subservient continent. Early in my teaching career, I saw the signs that a new perceived threat infiltrated our earnestly idealistic schools: Mandarin, to prepare to engage with the new superpower on the block. Arabic has appeared more and more—not, sadly, in a culture-wide peaceful engagement with the Arab world but in preparation to battle with and dominate rising economic powers in the Middle East. I won't be surprised when Hindi becomes the language all parents clamor to enroll their students in, should India be recognized as the next economic nemesis and socio-political maverick on the horizon.

Take the case of math. Once upon a time, math was foundational because it developed students' capacity for complex, abstract thinking. Sure, mastering arithmetic was helpful for managing daily life, but math was so much broader than the skills that culminate in a calculator. Math was introduced into schooling to develop logical processing, rational ordering, understanding abstraction and proportion...but industry won out, and the conventional sequence of mathematical studies created a path from the crib to NASA's labs. Mathematical competence has become a new dividing line in careers, and being conditioned as cogs in the machine toward universal domination has become the standard, not the exception among paths to rational genius. It's been a long way from al-Qarawiyinn to the University of Phoenix, and these shifts now prompt an identity crisis for higher education. Do colleges and universities serve academic ideals like the development of critical thinking and observation of our world? Or are they (as most of the marketing suggests) stepping stones toward the retention and expansion of socio-economic power?

It's quite the contrast from the case of the arts and humanities. While language and math have increasingly been valued, the arts, the humanities, and the skills that emerge from them like critical thinking, critical reflection, multimedia communication, and self-awareness, have been demoted. In part, this is because these skills are less-easily and less-clearly assessed by standardized examinations, but I suspect that it's mostly because these are the subjects that promote individuals' agency in creating, consuming, and transforming culture. *That* is as much a threat to the status quo for the American economy as external, rising powers. When funding is tight, these programs get cut first, and even in independent schools where arts and humanities programs thrive, parents are preoccupied with getting their students into Geometry by eighth grade and AP Calculus by junior year. Sure, they love seeing their students' talents celebrated on stages, in concerts, and in galleries. They're proud of their kids' creations, but if they're not on track to Harvard and executive leadership, they double down on the subjects that serve industry and push the arts and the humanities aside.

Many independent schools are founded as alternatives to the Academy of Little Cogs and genuinely intend to shape children differently, to prepare them to work and lead and live with clear values and commitments and passions. Except for a few schools that exclusively educate historically underserved populations, most serve privileged populations and prepare students to retain and expand their privilege. The juxtaposition of idealistic school missions with their shared context (the pipeline that our cultural definitions of education has created) is overwhelming. It's too big of a problem to even define, never mind address, but social and cultural transformation doesn't begin with broad, sweeping statements and ambitious changes. Transformation begins with the little things.

In my first job as a teacher and campus minister in an all-girls, independent Catholic school, I saw and contributed to meaningful change and enjoyed an ongoing education in constructing culture. With the start of each school year, I'd be finalizing the background details of major events and start to build teams of faculty and students to lead the retreats and design our weekly and occasional liturgies. My co-campus minister and I inherited a program that was strong and earnest, but, like all school programs, it got a little stale and needed a refresh to reflect the evolving commitments of both our students and faculty and the culture of the school.

Perhaps unlike the popular image of an all-girls Catholic school, we consciously, if subtly, defied the patriarchal norms inherent in Catholic schools and, whenever we could, enhanced the authority of women. To paraphrase the already badly paraphrased Gandhi, we tried to *be*—for our students, for their families, for the Church and the world—the change we wanted to see. We used language that was gender inclusive and prepared students to serve in roles of visible and meaningful leadership. We introduced or altered practices that widened the lane for conversation, that invited a dialogue or a moment to educate and reflect. We mined the school's traditions for facets that reflected the inclusive consciousness of the world we wanted to create. We gave the ambo to students and staff to deliver reflections in Chapel every week. We couldn't call it a "homily" or "preaching," but we didn't need to. It was evident that the person at the mic spoke from a place of critical reflection and spiritual and moral self-awareness. For the times when we needed a priest (the handful of masses throughout the year), we cultivated a short list of local clerics who knew us, who supported and shared our vision, and who wouldn't report us to the diocese for letting our headmistress deliver the homily or putting students serving as eucharistic ministers too close to action on the altar.

These commitments fueled our design of the retreat program, too. Retreats provided students at least yearly invitations to sit with their experiences, to step away from the routines and pressures of home. Traditionally, retreats intended to encourage pious engagement and get a glimpse of monastic life, but that view was rooted in an old theology, one that centered the patriarchal Church and put us all in various orbits around it. We drew on a new theology, one that put lived experience at the center of our reflection and invited students to look for evidence of their own growth, of the values and relationships they forged.

We offered—but didn't impose—language of the gospel and the Church's social justice teaching to facilitate that reflection. We curated a list of saints who exemplified this theology—not virgins and martyrs but prophets of social justice, even the ones that the Church didn't fully recognize yet, like Dorothy Day and Oscar Romero, and holy people who lived outside the Catholic world completely like Martin Luther King, Jr. and Thich Nhat Hanh. We wanted students to imagine themselves capable of stepping in the shoes of any of these people whose profound personal transformation impelled them to recreate the world.

We never asked students to conform to any particular approach to Catholicism. We tried to respond to the religious diversity of our students, not just box-checking their religious affiliations but also the range of attitudes toward and engagement with religious practice. We didn't make *statements*—we tried to ask questions that all students might want to engage, questions they could use to navigate their worlds. For students who were already deeply pious and even exclusivist in their religious outlook, we invited them to see the roots and practice of their faith in broader ways or from different perspectives. I like to think that we gave students not just an updated portrait but direct experience of a different kind of Church. If none of those thoughtful structures and practices worked, at the very least, they had a gay campus minister, a contradiction that took the shape of a middle finger to the heteronormative Catholic patriarchy.

I had a lot of doubts in those days about what I was doing—mostly because I felt like I was making it up as I went. Sure, I knew a lot of people working in campus ministries and chaplaincies, but I didn't fit into their models. I didn't want to be everyone's therapist and/or savior. I wasn't a cheerleader for Christ. I wasn't Social Justice Guy. I definitely wasn't the campus minister who oozed an "I really wanted to be a priest, but, you know, sex" vibe. Where did that leave me? I wasn't a true *minister*, because this wasn't a vocation for me...a distinction that was very hard to clarify with folx. Many a potential date walked away from me, puzzled that I was basically a professional Catholic but doing shots at eleven-thirty on a Thursday night at ManRay. I was passionate and sincere in my work; it just wasn't a *vocation* in the ministerial sense. I loved my work, but this lack of lifelong calling was the crack in the door that revealed, at least to me, my fraud. So if I wasn't a minister, what the hell was I doing?

Those doubts, shades of impostor syndrome, served as a kind of alarm warning me that I was straying from the path, away from what was comfortable because of its familiarity and despite its inconsistencies with our community's lived experience. Just because I didn't fit into preexisting roles didn't disqualify me from engaging, contributing to, and shaping the tradition. A tradition rooted in decaying ideas and practices is sure to rot, but I wanted my students to be able to cultivate a tradition that continually evolved to reflect the needs and gifts of the people who cling to it. We weren't straying from tradition—we were creating and shaping it. We were facilitating its evolution.

If my career in education responded to a call, it was a call to a life of facilitating. It was precisely *through* the work of teaching and campus ministry that I both developed fundamental skills for facilitating and expanded my comfort zone for and capacity to relate to diverse groups. I learned from the pros (experienced teachers) how to shape groups toward the best, if not always desired, outcome. With teenagers and colleagues alike, I learned how to read people and to see the question behind the question, to listen for the story behind the story. These aren't skills I could leave at work—they integrated into my DNA and threaten to resurface whenever I talk to people. Half-way through telling me a story, one friend turned away from me and jokingly, but pointedly, told me that she felt I was looking into her soul. Another laughed uncomfortably when, after learning of a career that took him farther and farther out into the world I asked with a half-smile and a furrowed brow, "So, what are you running from?" You can take the guy out of the campus ministry office, but you can't take campus ministry out of the guy.

I shared a vision with my colleagues not just of what our students could do and what our school community could be. We shared a vision for how the world could be different, and every mundane task we undertook looked toward that vision, from packing supplies in the van to communal response to sudden tragedy. That, I learned, is how change and transformation happen—envisioning a destination and taking deliberate steps toward it. My work as a campus minister, which has informed my whole career in education and beyond, was largely designing experiences for students to get a taste of what could be and to find a role in, motivation from, hope from that little taste. We enabled them not to just transform themselves; we empowered them to change the world. You may have noticed that not *much* has changed in the world or in the Catholic Church since I started teaching, but that doesn't mean that our work wasn't impactful. Our students carried these experiences into their families, into their religious communities, into colleges and workplaces, and while I won't live to see the cumulative effect of all those ripples, I do enjoy watching the ways they make a mark. One former student is now a leader in the movement to ordain women as deacons, organizing and designing experiences for people to get a glimpse of a radically inclusive Church...and to see their role in it, find motivation from it, derive hope for something new.

———————

When it comes to *Fiddler*, my deepest disappointment is that it depicts change as necessarily and exclusively painful. As a theme, this isn't exclusive to *Fiddler*. How many examples can you conjure of plays, movies, books, and other narratives that present change as a social *good*? Not easy or consistently joy-inducing, but *good*, a moment for growth, for adaptation, for redirection toward the world we really want to live in? I've seen that approach, and in the individual lives and collective efforts of students and teachers, I've seen it sustain and contribute to the transformation of people, communities, and the world.

The swell of pride and emotion I feel when walking through my years as a campus minister and the hope I reclaim that I first generated in that role fizzle a bit when I remember that we were one small school. It's not that I lose hope—it's more that I recognize that change in this direction will continue to trudge, to move at a glacial pace, because so few people are equipped with the tools and vocabulary to facilitate that change—and the patience to change one tradition at a time. Facilitators are the engineers of cultural transformation, but few facilitators are out there, and most of the good ones, including the best classroom teachers, are already underappreciated and under-paid. If we don't want to regress to the "normal" that delivered us to 2020, perhaps the next big language children need to acquire isn't Mandarin or Arabic, or even Hindi. It's the language of facilitation.

chill

"Connection doesn't happen on its own.
You have to design your gatherings for the
kinds of connections you want to create."
                    Priya Parker, *The Art of Gathering*

Priya Parker opens the third chapter of *The Art of Gathering: How We Meet and Why It Matters* with a succinct and unsubtle heading: "'Chill' is selfishness disguised as kindness."

For Parker, *chill* hosting isn't problematic because of the nature of chilling itself or because of its attractive absence of neuroses. It's problematic because it's an abdication of leadership. When this happens, she writes, "You don't eradicate power. You just hand the opportunity to take charge to someone else…You are not easing [your guests'] way or setting them free. You are pumping them full of confusion and anxiety." Sure, adopting an attitude of *chill* might sidestep conflict or the possibility of failure (failure to live up to one's own expectations or others' examples), but it's ultimately self-serving. Parker's advice is straightforward and elegant, if not simple or easy: "If you are going to host, host. If you are going to create a kingdom for an hour or a day, rule it—and rule it with generosity."

I don't typically love appeals to medieval political systems and patriarchal metaphors. I mean, is a "kingdom" even a thing anymore? How many monarchs today actually retain more than symbolic authority over the citizens of their realms? In this case, though, it's an easy demonstration of the kind of power that hosts wield but typically fail to recognize: governing authority. The ancient rules of hospitality are written into our bones, the product of centuries of social convention and psychological conditioning, and at some very basic level we understand and respect the authority of a person or group inside their established boundaries, the authority of a proverbial king (or queen) over his (or her, or their) castle (or condo). When it comes to gatherings, the hosting sovereign sets the parameters, models the customs, acquires and distributes resources, diplomatically navigates the gathered, and anticipates their needs and desires.

And how does the old saying go? With great power comes great responsibility. Parker distills this into three discrete goals for hosts: protect, equalize, and connect their guests. Still, Parker observes, hosts who approach the task with *chill* at the fore shirk their authority and fail their guests. In her analysis, *chill* functions as a safety net for folx who are uncomfortable with holding authority or even acknowledging power dynamics at play. It's a good thing that we live in a time of growing awareness of social power dynamics, but avoiding or denying the power one wields because of discomfort with the topic or with the very fact that one possesses power (especially if it is not earned or deserved) is, at best, disingenuous and, at worst, damaging to one's credibility and relationships.

In my experience, Parker is spot-on, but I think she misses an important companion to power at the heart of the problem: authenticity. It's not just discomfort with wielding power that breeds failed hosts—it's also discomfort with the expectation of fulfilling a prescribed template or mimicking the masters. Who can match the party prowess of Truman Capote or Anna Wintour, the crafty perfectionism of Martha Stewart, the diplomatic genius of Henry Kissinger or Madeleine Albright? Without significant time and practice, who could possibly live up to Parker's own projection of what comes with good hosting? The inclination toward *chill*, especially in an era dominated by stylized and idealized self-depictions in social media, reflects both a fear of failure, of not living up to the standards set by the most popular or most visible exemplars, and a lack of exploration and cultivation of one's own unique capacities and values.

An example that Parker cites to demonstrate the power vacuum that results from abdicated leadership illustrates this authenticity factor as well. In the opening session, Harvard Kennedy School of Government Professor Ronald Heifetz begins his course with an experiment.

> Instead of walking into the room and taking attendance or launching into a lecture, he sits in a black swivel chair in the front of the classroom and stares at the ground with a blank, slightly bored look on his face. Dozens of students sit in front of him. He doesn't welcome any of them. He doesn't clear his throat. He doesn't have one of his assistants introduce him. He just sits there in silence, staring blankly, not moving an inch.

Parker describes students' reactions, moving from a heavy silence and nervous laughter to stilted attempts at conversation and problem solving. After five minutes that seem, to the group, an eternity, "Heifetz looks up at the class and, to everyone's great relief, says, 'Welcome to Adaptive Leadership.'" Stepping out of his prescribed role, he disrupted everyone's expectations and rather vividly demonstrated what happens in the absence of leadership.

Heifetz's practice reminded me of a rather unique experience from grad school. I took a course on group dynamics rooted in a theory of the collective unconscious and how groups, and by extrapolation organizations, formed and functioned. The theory proposes, in short, that any group develops a collective unconscious, that members assume explicit and implicit roles within the group according to their personal valences, and that a group is vulnerable to dysfunction if its most essential aspects—its boundaries, system of authority, roles, and tasks—are unclear or eroded. The theory was (and remains) compelling to me. It resonated as much with my experience as a teacher and administrator as it did with my understanding of ritual and, more broadly, cultural construction. The four essential aspects of group life (boundary, authority, role, and task) constitute a kind of diagnostic tool, a starting point for understanding how (and how well) a group is (or isn't) functioning, whether it's a clique of tweens or the European Union.

Participation in a three-day group relations conference was a requirement of the course. The schedule moved us between sessions with the large group of about 150 people and sessions with smaller groups. The earliest large-group sessions had no theme or agenda. Instead, the "consultants," the conference's leadership team, designed different seating arrangements, giving us a chance to experience and observe what different kinds of proximity and juxtaposition eked out of our collective unconscious. The first and final sessions adhered to a traditional conference setup (a long row of consultants anchored by a center podium, facing straight-line rows of participants), but other sessions' seating variations included scattershot (chairs randomly placed with no attention to flow, direction, or focus), clustering (circles of small groups), and, my personal favorite, a single spiral starting at the center of the room. As the doors were opened, our only instruction was to take a seat. Virgo that I am, I arrived early enough to be able to watch others enter, assess the setup, and then choose how far into the spiral they'd squat. Anticipation about who would occupy the first seat at the center built steadily. *Who*, we wondered indiscreetly, *would have the gall, the gumption to claim the more visible end of the line* (though few paid attention to who might claim the last seat)? After about two thirds of the group was settled, a cisgender, heterosexual, White male took the prime seat (surprise, surprise) to some light applause and nervous laughter.

Instead of a topic to spark conversation in each session, or even an appointed facilitator, we just waited, gave ourselves over to the collective unconscious we'd been slowly revealing, and then…something always happened. Someone was moved to say something—an observation, how she was feeling, a response to something from a previous comment or even a previous session. Some people tried to be funny; some people actually were. Others were provocative, aggressive, even, in their comments. I found myself letting go of any cynicism and self-consciousness, trying to be fully present and open to whatever our collective unconscious needed from me. Despite this, I found myself ensnared in a grudge match with the lead consultant, calling him out among the large group for insensitivities that affronted me and many others in the conference, but no one remembered our sparring matches. Instead, everyone remembered the "big, black cock."

You read that correctly. You see, in addition to my small cohort and other students connected to our university, the conference included various individuals and groups from outside the school, including a cohort from another university who arrived with their advisor, a prominent voice in the academic group relations field and a consultant for our conference. They stood out. In every single session, at least one of them would provoke the group, framing their prodding as committing to candor and honesty or "leaning into discomfort." Because everyone loves being told, "You know what you need to do? You need to lean into discomfort." About half-way through the conference, about half-way through the spiral-seating session, and about half-way through my friend John's comments, one of these provocateurs, seated not far from the center, conspicuously put his coffee mug and notebook on the floor and wordlessly stood atop his chair, executed a full body, vertical stretch, and then just as conspicuously dismounted, picked up his notebook and mug, and returned to his seat.

Still mid-sentence, John was visibly pissed, not because what he was saying was so important, but because of this other guy's obnoxious intent to continue the pattern of disruption he'd already established. He'd already deliberately self-identified to the whole group as Black and as gay with a tone that almost challenged people to ally with or against him. He might've wanted to stir something up, but the unspoken consensus in the room was that he'd gone too far. He was *that guy*, the attention-seeker, the tantrum-thrower. Most eyes were still on John, feigning interest in the rest of his words and poorly disguising our collective disgust and shunning of the provocateur. John finished his comment, and as we returned to now-very-uncomfortable silence, I shared a few healthy eyerolls with friends scattered around the room.

A few minutes later, another member of *that guy's* cohort spoke. A cisgender, heterosexual, White woman, she said boldly and loudly, "I don't know why no one is talking about the big, black cock that was in the middle of the room." Now *I* was pissed. *Did I blink? What did I miss?* She went on, clarifying that she meant the provocateur and expanding her accusation to insist that our collective silence and non-reaction indicated our individual and collective discomfort in the presence of a gay, Black man. She was right to identify our general discomfort, but wrong about its source. Our discomfort stemmed from the sudden shift in the conference. What had started like a Jungian Quaker meeting, inspired by the unconscious instead of the Holy Spirit, had become an overly intellectualized and wildly polarizing *Lord of the Flies*. The incident of the big, black cock didn't just disrupt the session—it profoundly informed our experience in the time that followed. It was a pivotal moment for the entire group, and the emotional intensity of the rest of the conference was otherwise inexplicably high. Some saw the moment as proof that the entire experience was ridiculous; others felt it was a useful catalyst to keep peeling back our individual and collective layers.

A few weeks after the conference, word got around that *that guy's* cohort and their advisor arrived with the intent to disrupt. They intentionally poked and prodded—toward what end? I'm not sure. A group relations conference is a laboratory, a clinical space that enables experimenting, iterating, and testing hypotheses toward gleaning some insight into patterns and functions of human social behavior, but a scientific laboratory depends on controls that ensure the integrity of the data. Any tampering with those controls dilutes whatever might be gleaned and discredits the experiment. In this case, the integrity of the experiment and its data depended on each participant's adherence to the principles of the conference, each participant's commitment to be part of the experiment and not to bend it around their desires. The efforts of these rogue scientists, surreptitiously conducting an experiment within an experiment, didn't completely discredit the experience, though we did yield unpredictable results. On one hand, one might say that they heightened our understanding of the value of ethical adherence. On the other, they demonstrated the vital importance of authenticity and the havoc that inauthenticity wreaks.

While Heifetz's classroom experiment opened his students' eyes to the chaos and power-hunger that often simmer just below the surface of social engagement, the manipulations of *that guy's* cohort demonstrated exactly how social power gets snatched. For Parker's purposes, Heifetz's initial persona illustrated the "bad host," the host whose *chill* has advanced to *frozen,* but *that guy's* cohort illustrated "bad guests." The responsibility for a successful gathering doesn't depend solely on the efforts and forethought of the host; it depends equally on guests' ability to (ugh…here's that patriarchal metaphor again) be good subjects in the kingdoms they visit. That endeavor begins with self-awareness, awareness of what one brings to relationships or to a group and awareness of one's limitations. If a host is responsible for protecting, equalizing, and connecting their guests, then a guest is responsible for arriving with an openness to being protected, being equalized, and being connected.

controversy

I love a good scandal. Especially when it doesn't involve me. And especially when it comes with a healthy serving of schadenfreude. One of my favorite scandals in recent years came from the world of [gasp] professional sports. I know, right? Can you believe it? As *The New York Times* reported, the head coach of the Las Vegas Raiders resigned in 2021 after a trove of his emails surfaced, revealing that Jon Gruden "had casually and frequently unleashed misogynistic and homophobic language over several years to denigrate people around the game and to mock some of the league's momentous changes." Soon after the details were reported, Gruden announced his resignation on Twitter. Like a good twit.

> I have resigned as Head Coach of the Las Vegas Raiders. I love the Raiders and do not want to be a distraction. Thank you to all the players, coaches, staff, and fans of Raider Nation. I'm sorry, I never meant to hurt anyone.

Gruden quickly became a target of all sorts of vitriol. While I typically avoid adding fuel to fires, especially those raging among the cancellers of culture, a couple of aspects of this scenario really rattled me. I won't presume to speak for people who are offended by his derisive use of the word "pussy," denouncement of women referees, or his habit of swapping photos of women with his buds. I won't try to unpack his resistance to politically engaged players or his defense that he "never had a blade of racism" in him. I won't try to diagnose the toxicity that leaks from the intersection of White, cisgender, and heterosexual identities and that bolsters the confidence of people like Gruden who consider their actions unquestionable, their power undeniable, and their privilege entitled. The folx whom those arrows wound can respond from their own vantage points and let us all know how Gruden failed and how we can all do better. Here's what really rattled me: his use of the word "faggot," and the closing line of his resignation, "I'm sorry, I never meant to hurt anyone."

———————————

The first time the word *faggot* was hurled directly at me was my first day of high school. After another freshman grabbed my collar and pushed me against the wall of a stairwell, he spit the word in my face and then walked away. I was one of 1,500 at an all-boys Catholic school with such a big sports program that nearly every academic department included coaches who needed a class or two on their contracts to justify a full salary. My chemistry teacher was the head basketball coach (and because of his public mockery of an already vulnerable and targeted student, I just stopped paying attention to anything he said after I passed our first test on the periodic table). My economics teacher (who spent the first fifteen minutes of class updating us with how his stock portfolio was doing) was an assistant football coach. Yeah, it was a great learning environment for a young musical theater aficionado like me.

> In the emails, Gruden called the league's commissioner, Roger Goodell, a "faggot" and a "clueless anti-football puss" and said that Goodell should not have pressured Jeff Fisher, then the coach of the Rams, to draft "queers," a reference to Michael Sam, a gay player chosen by the team in 2014.

À la Carrie Bradshaw, I couldn't help but wonder, *Did he work at my high school?* While I was initially unsurprised by someone in the NFL being a Grade A jackass (my apologies to the jackass community if the metaphor offends any of donkey-kind), I got stuck on the way reporters in the *Times* and on NPR consistently characterized his offenses as "homophobic." *Phobic? What is he afraid of?* As a word, "homophobia" is wildly insufficient to capture the story it needs to tell. Whether it's effected by an NFL coach or some random asshole in a school stairwell, *homophobia* points to aggression and violence against people because of their sexual identity, not *fear of* them. A semanticist might remind us that an *irrational dislike or prejudice* defines the term, and that calling it a "phobia" only affirms the notion that there is something to be feared. And that is some Jenny Jones "gay panic" defense bullshit.

Am I to be feared? I mean, I don't think there's anything to fear in me or my actions (unless you find yourself in a trivia game that ignites my superhuman ability to quote *Murder by Death*, *All About Eve*, and *The Golden Girls*...in which case, make peace with your god and gird your loins). By treating it as a fear, we perpetuate the fine, American tradition of blaming the victims, and, instead of resolving the source of an aggressive prejudice, we leave the burden on queer shoulders. To attain some hint of equity, we're expected to demonstrate that we're harmless, that we're useful, that we're, you know, *people*. Deprived of civil rights and social acceptance, the dominant thrust of queer activism appeals to heterosexuals' sense of humanity, to trigger their empathy. And when straight people come around to (I hate this word) tolerating or even embracing queer folx, they expect affirmation and applause, whether or not their recognition of our humanity translates to committed allyship and meaningful action.

This tension was brilliantly lampooned in "Homer's Phobia," an episode of *The Simpsons* in which Homer distances himself from a family friend who is gay, voiced by John Waters. With gay panic creeping up his spine, Homer takes Bart on a tour of hyper-hetero activities to negate any influence John might have. His last attempt to straighten up Bart is a trip to hunt bucks at Santa's Village, but when the reindeer turn the tables and attack Homer, it's John who saves the day and inspires in Homer a new-found respect for...John. "Well, Homer," he responds, "I won your respect, and all I had to do was save your life. Now if every gay man could just do the same, you'd be set."

In recent years, some have replaced "homophobia" with "heterosexism." Stripped of any reference to fears, irrational or justified, *heterosexism* reflects the broad imposition of (heterosexual) assumptions that inhibits queer people's lives, liberties, and pursuits of happiness. Unlike its predecessor, *heterosexism* clearly identifies the source of the problem: heterosexuals. I use this term frequently, and doing so helps me rewire the corners of my brain and my soul where internalized prejudice continues to haunt me. To quote Liz Lemon, "Words are the first step on the road to deeds!"

How does it haunt me, you ask? Before I walk into a room of heterosexual people, I tremble. I consciously calm my breathing and remind myself to speak *as myself* (not to summon a deeper, more masculine tone in my voice). I scan the room and look for clues that suggest friendliness and allyship. Except in predominantly queer spaces, I struggle to believe that I belong, that I deserve to be there, that my voice and my input are welcome. As I listen to people speak, strangers or familiars, I dig between the lines to excavate hidden messages or patterns, potential insults to anticipate and arrows for me to deflect. I map out the minefields of interactions that might bruise, cut, or break me. Among strangers, I quickly self-identify as a gay man, whether in subtle gestures or explicit language, to forestall the inevitable remarks denigrating queer people, denigrating me. And, most diabolically, *I actually believe* that among heterosexual people, remarks denigrating queer people are inevitable.

Sure, these are *my* neuroses, but they spawned because of heterosexuals. *All heterosexuals? Really?* Yes, there are enlightened, loving, and justice-oriented straight people. Some of my best friends are straight. But, like global warming, my contemporaries didn't start it, but they sure haven't done enough to stop it. Real transformation begins with discrete, sustainable changes, choices that individual people make. So here's a choice every one of us can make: let's scrap "homophobia" from our vocabulary. Let's avoid hiding behind clinical language like "heterosexism" and call it what it really is: *hatred* given form as discrimination, exclusion, psychological torture, or violence. Modify it as "anti-gay," "anti-lesbian," "anti-bisexual," "anti-queer," "anti-trans," "anti-LGBTQ," whatever applies, whichever group is being targeted, but call it hatred.

———————

Mr. Flanagan was my tenth-grade English teacher. Not a member of the coaching squads, he was an actual expert in English literature and language, a masterful teacher, and an effeminate and fabulous gay man. What he lacked in height and heft he made up in color and flourish. When we couldn't make sense of the forms of modern poetry, distracted by the dispensing of conventional punctuation and grammar, he'd recite the poems with passion, with insight, and with joy. When we weren't brave enough to articulate what we really heard or felt, he pushed us until someone would break through... And if no one did? He exploded. It was scintillating.

"This Is Just To Say"

I have eaten
the plums
that were in the icebox

and which
you were probably
saving
for breakfast

Forgive me
they were delicious
so sweet
and so cold

He read William Carlos Williams' famous verses with intensity...slowing down to punctuate every word in the final stanza. Flanagan followed the last word with a long pause, giving every one of us enough time to figure out that this poem wasn't actually about fruit. Then, suddenly, he slapped his desk and exclaimed, "WONDERFUL!" When he looked around for a response to his question about what the poet was *really* talking about, we resisted, embarrassed (though, whether we were embarrassed to talk about sex or about being able to understand poetry—that was different for each). "Anyone? Anyone?" We all avoided eye contact. "SEX! He's talking about SEX!" he shouted with another slap on the desk. But, for me, the takeaway from that class wasn't that William Carlos Williams wrote poetry about sex. It was that the speaker, despite his gentle, coy, seductive language of apology, wasn't really sorry. I suspect most of the boys in class walked out mildly titillated after twenty minutes of talking about sex and poetry, but I walked out with a new insight: straight men are never really sorry.

"I'm sorry, I never intended to hurt anyone."

As a teacher and school administrator, I got to test a lot of different abstract principles and theories. *If you build it, they will come?* Only if there's free food. *The truth will set you free?* Perhaps, but it also hurts, so you'd better tell the truth with real people in mind. *Teenagers, like dogs, can smell fear?* Yes, yes they can. *Middle schoolers are the worst?* No, no they're not. But one principle got not just tested but proven every day, whether dealing with student concerns, faculty issues, or the all-consuming parent drama (seriously, parents, take the drama out of your children's schools!): *Impact is more important than intent.* From the banal to the seriously tragic, "sorry" was *never* enough, and individuals' or a community's capacity to reconcile and move forward depends on each individual's commitment to understand and address hurtful impact.

The problem with Gruden's apology, as Ryan Russell highlighted in an op-ed, is that it reflects the inaction and performative allyship of the NFL. Instead of exploring the best way to support players and staff when they followed Colin Kapaernick's example and knelt during the national anthem to protest systemic racism, league leaders and owners fretted about the effects on ticket sales. While they praised Carl Nassib for publicly coming out and promised support, they failed to confront or even consider the toxic culture that stops players from coming out in the first place. Gruden's apology fails to recognize his offense or even squeeze-in a vapid promise to *do better* or *work on himself.* He failed to recognize his impact and hid behind his intent.

––––––––––

When it comes to hatred, bad apples fall from rotten trees. Russell rightly criticized the NFL for excluding executives and owners from moral and professional scrutiny ("the real roots of the league's continuing disappointments") and identified the necessary next step: "[C]hange, inside and out and top to bottom. Every decision—from hiring coaches to signing players to funding and creating social initiatives—needs to be made with the serious and intentional desire to be diverse, inclusive and long-lasting." The lens that Russell proposes isn't radical or innovative (it's what my colleagues and I used to call "mission-driven decisions" and "mission-appropriate hiring"), and it echoes the reality that transformation begins in small, direct, and immediate changes—changes that Gruden and others successfully avoid with words like, "I'm sorry, I never intended to hurt anyone."

Gruden never intended to hurt anyone. Neither did the bully who slammed me against the wall in ninth grade. He didn't intend to hurt me—he intended to *intimidate* me. He intended to maintain the power and privilege that he enjoyed and to show me exactly how he would hold on to it. I wasn't part of his calculus—I was just an expendable plebe who happened to be on his path—but for over thirty years, I've lived with and carried the damage of that moment.

But I've also lived with the memory of Mr. Flanagan, who showed me that being a faggot isn't all doom and gloom. Because of the strictures of Catholic school-life in those days, gay teachers couldn't do much to explicitly advocate for us, but they found subtle ways to affirm us, lift our spirits, give us some semblance of hope and safety. They lacked the authority to transform the school's culture, but through their solidarity, they gave us an experience that was better than their own and helped us to love, not fear, ourselves. And Mr. Flanagan, one poem at a time, gave me a life-saving lesson: once in a while, when you read between the lines, you dig up something wonderful.

Dan Savage ruined my life
(it's not what you're thinking)

Within a few hours of the first day of classes at my all-boys Catholic high school in 1990, I realized two things simultaneously: I'm gay, and I'm not safe. The gay part was developmentally appropriate—with limited visibility of LGBTQ people in a generally heterosexist world, it's not surprising that I took a little longer than my hetero peers to understand my sexual identity. Over the course of elementary school, I experienced behaviors that would be called "bullying" today, and I chalked it up to the social dynamics of the community I grew up in. I guess I knew I was different, but I didn't have words to explain why or how. And then on the first day of high school, a classmate forcefully held me up by the collar against a stairwell wall and spit the word "faggot" in my face.

Throughout my high school years, my favorite classes were always my religious studies classes, so I majored in it in college. By the end of college, I was on track with a solid life plan: I would be the youngest tenured professor of religious studies in history. Or something like that. I started Divinity School and quickly got bored with systematic theology, so I shifted my focus to the comparative study of religion which prepared me well for my first job as a world religions teacher and campus minister at a small Catholic girls' school. It's part of a network of schools founded by an order of nuns with a single mission: to make known the love of the heart of Jesus. The school's mission and goals were holistic and notably respectful of religious diversity. I thought, *I am home*. I'd found my vocation—not just teaching world religions and organizing liturgies and retreats, but I had the opportunity to move the needle in the Church, to make my students aware that the Church isn't just the teachings from Rome, but the lived experience of every one of us, even a gay campus minister.

As the school year started and I met my colleagues, I never got the message to stay in the closet or to hide part of myself, but with students, I knew there was a line. There were things I could share with colleagues that I couldn't or shouldn't with students or their families. I thought about my gay teachers in high school (we didn't officially *know* they were gay...but we all knew). Years later, Mr. Austin, my French teacher, one of those teachers whom I'd stayed close to, described a network of gay teachers who identified potentially gay students and kept an eye out for us, like a subversive (and fabulous) cabal of guardian angels. But I also remember that another teacher was fired when an unhappy parent complained about him when he was outed to a group of students. And I remember that, after a few days of murmurs, nobody talked about it. I knew that the line was a good thing for me, and it was an unspoken pact between me and my colleagues. We all recognized that if word got to the wrong ears, my job was at risk—and it would put the school under scrutiny, possibly causing problems for my colleagues and even the religious order.

As an educator, I strived to highlight diverse and balancing voices to give students a rich understanding of their faith communities. My intent was never to bring down the Church; I am far too calm to be a revolutionary. Instead, inspired by John XXIII, who sought to bring in new light and fresh air, to enable the Church to engage the world, not shrink from it, I saw that my job was to help my students open the windows. Whatever the topic, whatever the curriculum, whatever the activity, the goals were always the same: for each student to find ways to understand herself and her location in the world, to be able to see and respond to the needs of others, and for her to have the tools to recognize God's love (or its absence) in the world. I used inclusive language in liturgies and retreats, and I developed programs with my own experience as a closeted and sometimes very frightened student close at hand, always coming back to the guiding mission to make God's love known in the world.

All educators begin from their own experience of being educated, and our experiences as students inform the roles that we play in our schools and with our students. As I began teaching and serving as a campus minister, I thought, *What didn't I hear that my students could hear from me? What couldn't my teachers do that I could do for my students? What did they need to know about me that I could never learn about my teachers?* My own teachers protected us from the shadows, and it was incomplete. I took seriously my responsibility to make—to be—a safe space for my students.

My classroom reflected this: typically, classroom desks were in a circle, but a few comfortable chairs next to my desk, a miniature rock garden to get one's zen on, and a candy drawer provided multiple excuses for students to stop by and strike up a conversation. Each year, I'd get at least one student lingering around my office, seeking opportunities to talk about, well... whatever...and the bell would ring in my head, and I'd think, *Oh, she's coming out. OK.* Sometimes it was the first chat, and sometimes it took a few months. Each found her words in her own time, and it struck me as an honor to be the first person, or at least the first adult, that she could talk to. I had the chance to give my students language that I was never given and reassurance that I never had. As my career progressed, my sense of purpose in life and work had crystallized: I would work to be the mirror and the window for my students and could try to move the needle in Catholic schools.

Then I went to Seattle.

The National Association of Independent Schools holds a conference every year, and in 2012, Dan Savage was a featured speaker. Dan Savage has been giving feedback and advice on a wide range of topics relating to love and relationships for decades through his columns, books, and podcasts. In 2010, Dan and his husband, Terry (like I know them personally), started the "It Gets Better Project," in response to a spate of suicides of queer teenagers. Dan explained that they'd hoped for maybe 100 videos from queer folks who would share their stories of how life got better, but within the first week, they had over 200 videos. Today, It Gets Better hosts over 60,000 videos from a wide range of people, including influential allies. Who could've imagined that the President of the United States would record a video to comfort and reassure queer teenagers who were struggling? Thanks, Obama.

Dan and I have a lot in common. We're both White, cisgender, gay men who grew up Catholic in Chicago.

OK, that's about it. Dan is an engaging speaker, he knows his stuff, and he's got statistics and data at his fingertips at all times. His talk: I laughed, I cried, it was better than *Cats* (the play, not the movie. Everything is better than the movie.). Everyone in the room was electrified and energized, and the wild success of the project was inspiring. After sharing his story, he took questions from the crowd. A woman approached the mic with a written question, and she explained that the person who wrote the question worked at a conservative religious school, and even rising to the microphone at this talk would risk her employment. Everyone in the room clutched their pearls—it was a collective gasp of horror and pity. A wave of collective disappointment swept through the room, like a loud murmur of "Ugh, how awful? How could you ever work someplace like that?" Except for the three of us from the Catholic school; we were like "Yeah, that sounds familiar."

She read the question, which asked something like "What advice would Dan give a teacher like the questioner, who saw herself as a resource and a role model for kids in that community who were closeted or questioning?" She knew they needed an ally, and everyone in the room seemed to nod along like "Yep, that's what we do." This time, the three of us from the Catholic school joined in the reaction. This was one of the reasons that kept us in Catholic schools: we provided an outlet, a safe space, and an alternative to understanding who the Church is. And we wanted to know what more we could do. So the questions stood: What advice would Dan give to a teacher in that position? How could we help our students?

Dan took a moment, cocked his head, and said, "You're not going to like my response." His advice was to get her resumé in order.

We all thought that working in an environment like that was a way to send a message to kids that they were safe, but in reality, he explained, the message we sent was that it's OK to leave part of yourself at the door on the way into work.

I had never thought of it that way. And in that moment, Dan Savage ruined my life.

If I was sending the message to students all those years that it's OK to leave part of yourself behind, what else was I telling them? By this time, the campaign for marriage equality was succeeding in many states and paving its way to the Supreme Court, but with each state that recognized equality in marriage, there were reports of teachers in Catholic schools being fired, of schools and orders under scrutiny and wrangling with local dioceses. I wasn't married, so my sexual orientation wasn't a matter of public record, but what about my colleagues and friends who were married? I couldn't help but wonder, was the Church's stance on gay marriage keeping *me* from getting married? Did I love my job more than I loved myself? Was I complicit with an unjust institution?

After Dan ruined my life, and after a whole lot of discernment, I got my resumé together, and I found a new job that took me to an Episcopal school on the West Coast, and the line of questions that he opened up for me continues to resonate and challenge my path. My first official action as middle school principal was to put up a Safe Space poster in my office. It's a simple act, one that thousands of teachers do at the start of the school year. For me, though, it was empowering, even rebellious. I'd spent over a decade avoiding identifiers that would shine a big pink light on me, thinking this deflection would keep me safe and able to care for the students who needed me, but I didn't recognize that my self-preservation compromised my students' safety. I'd always been proud that students would turn to me for support, but the fact that students had to tip-toe into conversations about sexual identity with me, that there was any question that I wasn't a safe space, now shames me.

Dan also opened my eyes to the ways that I'd been creating safe spaces for students and colleagues but never had one myself. While our straight and cis colleagues were feted in school communities with news of a wedding or a baby, my queer colleagues celebrated privately. We strategized to ensure that news didn't reach the ears of conservative families and a prying diocese. When I got engaged, though, the news was met at my Episcopal school with celebration, not strategy to keep me safe. Yes, I still identify as Catholic. Yes, I'm still on the path I outlined at my Divinity School graduation—I still dream of being a lounge singer with an NPR talk show. And yes, I continue to pursue paths in interreligious dialogue, Catholic education, and queer activism, but now it's with my whole self.

The climate in Catholic schools hasn't changed much, but I have reason to hope. In 2019, a Jesuit school in Indiana defied the order of its diocese and refused to fire a gay teacher. And the Jesuits backed up the school. This is the first time I'm aware that an order stood up to the diocese and the Vatican in defense of its LGBTQ employees. The story of an incoming student at my Jesuit alma mater floated around Facebook—his father pulled all financial support when he learned that the kid is gay, making it impossible for him to go to school. The student resorted to a GoFundMe page to try to cover the cost of tuition in time for the payment deadline. I reached out to the university and shared the post to find out what they knew and how they were ready to help this student. The university was already in touch with him to make it work. And late in 2023, despite resistance in various corners of the Catholic world, Pope Francis opened the door for priests to bless (if not sacramentally marry) same-sex couples. What does that have to do with schools? Well, for the first time in my life, I can imagine a gay couple celebrating a wedding, or rather a blessing ceremony, in my high school's chapel.

But the most profound insights that stemmed from the moment that Dan ruined my life are these. First: when it comes to the Church, it might be getting better, but it's not my responsibility to stick around and make it happen. He helped me to see that if an asshole stubs his toe while kicking me to the ground, I don't owe him a Band-Aid. Second: my identities inform each other. They're woven together. Being gay impacts how I am Catholic and my engagement with practice and spirituality. But being Catholic also impacts how I am gay. And I don't just mean a constant strain of guilt. Catholic faith challenges me to keep my eyes open to the dignity of all creation. It helps me to find and uplift and care for all that goodness. Most importantly, it affirms my full self, as God created it, even if the institution doesn't...yet.

So, Dan, thanks for ruining everything.

grateful

For ritual nerds like me, envisioning the origins of longstanding practices, understanding how they changed, and imagining how they might continue to evolve is a favorite pastime. The roots of most religious customs extend back centuries (or even millennia), so reconstructing their beginnings relies on assembling historical data and reviewing relevant legends and narratives with a healthy hermeneutic of suspicion (in other words, a skeptical lens). Thanksgiving, though, is a rare observance that both straddles the realms of "secular" and "sacred" *and* that originated in recent-enough history that its evolution is well documented and accessible.

Despite this, the dominant narrative of the source and purpose of the holiday has effectively (if not completely) buried competing stories that are less flattering to European colonists and their descendants. You know the deets: Pilgrims and Indians become friends and share a turkey, blah blah blah. It's a narrative that survives not on its own merits but because people choose to retell it, to institutionalize it, to formalize it, and to nostalgize it. It survives because everything from federal, state, and local decrees to second-grade arts-and-crafts projects and the Macy's parade reinforce the myth, deepen emotional connections to it, and blur the lines between fact, fiction, and propaganda. It survives because it projects an America that too many people want to see, despite (or maybe because of) reality.

Recognizing the discrepancy between the Pilgrim myth and

the reality of colonization and genocide has been a very slow burn over the years, and few non-Native Americans, myself included, really understood why Indigenous folx observe a National Day of Mourning instead of Thanksgiving. Twenty-twenty, though, added plenty of fuel to the fire to confront, adapt, or eliminate practices that perpetuate systemic and baked-in injustice. Some encourage Americans to "decolonize" Thanksgiving by debunking the harmful fictions that have been added to the holiday and excavating the truth. One marketing firm, the Martin Agency, even promoted a pithy, six-step guide to decolonizing Thanksgiving: Learn the real story of Thanksgiving; Find out whose land you're on; Ask how you can serve local tribes; Decolonize your dinner; Share a blessing of gratitude; and, Share what you've learned. Others say that decolonizing Thanksgiving is impossible, that its observance is too firmly rooted in the myth, and, if it still fixates on telling or retelling a story about the encounter between Indigenous people and European colonizers, I have to agree.

I think there's a third option, though: scrap the story altogether and excavate the *actual* roots of the observance. Until the Civil War, days of thanksgiving were proclaimed by presidents and governors at various times and in response to various events, but it wasn't until the mid-19th century that the idea of a fixed date for a national observance emerged. During the Civil War, President Lincoln proclaimed the last Thursday of November (a curious designation in itself, no?) as:

> "...a day of Thanksgiving and Praise to our beneficent Father who dwelleth in the Heavens. And I recommend to them that while offering up the ascriptions justly due to Him for such singular deliverances and blessings, they do also, with humble penitence for our national perverseness and disobedience, commend to his tender care all those who have become widows, orphans, mourners or sufferers in the lamentable civil strife in which we are unavoidably engaged, and fervently implore the interposition of the Almighty Hand to

heal the wounds of the nation and to restore it as soon as may be consistent with the Divine purposes to the full enjoyment of peace, harmony, tranquility, and Union."

Lincoln's proclamation, written by Secretary of State William Seward, is a masterpiece of civil theology, tugging simultaneously at the spiritual, moral, social, and heart strings of the American public in an effort to unify a nation at war. Fixing the date and institutionalizing the observance also inspired the creation of a distinctly American harvest observance and invited the projection of what "America" should look like. The legend of a friendly harvest meal shared by the Pilgrims and the Wampanoag provided a convenient, seasonally appropriate story that provided a distinct source and evolved into a nearly sacred story that made European colonization look like a much-welcomed invasion. Perhaps the pinnacle of this projection was Norman Rockwell's famous "Freedom from Want," part of his "Four Freedoms" series for *The Saturday Evening Post* published during the Second World War, but he was neither the first nor the last artist to idealize the observance. Hollywood expanded the ideal and turned it into a day for casual family intimacy: Playing football with Dad while Mom tended to the oven. Tender, memory-making moments and much-loved or much-feared recipes. Important conversations and revelations—every time there's a Thanksgiving scene, you just *know* someone is going to drop a bomb, right? *Grandma, I'm gay. Could you pass the mashed potatoes?*

As a kid, I remember the decor in school shifting rapidly between Halloween and Thanksgiving. Carved pumpkins were replaced by caricatured turkeys. Witches' hats were trimmed and buckled into Pilgrim chic. In kindergarten, we traced our hands and transformed them into turkeys (the thumb gained a wattle, other fingers picked up feathers), and once we could manage scissors and construction paper, we made and wore "Pilgrims' hats" and "Indian headbands."

We learned that the name of our hometown was an Algonquin word, meaning "beautiful land," but we didn't learn anything about Algonquin history, language, or culture. Or the fact that nobody could actually verify the word in any Algonquin dialect. Or the fact that the name was picked by a White woman, the wife of one of the guys who developed the suburbs and economic corridor between Chicago and Fort Howard at the Green Bay.

We learned the name of the people who lived in the area before Europeans, but we never learned that *Potawatomi* was a reduction of the name they used to call themselves, *Bodéwadmiakiwen*. I was seventeen before I learned that the name of my beloved Chicago was itself a French bastardization of the Bodéwadmiakiwen name for the area. *Shikkakua*, which translates roughly to "the place with stinky onions," invoked the wild garlic that grew in the marsh where the Chicago River splits into north and south branches.

We learned about that magical "first Thanksgiving" between the Pilgrims and the Indians, but I was eighteen before I understood that labeling Indigenous people as "Indians" wasn't just a charming quirk of history but a racist, conflationist designation, and twenty-two before I ever heard the name "Wampanoag."

I was forty-four before I realized that my delimited education made it far too easy for me to look the other way in the face of statistics about the poverty of Indigenous communities, about the lack of adequate health care, education, and economic autonomy, about the ongoing lack of access to resources, about the tragic incidence of missing and murdered Indigenous women...in short, about the ongoing consequences of a genocide I was taught to ignore.

———————

My move from Washington, DC, to Washington State in 2015 prompted a cross-country drive and the opportunity to visit places I knew I'd never visit otherwise. I stopped in Welcome, MN, to find Hulseman Street, evidence of my own ancestors who arrived on the plains in the mid-19th century. I stayed a night in Sioux Falls so I could visit my grandparents' graves, part of an extended plot that includes my paternal grandfather's family. I stopped at Wall Drug two hours after the Supreme Court legalized same-sex marriage. Unsurprising spoiler: there were approximately 73,402 types of jerky to sample but exactly 0 pride flags available at Wall Drug. I stayed a night near Mount Rushmore after visiting the monument. I took a scenic route through southern Montana and into Wyoming so I could put my feet on the ground in Yellowstone.

I admit, my intention was a sentimental tour of Americana, but my cross-continental pilgrimage was tempered by a few impromptu history lessons and some very-welcome unlearning. When I needed to find a bathroom, I found myself absorbing the history and culture communicated through the Atka Lakota Museum, and I'd never thought to visit Wounded Knee until a roadside sign caught my attention on the way to Rushmore. Up to that point, the Indigo Girls' cover of Buffy Sainte-Marie's anthem, "Bury My Heart at Wounded Knee," was my sole point of reference, so after I parked I searched for some background on the site. I walked toward a small, fenced cemetery overlooking a mostly empty expanse of grass and was greeted by a guy who clearly spent the bulk of his day waiting for tourists to stumble across the site. He didn't smile, but he was kind, asked me where I was visiting from, asked me if I'd ever been there, and asked me if I wanted to buy a handmade dream catcher for eight dollars. I bought two, mostly to assuage the guilt that was steadily rising in me.

As I passed through the arched gate into the cemetery, he ambled down the hill to wait in the shade for the next visitor, and I fixated on the awkward cross at the top of the arch. The cemetery was long and narrow, bordered by a chain-link fence that hosted a series of scarves or strips of fabric, some quite faded and wind-worn, that lifted and fell with the gusts of wind that would sweep through. Left by people who'd come to honor the dead, like other memorial practices of stacking rocks on gravestones or leaving flowers, they served as a reminder to me that someone else was here first and that I would not be the last. I slowly stepped toward the large marker at the center, a short obelisk awkwardly capped by a stylized urn that communicated to me what I hadn't realized yet, that this marked the mass grave of over 300 Lakota adults and children who died there at the hands of US Army troops in 1890. I was one more under-informed tourist who stumbled onto sacred land and who would leave it behind, follow the highways that crossed the plains, the hills, and the mountains, and pay homage to four dead White men whose faces mock the Six Grandfathers whom the Lakota saw embedded in the rock's formations.

I arrived at Mount Rushmore late in the day, not long before the sun started to set—the air was clear, and the contrasts between light and dark, between purples and blues, between land and sky were dynamic, almost electric. A visitor's center funnels tourists from the parking lot through the Avenue of Flags, a loggia of sorts whose columns are flags from the fifty states, one district, three territories, and two commonwealths that comprise the United States of America. The Avenue ends with a series of plazas and an amphitheater that provide various vantage points and places to sit and contemplate the monument. It's a well-designed space that keeps visitors focused on the mountain, builds momentum, and inspires deep emotional engagement.

Before following the Avenue and descending the plazas, I took a moment to sit on a ledge, in part to take in the view of the mountain and the design of the plazas but mostly to people-watch. And to identify the source of the ice cream that dozens of people enjoyed. I stood out. College kids on a road trip, families on summer vacations, a busload of foreign tourists—most of the people around me arrived in groups, while I was alone, and, except for one promising group of middle-aged women who I was pretty sure were lesbians, my gaydar was silent. Despite being the end of a long day of driving and sightseeing for all of us, everyone seemed irritatingly buoyant and electrified by the national pride in the air. My visit to Wounded Knee, though, inoculated me from the swell of patriotism that seemed to consume the people around me.

I mourned the devastation to the mountain.

I mourned the absence of Indigenous nations among the flags.

I mourned the success of monuments like this that manipulate people's best instincts toward blind patriotism.

At various times over the years, I've heard people call for the removal of presidential faces from Tunkasila Sakpe Paha and closing the visitor's center. I appreciate the intention, but, like "decolonizing Thanksgiving," it's a symbolic gesture whose impact or emptiness can only be measured according to the personal transformations produced. It's a cosmetic makeover that ignores questions of foundational and structural integrity, questions that can only be pursued and resolved when people make discrete choices to reject harmful narratives, to deconstruct the assumptions they've inherited, and to design a path forward. It's not just decolonizing—it's deconstructing and reconstructing how we understand ourselves, others, and the world we share. How, then, might we start to deconstruct and reconstruct Thanksgiving?

First, return to Lincoln's original impetus for instituting a national observance. With fellow citizens quite literally and brutally tearing each other apart, the common ground Lincoln identified was bordered by the all-consuming grief that emerged from "our national perverseness and disobedience," the desperate need for healing, and a common vision of "peace, harmony, tranquility, and Union." Today, Seward's words are startlingly relevant, aren't they?

Second, eschew the harmful narrative. Just stop talking about Pilgrims and Indians. Stop imitating a feast that never happened. Stop. Just. Stop.

Third, lean into gratitude. I often turn to Anne Lamott to remind myself what this means. In *Help, Thanks, Wow*, she writes:

> Gratitude begins in our hearts and then dovetails into behavior. It almost always makes you willing to be of service, which is where the joy resides. It means you are willing to stop being such a jerk. When you are aware of all that has been given to you, in your lifetime and in the past few days, it is hard not to be humbled, and pleased to give back...
>
> You breathe in gratitude, and you breathe it out, too. Once you learn how to do that, then you can bear someone who is unbearable. My general-purpose go-to mystic Rumi said, "There are hundreds of ways to kneel and kiss the ground," and bearing the barely bearable is one of the best.

Gratitude is an essential human response that we've used to repair injuries, to relieve doubts, to inspire joy, to revel in the sacred, and to celebrate human relationships for as long as we've been a distinct species, but it doesn't just *happen*. It emerges when we develop a vocabulary for recognizing and responding to the people, the environments, the resources, and the experiences that shape us. It summons the best of ourselves to the surface. And if we can really return the "thanks" to Thanksgiving, it might even open a door to the peace, harmony, tranquility, and unity we desire.

lead

"Historically, pandemics have forced humans to break with the past and imagine their world anew. This one is no different. It is a portal, a gateway between one world and the next.

"We can choose to walk through it, dragging the carcasses of our prejudice and hatred, our avarice, our data banks and dead ideas, our dead rivers and smoky skies behind us. Or we can walk through lightly, with little luggage, ready to imagine another world. And ready to fight for it."

from Arundhati Roy, "The Pandemic is a Portal"

Amidst the flurry of baking and home projects, and once I ran out of things to watch on Netflix, quarantine gave me the impetus to return to books I'd read long ago. One of my favorites to revisit was *Summer for the Gods*, Edward J. Larson's Pulitzer Prize-winning account of the 1925 trial of John Scopes for defying Tennessee's ban on teaching the theory of human evolution in state-funded schools. I first stumbled across it as a young grad student. Buried in research about the Hays Code (that governed the production of films) and the House Committee on Un-American Activities (the congressional witch hunt that sought to root out communists from the American government), I just could not comprehend how American society could produce and permit such severe regulation of artistic output, foment such fear about people's political philosophies, and just look the other way as thousands of people were marginalized, stripped of their dignity and civil liberties, and derailed from their careers on the basis of propagandic and wildly irrational fears. *That could never happen again*, I surmised. Silly, silly Bill.

Larson's account of the trial was riveting for me—not because of the event's inherent drama that *Inherit the Wind* captured. The trial itself was a spectacle that never intended to highlight the intersection of faith, science, civil society, and public education. Though it prompted some legal debate on the free exercise of religion clause, the trial wasn't a demonstration of extraordinary jurisprudence. Instead, it was a platform for the egos of William Jennings Bryan and Clarence Darrow, a launching pad for a small town trying to get on the map, and a salacious "trial of the century" for journalists whose currency was scoop and sensation. Larson frames the jousting between Bryan and Darrow as the penultimate contest between two great titans and standard-bearers for emerging wings of American culture, fundamentalists and modernists. Not unlike other meta-pissing contests between privileged, straight, cis, White men, the players didn't anticipate (or didn't care about) the fallout. Instead of elevating the national dialogue about civil rights and education, the trial reduced the debate to polar extremes and contributed to increasingly tribal social divisions that now threaten the project of American democracy altogether.

Returning to the book in the context of 2020, I'm more aware of the broader conditions that produced the Scopes trial, a historical context with eerie parallels to our current context. The early twentieth century included a series of wars that tested the imperial and economic reach of Europe and the US and that left the Middle East both impenetrable and vulnerable. A pandemic with contested origins prompted a global public health crisis that was quickly politicized and exposed the chasm between rich and poor. Particular companies and sectors wielded disproportionate influence over American governance and social engagement. Movements emerged to respond to systemic injustice, segregation, and marginalization, to demand rights for women, for immigrants, for people of color, and for economically disenfranchised and under-resourced communities. Panic in response to widespread abuse of an intoxicating substance sparked moralistic debates and wide-reaching reactionary laws and bolstered an underground infrastructure for a shadow economy. And instead of coming together as citizens to discern a constitutional vision for navigating such upheaval, Americans soldered religious, economic, and cultural identities into opposing (and frequently internally feuding) tribes.

We haven't made much progress in the debate between science and religion. Even characterizing it as a debate, I risk reinforcing the notion that they're essentially incompatible. Though most folx are somewhere in the let's-get-along mainstream, the camps are still dominated by extreme and extremely loud minorities: in one corner, the fundamentalist Christians who deny the insights of science, and in the other the fundamentalist rationalists who deny the insights of religious experience. What *do* the extremes have in common? They deny the rest of us the promises of a pluralistic democracy. Social media gives us front-row seats to the ways these convictions seep into and poison discrete relationships. Established friends, respected colleagues, and loved family members now sling accusations of idiocy at anyone who doesn't support their full platform. Folx who once sought common ground with each other now wish all sorts of immediate and ultimate harm on each other. Maybe these extremes were simmering just below the surface the whole time—they emerged in the 1920s and are breaking through again. I just didn't anticipate the ways vitriol, rabid, and easily triggered hatred, and the dissolution of trust and optimism would come with a global crisis. I couldn't have imagined that nationalism that would roar so hideously from different corners and seek out exclusive—not common—ground.

This is a lot to take for an introverted optimist, but I'm buoyed by a couple of things. First, I'm critically aware that we've been taught or conditioned to accept inevitability, to believe that history is history because it was inevitable. In the family of cynicism, inevitability is a sibling to fatalism, that all-too-attractive beast who spawned hits like "Everything happens for a reason," "It is what it is," and "There just aren't enough workers." Each of those quips seeks to soothe us, to help us let go of the problems of right-and-wrong that nag and haunt us. I've adopted an alternative to inevitability: agency. I recognize and emphasize that we are equipped with the capacity to name our experiences and understand how they impact the ways we navigate the world. This makes it easier to counter the inevitablists with nuance: "Everything happens because someone made it happen," "It is because something else was," or "There just aren't enough workers who will degrade themselves for unlivable wages and undignified conditions."

Second, I've had a front-row seat to meaningful and visible change that has the potential to veer us away from cynicism and away from combative tribalism. I've been engaged in a fascinating dialogue between leaders in higher ed, health care, and business to discern what Glenn Llopis characterizes as a shift from the dominant ethos of *standardization* (that sacrifices humanity to the gods of efficiency and profit) toward one of *personalization* (the radical notion that the person is the starting point for constructing the systems and structures that help us navigate the world). Llopis prompted this dialogue well before the pandemic consumed us and the deaths of Ahmaud Arbery, Breonna Taylor, and George Floyd enraged us, but the experience of 2020 only magnified the need to reconsider the world we've constructed. That reconsideration means examining and clarifying the purpose of each industry, of each organization, of each individual.

At Llopis' third Leadership in the Age of Personalization Summit, he kept returning to five questions to facilitate our reflection and ability to identify and effect needed changes: Who do you let in? How do you see those you let in? Who do you let them be? What do you let them do? How do you let them do it? In the dialogues that proceeded from these questions, I kept returning to agency, mindset, and purpose. I heard, across sectors and across different individuals' experiences, consistent hunger for reclaiming the human aspect of work (agency), for reframing how we and others understood our missions and capacities (mindset), and for charting a meaningful course toward ethically sound and sustainable desires (purpose). Some folx shared insights that should've been obvious to all of us ("If you're not evolving as an individual, you're not capable of evolving anything else"). Some shared experiences that demonstrate and amplify a call to recognize that difference is the norm, not the exception. Some used their wit to reveal deep wisdom ("Never had a fight that a calculator can solve" and committing to move away from the world of "male, pale, and stale").

One question from that dialogue lingers for me: How do you ask others to bring their authentic selves to work when you don't know who they are? This taps into my experience as an educator. I really saw the most fundamental purpose of my work as inculcating in students the skills and language they needed to recognize their and others' gifts, limitations, and needs, but the reserves of energy and motivation that I relied on dried up because I wasn't able to bring *my* full, authentic self to work. *How can I ask students to be their fullest and best selves when I've chosen to leave part of myself at the door?* This points to a related question that leaders need to address: How do you ask others to bring their authentic selves to work when you don't know who *you* are? It's too easy to hide behind abstractions like "the great resignation" and avoid making the changes (and the sacrifices) necessary to really make work person-centered, to really make schools student-centered, and to really make health care patient-centered.

In 2023, Llopis invited me to offer a keynote at the fifth Leadership in the Age of Personalization Summit. Resilience was the focus of the conference, and I found inspiration in the most important cultural moment of the last forty years: Beyoncé's *Renaissance* album. The album is a love letter to the LGBTQ community which spawned House music and the Ballroom scene, and Queen Bey collaborated with a number of iconic queer artists like Kevin Aviance and Big Freedia. Specifically, though, the moment I focused on arrived with "Break My Soul," an anthem floating over the bassline of Robin S' "Show Me Love" about surviving and even thriving in a world that isn't made for you. Six weeks after the single was dropped, "The Queens Remix" of the song appeared, floating Beyoncé's lyrics over "Vogue," marking the first public collaboration between Madonna and Beyoncé. In the original version of "Vogue," Madonna recites a litany of classic Hollywood stars, but in this remix, Beyoncé recites a new litany, starting with "Queen Mother Madonna" and going on to name twenty-nine Black women musicians and the legendary houses of the Ballroom. In the realm of pop culture, this was a revolutionary moment.

Before and after Stonewall, queer people of color had been excluded from not just the White-dominated world and straight-dominated world but also from the White-dominated gay world. So they created their own scene, including the Ballroom, which included competitions between the Houses in various categories and a distinctive style of dance—voguing. Voguing emerged when dancers strung together the poses of models and classic Hollywood stars, the ideals of White beauty, but by inhabiting and reinterpreting those poses, they deconstructed the power held in those images and empowered themselves, if just for a moment on the dance floor.

By the late 1970s and early 1980s, Ballroom culture started to spill out of its enclaves, around the same time Madonna emerged as an artist in NYC. When "Vogue" came out in 1990, she was already a global pop phenomenon, and from the start she used her platform to highlight marginalized groups, including LGBTQ folx and people of color. "Vogue" intended to shine a long-overdue spotlight on the artistic genius of the Ballroom with a song uplifting the dancefloor as a model for empowerment in a world not made for you. It catapulted Madonna even farther into the stratosphere, but the folx in Harlem were left out of the profits she reaped from that success. Worse, instead of revering and honoring the creators of the Ballroom, "mainstream" (aka White) culture attributed the whole idea and dance form to Madonna. Over thirty years later, Beyoncé wrote the next chapter of this story. She retrieved Madonna's original intention, but instead of honoring Hollywood glamor, the ideal of White beauty, Beyoncé honored both the Black women who paved the way for her and the Legendary Houses that inspired Madonna, Beyoncé, and thousands of others. What unites all of this—the Ballroom, "Vogue," and "Break My Soul"—is a powerful insight at the core of each: how to survive and thrive in a world not made for you.

"Break My Soul" gave me new language to understand my own burnout. After leaving Catholic schools behind to work as a middle school principal in an Episcopal school, my mom died two days before school started. My sister died a year later, and four months after her and after a long decline, my dad died. Meanwhile, alone in Tacoma, I'd wake at 5am to be in the office early so middle school parents could dump their burdens on me, and I'd stay late most days so my colleagues had plenty of time to dump their burdens on me. I lost 30 pounds from anxiety and sleeplessness, but everyone told me I looked great. My safety net of family and friends was thousands of miles away. My soul was broken.

But then I fell in love with someone who reminded me to be kind to myself. He opened a door, and I catapulted through it. After resigning, I took a year off to heal and figure out what would come next. With distance, I realized that I had built a career of making safe spaces for others, but never had one myself. With that insight (and a lot of yoga and mindfulness, and a thriving relationship), I was ready to do things differently and build work around me. I returned to my first love, ritual, and my work is now focused on creating different kinds of safe spaces and transformative moments that make people really happy: weddings. But I work from a safe space, too, and draw on my unique mix of experiences and expertise to make the process meaningful. I tell clients that a wedding is an opportunity to change the world—they don't *have* to perpetuate outdated, misogynistic, heteronormative, classist, and racist practices just because they saw it on Pinterest or because their parents or the Wedding Industrial Complex told them to do it. By creating a ceremony that reflects *their* experiences, identities, and values, they can give the people they love a different idea about what a wedding can be. That creates a ripple effect, hopefully toward creating a world where our practices and institutions look like us, not where we conform to old structures.

After a career of adapting my life to work, now I can adapt work to my life. Sometimes, I still don't know what to do with all this freedom, and I find myself panicking that I'm not doing enough, that I'm not doing it right. Those instincts don't go away quietly, but they don't diminish the freedom and self-possession I feel and the confidence and creativity that are unleashed when I can lean into *my* vision, mission, and strengths; when I can freely identify and bring a queer lens to my work; and when I can set my own schedule and build my calendar around important events in my life—events I used to give up because of work, like holidays, vacations, or Beyoncé and Madonna concerts. Recognizing that freedom has given me an unexpected gift: a bolstered capacity to bounce back.

I was able to make this professional transition because I could afford to do it (and because my husband has amazing health insurance). I'm also White, cisgender, and educated. While I experience discrimination and hatred because of my sexual identity, I still enjoy a whole lot of privilege in this world. Most people are stuck in the world of standardization without the kind of access, stability, and supportive professional networks that I have. Most folx depend on traditional models of work for access to things like, you know, food, shelter, and health care, so they depend on others—leaders, power-wielders, influencers—to make those changes.

The changes needed and desired in society begin with the changes needed (and not always desired) in individuals who hold the reins. In "The Pandemic is a Portal," Arundhati Roy framed the pandemic as a tragedy and, importantly, as an opportunity to shed the layers we need to shed and shape the world we want to live in, fueled by a newly magnified awareness of our grief and vulnerability, of the fragility of our lives and our planet. We can rebuild the world into a better one—not perfect (is "perfect" really a thing?) but one in which we do not devolve into tribes, in which national conversations are not driven by pissing contests among the stale, pale, and male set, in which we start with the *person* to build our homes, expand our common grounds, develop our industries, and construct our worldviews. We just have to dismantle the hurdle of inevitability, reinforced by reticence and our grips on power. Leadership limited to telling everyone else what to drop and what to pick up won't dismantle that hurdle—intentional, personal transformation will.

travel

Once upon a time, I racked up frequent flyer miles on multiple airlines and stamps and punches in my passport. I navigated airports with ease and confidence, and I judged people who fumbled their way through the security screening—subtly, though probably not as subtly as I imagined. I prided myself in the efficiency and forethought of my packing. I honed an instinct for finding the best pre-flight Bloody Mary in each airport I frequented like I was a dowsing rod in human form.

As a young teacher, I'd wrap up the school year and traipse off to another part of the country or the world. I once spent a month in Italy, bouncing from Milano to the French border and down the coast as far as Assisi before looping back for my departure from Malpensa. Another year, my mother's plan for a full-family photo prompted a big gay road trip with two friends from Boston through Canada to Chicago and back. After a vacation to Czechia with my partner at the time, he flew home from Praha and I hopped a train to start a three-week journey through northern Europe and Scandinavia during which I bought the cutest shoes I've ever owned in Oslo, met a very charming Bosnian in Göteborg, and realized while standing before a Rembrandt at the Rijksmuseum in Amsterdam (after a visit to a coffee shop) that I really wanted to be single.

When I learned how to order something in the local language, I'd commit to finding the best one in the region—both to be able to tell people "I discovered the best *pain au chocolat* in Paris" and, in case I couldn't pronounce anything else correctly, to ensure that I'd have at least that thing to eat. *Prendo gli gnocchi al pesto e un bicchiere di vino bianco* fed me for a week in Liguria. Though I really wanted something with vodka or whiskey, I drank a lot of øl in København. Sometimes I'd get cocky and decide I didn't need a translation. *Yeah, I know enough German*, I thought one afternoon at a sidewalk café in Berlin, and I ordered a coffee and a slice of cheesecake. The server covered his smirk with a smile and returned five minutes later with a bowl of rice pudding that must've been from the *kindermenü*. For the rest of the trip, I dined with my new best friend, my German-English dictionary. Oh, but I really did find the best *pain au chocolat* in Paris.

When it came to accommodations, I strayed from the well-worn paths of hostel-hoppers and Rick Steves devotees in favor of stumbling onto (and, frequently, into) quirky, unusual settings, though I never knew where on the spectrum from luxury to basic shelter I'd be sleeping. In a pie-shaped room in San Remo, I slept in a twin bed with a tiny table on one side and a toilet on the other. My hotel in Milano was a modernist's dream—concrete floors and walls, a bathroom entirely covered in copper, and a bed, the only piece of furniture, in the middle of the room—while a room in Roma made me feel like I was in a period drama about the Borgias. Each room at my hotel in København was designed by an artist. Mine was about 180 square feet (16.7 square meters), featured a lovely, tall, east-facing window, and was painted WHITE with black and bright yellow (like, the yellow you see when you look into the sun) accents. I didn't sleep for three nights. I knew enough to walk away from the "upscale hostel" in Genova where the reception staff definitely weren't doing something highly illegal. I also knew enough to trust the charming old woman in Assisi who didn't speak a lick of English (nor I a lick of Italian beyond ordering gnocchi and a glass of wine). She was the only one home when I arrived, and, with a smattering of words I sort of understood and animated expressions I definitely understood, *signora* led me out of the medieval house that hosted her family's little B&B and up the steep cobblestone to the other medieval house that included my room. She returned an hour later with an espresso and a pastry, and the next morning's breakfast nearly made me weep (it was... so good).

Travel isn't always a fairy tale. The farther I traveled, both geographically and metaphorically, the weaker my instincts for self-preservation and cultural engagement, which I thought were so well-honed. When I arrived in Milano for the first time, my passport slipped out of my pocket. Later that day, a note from a mysterious stranger was left for me at my hotel. I called the number provided and arranged to meet him in the café inside a metro station nearby to retrieve it. A trio of *ragazzi* who kindly offered to direct me to my destination in Firenze picked my pocket; that they only snagged a map of the city and twenty euros was little comfort. Somewhere in southern Germany, I stepped off a train for some fresh air, but as I closed my eyes and inhaled, the train slowly pulled away (with my bags and passport). I lost a debit card and sixty euros, including the taxi fare to return to my hotel, to a cute boy on a dance floor in Berlin who got close, emptied my pockets, and disappeared into the crowd (I only realized what happened when I slipped on my driver's license, which he kindly left behind). While walking the Via Dolorosa in Jerusalem, a group of Palestinian children spit on us and tossed little pebbles at us. Deciphering the maps, ticketing, and routes of the Tokyo subway system sparked in me a complete meltdown in Shinjuku Station. In Taipei, our Taiwanese friend didn't understand why another American Bill and I were startled to be disrobing for full body massages in the same room. With a look that communicated, "Well, this might as well happen," we proceeded with an unspoken understanding that what happened in Taipei would stay in Taipei. And worst of all? Pigeons. A battalion of *piccioni* divebombed me as I exited the cathedral in Lucca, one brief battle in a lifelong war with the species.

With time, perspective, and a little empathy (except for the pigeons #godsmistake), nightmare scenarios evolved into good stories that highlight my sporadic ineptitudes and the unpredictable and overwhelming kindness of strangers. The fella who returned my passport was friendly, but anxious about bringing the found passport to the hotel or the police. "Because I'm Arab," he explained. "Arabs aren't treated well in Italia." That train in Germany only stopped when a stranger planted across the aisle on the journey saw me stranded on the platform and ran for a conductor to halt the train. A sympathetic woman outside the club in Berlin gave me a cigarette and five euros for a taxi. After softly but directly reprimanding the spitters, our tour guide described the degraded conditions under which Palestinians lived in their ancient capital. A commuter who saw my panic at Shinjuku helped me with the ticket kiosk and pointed me in the right direction. That massage strengthened our friendship, bolstered our comfort and trust in each other, and wasn't the last time we found ourselves naked together (relax—a few days later, the hot springs resort we visited restricted all clothing in the pools). After describing the avian assault I'd survived, the host of my B&B in Lucca laughed with me and recommended the squab at a local restaurant.

I'd been warned firmly and repeatedly by French teachers over the years of the "Ugly American" stereotype. Showing us slides of his many travels during one of our Friday *jours culturels*, our weekly slideshow tours of the Francophone world, Monsieur Austin described the engineering hidden by the soaring arches of a church and the magnificent colors of its windows. "Oh, look," he said, pointing out the McDonald's burger wrapper crumpled on the street in front of the cathedral, "an American has been here." At home, I might carelessly leave trash in my wake, but, mindful of Monsieur's disdain and fueled by a lifelong reliance on obsessive-compulsive behaviors, I developed a habit while traveling of minimizing my waste through a kind of nervous origami. I'd trap crumbs and residue inside used napkins or wrappers and tightly fold them into strips that could be folded into bows or knots and store them in a pocket of my bag or shorts until I could find a proper receptacle. Nowadays, during our occasional nosh from the Starbucks drive-thru, I catch my husband looking at me with a mix of wonder and deep, deep concern, while I mindlessly fold and twist straw-wrappers and napkins and pack them Tetris-style into a single bag. Travel changes a person.

When we got married, my husband and I ventured to Arizona (for the wedding), to Florida (to board a cruise through the Caribbean), and returned to Seattle via Philadelphia where, thanks to a missed connection, we got a bonus night in the City of Brotherly Love. Instead of squatting at the airport and agitating for an earlier flight, we interpreted our delay as a wedding present from the universe and spent the afternoon at the Philadelphia Art Museum. Soon after we returned home, though, we started hearing news that a mysterious and dangerous virus was spreading quickly around the world. In the previous month, we'd been on every possible form of transportation (well, except for helicopters and rickshaws, but pretty much everything else). We'd moved through every kind of public setting in multiple regions around the continent. We mingled with people from all over the world. *It's a virus? How is it spreading? Is it still hypochondria if I think I'm really sick?* The muscles and instincts I'd developed through decades of delightful (and privileged) travel quickly atrophied. Airports, once an infrastructural reminder of our immediate connection to a world only imagined by my ancestors, once a symbol of the progress of the industry and interdependence of our species, once a happy place that promised both escape and return, suddenly presented the worst possible threat to my physical and emotional well-being. *Will I ever travel again?*

Yes. Sure, I'll travel again for necessity (to visit family, to see friends, to connect with colleagues…) and for pleasure. On this side of 2020 and in this phase of my life, though, I appreciate travel not because of where I've been but because of who I've become because of it. Each experience of travel changed me—actually, each experience of travel gave me an opening to change, to shed a layer I wanted to shed, or to develop a new habit. Each experience set me before a mirror to see plainly and clearly my strongest skills and my biggest blind spots. Each experience gave me the chance not just to know myself better but to like myself a little more.

I didn't change just because of my proximity to beautiful and interesting places. This isn't the inevitable product of travel—plenty of people journey thousands of miles each year and don't see a mote of growth. Changes in me were the result of my experience of vulnerability, of being the foreigner, the stranger in a strange land. It humbled me and, stripped of language and constantly fifteen paces behind local cultural expectations, left me with nothing but my capacity to connect with other people. As much as I relished solo travel, it was never an isolated experience. If I overcame debilitating fears or self-doubt, it was only because strangers along the way recognized and responded to my needs with open minds and open hearts (and, sometimes, open wallets). They didn't know it, but each led me one step closer to my best self. I'll travel again because I still have work to do, layers to shed, and habits to perfect. And because I want to find the best red bean bun in Taipei.

witness

I made a mistake. Instead of going directly to City Hall, the starting point for a demonstration against the Russian invasion of Ukraine, I got off the bus near Seattle Center, thinking I'd intersect crowds, or at least handfuls, of people preparing the outdoor amphitheater for the rally, the culmination of the mile-and-a-half march from City Hall. No one was there beyond the typical smattering of tourists and the locals managing, feeding, and entertaining those tourists. *I've made a huge mistake*, I said to myself à la Gob Bluth. *Now…which way to City Hall?* I didn't know Seattle well enough yet to travel by instinct. Instead, I pulled out my phone, found City Hall and my location on the map, and started walking. I was tentative, not sure which of the avenues the march would follow. Then a blur of blue and yellow flew past me, and I exclaimed to myself, *Follow those Ukrainians!*

I found myself working hard to keep up with a family, a pair of brothers who led the group at a brisk pace, each cloaked in a Ukrainian flag and carrying a wooden pole that draped another oversized flag, followed by a woman married to one of them and their two tweenagers. As we waited for the light to change, I asked the woman if I could take a photo of her daughter's sign, and in lieu of saying "yes," they just snapped into a practiced pose. The daughter lifted her handmade sign, a piece of blue cardboard with letters drawn by lighter markers pleading "SAFE THE WORLD FROM NUCLEAR WAR." Her brother turned out slightly, framing one side of the earnest and misspelled message, and their mother grabbed the flagpole from her husband and framed the other side.

Within a couple of blocks, I realized that I'd found myself in a privileged position. Following them, I was able to take in the reactions from passersby. As we marched briskly forward, some other pedestrians reacted with smiles and cheers, drivers with honks of their horns or shouts from their windows. Such impromptu enthusiasm and camaraderie made the ones who didn't react somehow conspicuous, somehow suspicious and complicit in their silence.

I felt like a volunteer staff photographer, keeping a minimal distance in their stead and snapping pics of the bright blue and yellow flags as they flapped through downtown Seattle. We neared an intersection, and the red light allowed my adopted family to merge with two other families waiting to cross. They greeted each other with familiar hugs and bright expressions, and they continued the trek to City Hall, where they'd merge with hundreds of other families, hundreds of other flags around shoulders and on improvised flagpoles, hundreds of signs made by children's hands.

Walking at a slower pace as we approached them, two women found themselves immersed in the group, visibly delighted with being surrounded by these overnight activists and just as interested as I was in the kids' signs. When a passing driver honked and shouted support, the group waved in thanks and cheered back at him. I caught the two women sharing a smile, feeling the same thing I was: happy, inspired, relieved that people cared.

————————

Why do we use raw noise to show our support? Think about it—the applause that Lady Gaga lives for is just us slapping the most percussive parts of our bodies to make loud sounds. We shout indiscernible and etymologically curious phrases like huzzah, yahoo, yippie kay yay, hoo-ah. The greatest demonstration of support is a standing ovation, which pushes the applause and the shouting to the max. When performers perform, when the defeated rise, when we are filled with so much joy or rage or determination, we jump up, stamp the ground and clap our hands, we scream. It's primal, isn't it? It's one of those primal instincts that, even after a couple of hundred thousand years, Homo sapiens are still reduced to when we know wonder, when we stand in awe, and when we want what we don't have.

When the proverbial "they" said that history repeats itself, I didn't think "they" meant it would happen during my lifetime. Most of my understanding of history was shaped by my undergrad experience, particularly my exploration of the history of anti-Judaism, antisemitism, and the Shoah, and one insight from those studies continues to shape my worldview: persecution is cyclical and predictable. Political, economic, social, or natural calamities are always followed by persecution of people on the margins. They either get blamed for the calamity, or they are identified as competition for resources; either way, they're degraded and dehumanized, making it easier, more palatable and socially permissible to isolate them, to make them bear the brunt of collective rage, or to eliminate them. In medieval Europe, anyone deemed an essential outsider was especially vulnerable in the wake of volcanic eruptions, outbreaks of plague, or agricultural blights. With the Renaissance, Enlightenment, and Modern eras, that instinct, an extrapolated mob mentality, just morphed into institutions and systemic oppression. To me, the most disturbing and irrational examples are the vicious fictions of "host desecration" and "blood libel," but I was always struck that Jews suffered these accusations—and often official prosecutions and unofficial, mob-fueled pogroms—in the wake of some other disaster.

Knowing where the patterns and cycles of anti-Judaism and antisemitism led, recent history makes me very nervous. Minority groups with recently achieved visibility, status, and legal protections in the US have been under fire from groups on the social and political "right" (and I use the term very narrowly). The most vulnerable among the most vulnerable are targets for slow but steady erosion of hard-won rights. Six decades since the Voting Rights Act, African Americans and economically disenfranchised people are targeted for political isolation through gerrymandering and disruptions that make it just that much harder to vote. Fifty years after *Roe v. Wade*, diabolical and long-term political strategies secured the erosion of women's legally protected autonomy over their bodies. Five decades after the Stonewall Riots and almost a decade since *Obergefell v. Hodges*, queer people might be able to marry, but access to and equity in employment, housing, and health care is, at best, dangerously inconsistent. Now, activists on the right have fixed their crosshairs on transgender folx and drag artists, the most vulnerable among the most vulnerable, and using children as the first hurdle in a culture war. Just more than a century ago, an influenza pandemic killed 50 million people; now, we've emerged from a pandemic that has already killed nearly seven million. What comes next?

In terms of the achievement of human rights around the world, we've come a long way, but to assume that those rights are secure and irreversible is hubris. In Jewish history, the late 18th century is characterized as an era of emancipation because, country by country, Jews achieved full citizenship in most of Europe—an unimaginable feat just a few generations previous—but with the dawn of the modern era and the rise of the nation-state, Europe also cultivated the language and institutionalization of pseudo-scientific racism. What had been hatred of the religious other (anti-Judaism) became the dehumanization of an entire group of people according to the construct of race (antisemitism), and when Europe experienced the collective fallout of a global war, pandemic, and economic depression, Jews were once again—but so much more—vulnerable. Spikes in what we'd now call "hate crimes" and gradual legal disenfranchisement, all justified or at least normalized with the language of science, paved the way for Nazis and their collaborators to isolate and eliminate Jews, Roma, Sinti, disabled people, homosexuals, and political opponents. Through this lens, if Putin's invasion of Ukraine echoes Hitler's invasion of Poland, things portend especially badly for folx on the margins.

When we neared City Hall, a detail of police on motorcycles was ready to go, waiting for the cue to slowly move forward and secure the path to Seattle Center. I stopped and waited on the curb, letting my little adopted family disappear into the swarm of people assembled behind a blue banner with yellow letters, announcing WE SUPPORT UKRAINE. I watched most of the column pass me and tried to take in all of the messaging, all of the emotion, all of the solemn rage.

I slipped into the crowd, steadily moving toward the Space Needle. Everyone wore some form of blue and yellow, many held homemade signs. Some showed up with friends, some as family units. I noticed that I was different from most of the solo flyers, who had *cameras* (real cameras, not just smartphones) and darted up and down the column, seeking out powerful and provocative statements. I guessed most of them were journalists or professional photographers eager to document this particular moment in history and found myself suddenly paranoid. *Do they think I'm a spy?* I was just a guy walking along in the crowd. I don't look Ukrainian. I carried no sign or flag. *Did anyone notice my blue sweater or my yellow socks?* I joined in chants I could understand and smiled politely and supportively when the group slipped into Ukrainian. *Maybe I should've brought a sign.*

NO FLY ZONE!
HELP UKRAINE!
STOP THE WAR!

———————

At one intersection, loud and aggressive honking came from traffic stopped on either side, but the honks didn't seem to conform to the light and rhythmic honks from earlier passersby that seemed to say, *We're with you!* These honks sounded more like, *What the fuck?* Marchers only responded with smiles and cheers in response, either unaware or unbothered by the possibility of the collective passive aggression of Seattle drivers. I remembered a demonstration in New York against the war in Iraq—I was shopping in the Flatiron District and delighted to see a parade of protestors coming down Broadway. When I realized that they'd momentarily be blocking my path, with full shopping bags in both hands, I darted across the banners at the helm. Once across, I felt an immediate pang of shame. *They gave up a day to demonstrate and stop traffic in Manhattan*, I thought. *The least, the very least I could do is to stop for two goddamned minutes to listen, to watch, to think…*

We approached the Giant Red Twin Popsicle, marking the final stretch of the march. The night before, I'd thought about finding a Pride flag to carry to show solidarity with LGBTQ Ukrainians…but I forgot. I flipped through the photos I'd taken, I looked around, hoping to find one or two Pride flags: nothing. I checked my gaydar: nothing. I couldn't get *too* judgy, though, as my great attempt to communicate solidarity was to carry a Pride flag. Lackluster at best, and I forgot. *Where are the gays?*

I'd heard some reporting on NPR about the State of Israel's complicated position in this conflict. On one hand, they're morally opposed to the invasion and to Putin's unsubstantiated claim that he's defending ethnic Russians from genocide. On the other, Russia's friendship (or, at least, lack of animosity) is crucial to Israel's survival. Oh, and, over the course of the last few hundred years, Jewish communities suffered systematic and random persecution in Ukraine. That's not so different from most regions in Europe, but by the 19th century, about a third of European Jews lived there. By the end of World War II, the Jewish population in Ukraine had reduced from nearly 900,000 to fewer than 20,000, a terrible fact that, many historians argue, could not have happened without local collaboration. In this light, I can understand why Jews and even the entire State of Israel might hesitate to enter the fray. If nothing else, people need a moment to bolster themselves when attempting to love someone who hates them.

Maybe this points to a parallel insight about queer folx. Private, same-sex relations (also known as "gay sex") in Ukraine might be technically legal since 1991, but exclusion from fundamental rights like marriage and adoption are indicators of the fragile social climate for LGBTQ people there. Maybe the gays have stayed away because of the history and current reality of heterosexism in Ukraine. Then again, maybe we're just distracted by the bigots in our own backyard who are targeting trans youth, picking fights about who can and can't play sports, and clogging the judicial system with attempts to erode very hard-won legal protections for queer people. Maybe we're preoccupied with the Florida state legislature who have collectively decided to stoke heterosexism and hatred in an election year by, once again, painting LGBTQ people as predators, by criminalizing allyship, by returning queer kids to invisible and even more vulnerable status in the classroom. Apparently, Anita Bryant's legacy is stronger than we thought.

What is it about conservative cultures that makes sexual difference such a target? It's not just stereotype threat, and it's not paranoid to suggest that I can reasonably assume that a socially conservative dish comes with a big, fat helping of hatred for queer folx. Why do *these* people hate me, but *those* people don't? Is this actually a symptom itself of some other cause, a ripple effect of shared national or cultural trauma? Does each invasion, each drought, each economic collapse arrest the collective social development of a group?

In *My Grandmother's Hands*, Resmaa Menakem explores inherited, intergenerational trauma and offers a distinct starting point for understanding and healing from racism. We know now that trauma has a biological impact and that it is passed on and becomes so familiar that it passes for family norms or culture.

> Historical trauma, intergenerational trauma, institutionalized trauma (such as white-body supremacy, gender discrimination, sexual orientation discrimination, etc.), and personal trauma (including any trauma we inherit from our families genetically, or through the way they treat us, or both) often interact. As these traumas compound each other, or as each new or recent traumatic experience triggers the energy of older experiences, they can create ever-increasing damage to human lives and human bodies.

Most of the book focuses on the experience of African Americans, but Menakem invokes a little historical empathy, too, asking readers to consider the Europeans who colonized the Americas and enslaved Africans. He asks,

> Isn't it likely that many of them were traumatized by the time they arrived here? Did over ten centuries of medieval brutality, which was inflicted on white bodies by other white bodies, begin to look like culture? Did this intergenerational trauma and its effects end with European immigrants' arrival in the New World?

It's a halting and haunting question. And for those of us who feel culturally, philosophically, and morally enlightened or progressive, it's also a call to compassion, even for—especially for—people who hate us. It doesn't excuse conscious choices that directly or systematically harm a group of people, but it does remind us that, underneath layers of bigotry, there are layers of pain, generations of pain. And, underneath all that pain is a person, sometimes buried so deep their humanity is nearly undetectable. We may think of ethics and choice in the domain of the conscious Homo sapiens individual, as pertaining only to navigating discreet relationships with others and the world. It's easier to believe in our own autonomy (and to cleanly and directly blame others) that way, but now we know that we have inherited and will pass down choices that have harmed others, that harm ourselves. Ethical discernment is part of our biological and evolutionary development. Our choices, quite literally, shape future generations.

Cultures like Ukraine, rooted in regions rich in natural resources or of important geographic and commercial intersections, have been shaped by millennia of aggression from neighboring powers. Could this be a clue as to why marginal groups are so vulnerable in the region? The insight doesn't excuse the history of antisemitism, the targeting of Roma and Sinti, the ongoing persecution of queer people. It certainly doesn't excuse the current denial of Black and Brown people, fellow refugees fleeing a war, from boarding trains and accessing borders. Instead, the insight magnifies these choices. How we respond now, how we treat each other now, will instruct generations to come on how to achieve (or how to disastrously miss) a true and lasting peace.

I'm reminded of *This Land Is Mine*, Nina Paley's dark and satirical depiction of the history of Palestine, a history of constant successive invasions by bands, emerging nations, and empires who hid their thirst for power and resources behind the veil of political or religious hegemony. We could probably imagine a similar depiction for Ukraine, trampled and tossed around from empire to empire for thousands of years. I could even imagine a similar attempt to capture the persistent persecution of queer people. Couldn't you? Gloria Gaynor would belt "I Will Survive" while an animated drag queen lip syncs through successive threats. Medieval and modern torture devices would give way to the restriction of access to fundamental services, civil rights, and health care, and then, finally, to battery by legislation. *I'm just a bill, yes, I'm only a bill…* The important part of the story wouldn't be the constant persecution. The important part would be the survival of that drag queen. Instead of the Angel of Death consuming the world as in *This Land Is Mine*, it would end with the drag queen standing up after being beaten by the "Don't Say Gay" bill, putting on a new wig, and touching up her lipstick.

Since the early 20th century, the early days of the movement for LGBTQ civil rights (it didn't begin with Stonewall, folx!), one goal queer people have shared is survival, but maybe it's time to shift gears, to shift our ambitions. Now that we've got some modicum of legal protection and security in some parts of the world (and apparently more firmly in some parts of this country than in others), maybe it's time to cultivate compassion for others who have also been used as punching bags by more powerful others, even if, especially if they hate us.

I turned to my left and felt my dander rise at the sight of a Blue Lives Matter cap. Within a few blinks, I decided that the (from what I could see) straight, White, cisgender man wearing it was an asshole. *So much for compassion, Bill.* I laughed at myself, at my moral inconsistency, at the fact that I'd been spending so much time checking my and others' privilege that I forgot to also check my proclivity for quick and brutal judgments.

———————

GLORY TO THE HEROES!

Huh? That one confused me. *The heroes?* To my overly sensitive pacifist ear, invoking heroism is a complement to glorifying war, to glorifying and perpetuating violence, the violence that killed them in the first place. *Maybe it sounds better in Ukrainian.* The last march I was in was (mostly) silent, a long walk through Seattle in the wake of the murders of George Floyd, Breonna Taylor, and Ahmaud Arberry. *Were they heroes? Their deaths weren't particularly glorious.* I've walked in various Pride parades over the years. Pride parades have drifted far from their original (and, ostensibly, still core) purpose to demonstrate, to advocate, and to protest in a society that denies our lives, liberties, and pursuits of happiness. Now, most of the big-city parades look like decadent marketing conventions. *How would that sound in a Pride parade*, I wondered, *"Glory to the heroes"? Who* are *our heroes?*

As the column of demonstrators moved into the park, we trapped drivers in a parking lot and passed a sprinkling of people, families and tourists who took advantage of the sunshine and warmth to spend the day in the shadow of the Space Needle. Some took their phones out to snap pics, making me wonder how many of us would pop up on some stranger's Instagram or Twitter feed, how many of us would be deleted on the way home, how many of us would remain to be stumbled over months, years later.

NO FLY ZONE!

We arrived at Seattle Center echoing the leader's chant, but I had to admit to myself that I didn't really understand this one. I reminded myself to Google it later. Moving through the pedestrian boulevard toward the amphitheater, we passed a violinist really rocking out with a recorded accompaniment.

Usually, his music and charisma would rake in a few bucks from passersby, but with a steadily moving parade of blue and yellow dominating his stage, I wondered if he was pissed that no one was going to drop a dollar in his violin case, or if he was so enthused *because* of his support for our cause, or if he noticed us at all.

STOP PUTIN NOW!

Music blasted from speakers along the amphitheater's stage to spur a festive mood, but the area was quiet, solemn. Fifteen minutes after I arrived, so many bodies continued to spill into the amphitheater that the emcee asked the crowd to squeeze in, to make more room. As I found a spot in the shade, a guy walking past said to his friend with more than a hint of sarcasm, "Maybe they have a speaker system so everyone can actually hear this time." *There's always that guy, isn't there?* The emcee tried to vamp, clearly eager to get the program going and overwhelmed by the numbers of people still filling the knoll. A children's chorus was assembled on risers, where they waited patiently while various officials gave rambling speeches and led anemic chants. "Last week the skies cried," the emcee announced, attempting to stoke a little hope. "The weather, or God," she said, "is on our side." A man stepped forward to sing the Ukrainian national anthem with a powerful and graceful tenor voice over an almost campy orchestration. Many around me sang along, and the crowd applauded brightly for him. The emcee spoke of her pride in this moment of being a Ukrainian and an American, and the US anthem started to play. Within a few bars, I noticed my right hand floating up to rest over my heart and my mouth moving as I sang along. *When did I get so patriotic?*

The emcee asked the crowd to take a minute to honor thirty-seven fallen heroes, and we all fell silent. Well, all but one couple over my left shoulder who got my and several others' sharp and judgy glare. Three seagulls overhead cawed and broke the silence, applause followed. The emcee returned to the mic: "Heroes never die." *Heroes never die.* An official from the Ukrainian consulate did his best to spark a fire in the crowd, but his passion and desperation were stymied by the barriers of language.

FIGHTER AIRCRAFTS TO PROTECT THE SKY!

It lacked rhythm and pith, but when it didn't catch on, almost as if someone whispered a correction in his ear, he tried again.

MORE FIGHTER JETS!

———————

I went to see and be seen. I went to listen, to learn, to think. I wanted to witness history, but I didn't expect to *be* history. I didn't expect to see myself reflected in it or to see a part for me to play. I'm not bearing arms or rushing to provide assistance at the front. Honestly, I'll probably do little more than keep up with the news, donate to relief or refugee organizations, and engage in heated dialogues about whether this or that should happen, but being a witness means opening my eyes and mind, choosing to be impacted, choosing to transform. We're not stuck with the way things are, and we're not stuck with our primal instincts. We always have a choice, and our choices are the only way we're going to bend the moral arc of the universe toward justice.

III.
PRIDE

———————————

.

pride

"This could be the first funny revolution," Lou said. "Aren't these guys great, Bunny? Lily Law should never have messed with us on the day *Judy* died. Look, they've turned the parking meter into a battering ram."

...

The riot squad was called in. It marched like a Roman army behind shields down Christopher from the women's prison, which was loud with catcalls and the clatter of metal drinking cups against steel bars. The squad, clubs flying, drove the gay men down Christopher, but everyone doubled back through Gay Street and emerged behind the squad in a chorus line, dancing the can-can. "Yoo-hoo, yoo-hoo," they called.

Lou and I stayed out all night, whooping like kids, huddling in groups to plan tomorrow's strategy, heckling the army of cops who were closing off all of Sheridan Square as a riot zone and refusing to let cars or pedestrians pass through it.

I stayed over at Lou's. We hugged each other in bed like brothers, but we were too excited to sleep. We rushed down to buy the morning papers to see how the Stonewall Uprising had been described. "It's really our Bastille Day," Lou said. But we couldn't find a single mention in the press of the turning point of our lives.

Edmund White, *The Beautiful Room is Empty*,
pp. 226, 227–228

In the final chapter of his semi-autobiographical novel about coming of age (and coming out) in 1950s and 1960s America, White's narrator paints quite a picture: a kickline affronting riot shields, adrenaline-driven solidarity, and utter hopefulness confronting a world that doesn't want to talk about the most important moment in his life. There are a few problems with White's description of the Stonewall riots, including the suggestion that they began the day that Judy Garland died—it was the day of her funeral—but, more importantly, his description is incomplete. Thousands have told and retold (and mistold) the story—no description could be complete, could it? A description is limited by what we can see and hear and feel—and when someone asks, or when no one asks, we piece together what we can. Putting together the pieces of the Stonewall puzzle is complicated by the question of who owns the narrative. To some, Stonewall looked like the liberation of gay White men; to others, it was a rebellion of transgender folx and drag queens, mostly people of color, finding strength to resist for the first time. It depends on not only who is telling the story, but also who is hearing it, who is seeing her/him/themself reflected or rooted in it, who is claiming the legacy of resistance to the raid of a small bar in the Village on the night of Judy Garland's burial.

I read *The Beautiful Room is Empty* in college in the late 1990s, and it was my introduction to Stonewall. At the time, I could count on two hands the number of students who were out on campus. I didn't feel particularly unsafe—no more unsafe than in any other environment—but while away at school I also didn't have access to gay culture. During summers, I'd return home to Chicago and find ways to sneak down to Boystown, find the bars that didn't card, and, well, do all the things that nineteen-year-old gay kids do. The summer after my first year in college, I'd already planned an elaborate ruse to explain why I'd be out of the house all day one Sunday in June when my sister, Patty, called and invited me down to her place in the city and to join her at the Pride parade. By the end of the day, I had shared my sexual identity with Patty (the first person in my family) and my mother had started the silent treatment on her for taking me to, what she called at the time, "that lesbian thing." It was a quick and double-edged lesson: on one side, Pride was all about naming myself and finding others who would help me along the way. On the other, though, claiming my identity would spur consequences. When I was introduced to the phrase "Politics is personal, and the personal is political" in grad school, I understood it through the lens I acquired by coming out.

June 28, 2019, marked the fiftieth anniversary of the start of the Stonewall riots in New York City. This anniversary was preceded by years of slow but steady success toward achieving equality for queer people in the US, including pivotal Supreme Court decisions like *US v. Windsor* and *Obergefell v. Hodges* and growing representation in various media. Throughout that year's "Pride season," companies capitalized by rebranding themselves as Pride-centered organizations, but walking through a mall during the month of June didn't feel particularly celebratory. While companies might've intended to magnify the significance of a milestone anniversary, the result was just an obnoxiously rainbow jungle that, instead of highlighting the significance of the milestone, shone a light on hollow corporate performances of inclusion despite policies, practices, investments, and financial support of politicians that actively eroded equity for LGBTQ folx.

A year later, with all the energy swirling from the fifty-first anniversary of Stonewall and the fiftieth of the first official Pride march, it was easy to get sentimental about these milestones, but two things bothered me. First, while there was much to celebrate, 2020 provided ample reminders of the work still to be done. We saw a rise in hate crimes against queer people, not to mention increasingly aggressive and insulting rhetoric from multiple directions. We saw state legislatures move to restrict voting rights and target transgender people (particularly, and most disgustingly, trans kids). Those voices have only gotten louder and harder to drown out, making me all the more grateful for and inspired by folx who speak up, who brave the backlash, and who shout from the rooftops the injustices perpetrated against queer folx and other marginalized and vulnerable people. Still, the fact that we, or anyone on our behalf, has to shout to assert basic human dignity tells us that the work is not and may never be complete.

Second, I felt that consumer culture co-opted Pride, perhaps irreversibly. In the 1980s and 1990s, it was a risk for companies to be present at Pride festivals—it was a statement. But since then, too many parades have been miles-long advertisements of flashy and well-stocked floats for banks and airlines and other businesses hoping to build their credibility as inclusive and queer-friendly companies, relegating the activists and churches and synagogues and PFLAG chapters to filler status along the route, a shift brilliantly skewered in *Saturday Night Live*'s Pride song, "It's Pride Again." The most dangerous consequence of this is that marketing efforts not only *tell* a story—they *frame* a story; they shape the worldview of the engaged audience. Too many corporate presences at Pride events have shady histories (to both overgeneralize and understate) when it comes to support of their queer employees both in business culture and in public policy, but they have the resources to tell a story. The story I heard, though, wasn't *my* story—actually, my story didn't seem to fit into the worldview of any of those ads.

As an antidote to this, I found myself in a pattern of daily reflection on people, events, and experiences that shaped *my* story, influenced how I thought about myself and the world around me, provided a bridge during lonely times, and gave me language for the joyous ones. It was a simple practice: throughout the month of June, set aside half an hour, re-watch a few clips or look up some information or flip through an old book, think critically about how I've been shaped and challenged and supported in my life, and be grateful. This became my way of personalizing Pride. I tailored it to my style and needs, I didn't try to claim someone else's perspective or experience as my own, and I shared it with my friends on social media. Sometimes, friends responded with gratitude—my reflection triggered a happy memory or introduced them to a new idea or figure—which was lovely to see, but the practice was really one of discernment for me, to help me articulate who I am, what my identity means for me, and what I need and desire.

Things have changed since then. I returned to these reflections in the wake of the COVID-19 pandemic and the murders of George Floyd, Breonna Taylor, and Ahmaud Arbery. For two years, the Pride celebrations, parades, and festivals we used to know and love (or at least tolerate) had been rightfully canceled, though, with the resumption of something-like-normal for many due to rising vaccination rates, the spaces that tied "the community" together came back to life. Those spaces we've created to be safe, to be ourselves—all those spaces that evaporated when the world shut down—reopened. Bars, restaurants, gayborhoods, community centers, choruses, athletic leagues, chosen families, support groups…I wondered whether and how those spaces would reflect the things we endured, the changes we navigated, the scars we bore, the mistakes we made. I wondered whether we'd resist the narratives imposed on us and instead construct our own stories and really listen to the stories we have the privilege to hear.

Gay men faced a plague forty years ago, another plague that was ignored and played down, that seemed to target an already vulnerable group, that was treated by leaders and neighbors alike as a justified punishment or at least a natural consequence of the "lifestyle" we lived. The AIDS crisis added urgency and fuel and anger to the movement for equal rights that started well before Stonewall, and that led us to equal marriage in the US. Queer folx established safe neighborhoods, those "gayborhoods" through which our Pride parades once traveled, and spurred economic revivals and returns of services to neglected urban areas. As that crisis relented, queer folx were visible in a new way. Harvey Milk's legacy and murder revealed a need for queer representation in local and national politics. Ellen came out. *Will & Grace* joined the prime-time lineup. When I joined the Boston Gay Men's Chorus in 1999, though more and more folx started to see themselves reflected in public institutions and visible in our culture, coming out and *standing* out, claiming our space, was still a political act.

After an experience that rocks us, we search for what's steady, and I'm optimistic that we will be able to discern both what's at the core of our celebrations and identify new ways to visibly and meaningfully mark Pride. As we look to future Prides, could the parties and interfaith services and parades and brunches and performances shift away from highly externalized celebrations toward something more personal? Instead of waiting for advertisers to tell us what to be proud of, we can do that for ourselves. We can take ourselves seriously and look at our lives critically. We can open our minds and hearts to a few minutes of reflection. We can tell each other about the people who shaped us, about the experiences we've had and the insights we've gleaned. We can articulate our own desires and needs. In short, we can make Pride personal again.

The essays that follow don't constitute *the* Pride story, and they are not an attempt to be exhaustively inclusive or broadly researched. In fact, stepping back, I can see that many of the people and experiences I've identified add to a stereotype of gay men of a certain age. I've never thought of myself as an old, campy queen whose every reference calls back to a diva or a script, but if the shoe fits, I'll gladly try it on. Besides, isn't it the ordinary things that open our eyes to the deepest insights? Isn't it always "a quiet thing," as Liza sang, that changes us most profoundly? I love to swim in the world of high art and philosophy, but it's the popular culture and the very ordinary media that grab me, that stick with me. In fact, I find great comfort knowing that the things that once made me stand out are the things that now make me feel quite ordinary because they are the things that connected and continue to connect me to people I admire and love, even people I've never and will never meet. They may not all be "high art," but they are building blocks for my corner of the world.

So, no, this is not the Pride story. It is part of my story.

belters

One evening in October 1963, three monumental divas converged on *The Judy Garland Show*. I suspect that most gay men watching the broadcast went gaga, seeing on one stage together the towering fifty-five-year-old Ethel Merman (who never needed a mic), forty-one-year-old Judy Garland (at one of her many peaks), and a baby Barbra Streisand, just twenty-one and launching a new show on Broadway, *Funny Girl*. The episode includes a stunning duet between Barbra and Judy, which has since become the standard for blending standards and the original on which all gay men at piano bars modeled their money notes, but it also features a "surprise" interlope from Ethel Merman that sparks some charming exchanges and builds to the trio belting Ethel's classic "There's No Business Like Show Business."

I first saw the episode at the apartment of a friend of a friend when I was twenty-two. A group of us left the bar where we'd been watching and singing along with iconic numbers from poor-quality videotapes, lured back to this guy's apartment with the promise of watching Judy's full Christmas special. While he was searching for the right tape, the rest of us were mesmerized by three schticky divas that presented an anti-*Valley of the Dolls* trio. It's one of those particular moments that I can still hear and feel, a moment when I, finally, found myself at home. With abandon and without reservation, I'd stumbled into the realm of other gay men who proclaimed their love of performers, their encyclopedic retention of Broadway lyrics and ancient gossip.

Years later, I'd live in a house that was once the Napoleon Club, home to a piano bar where Judy and other stars would party after out-of-town openings. Once I heard a story about Judy dancing and singing on top of the piano that sat where my dining table stood, followed by a story about a guy getting his first hand job in the spot that hosted my refrigerator. But that chilly night in an overheated apartment in Boston, surrounded by strangers who shared little more than a sexual orientation and a disposition for classic songs, I claimed my identity as a Friend of Judy.

"Friend of Judy" is an old disguise, a covert term that preexists the common parlance of "gay" to refer to homosexuals without sounding too clinical, but as a historical artifact it highlights the role that Judy played in gay men's lives. She sang a story and lived a life of heartache, a story that resonated with the experiences of gay men, and she openly advocated for her gay fans in a hush-hush era. Like Judy, Ethel and Barbra were unconventional stars—their talent didn't depend on conforming to fashionable looks or styles; instead, fashion conformed to them. And their talent wasn't conventional, either. With big, brassy tones, none of them was going to be recruited by the Metropolitan Opera, but that didn't ever stop them from singing loudly and proudly.

In the schtick of the episode, they joke about their niche as belters, and Barbra was the newest member of this unique little club. The most remarkable aspect of the trio belting together reveals something about why belting is so powerful, both as a performance technique and for the belters themselves. Watch Ethel's, Judy's, and Barbra's physicality while they sing—the song takes over their bodies. Even the arms of the initially shy Barbra start to flail as her voice expands. Belting is an unabashed action. You can't do it if you're reserved, constrained, or afraid. You might slip a pitch, but with enough breath and gumption, you can recover the note and make it soar over a full orchestra just off stage. From this angle, it's no surprise that gay men were drawn to them. Admiring and imitating Ethel, Judy, and Barbra—their unabashed-ness, their courage to take the risk, to tell the hard story, to sing the notes loudly and proudly—was a step in building the courage to claim their own identities, to claim rights, to claim dignity. I think this is the real reason I started belting along with Ethel when I was fourteen and first discovered I could carry a pitch. I wasn't ready to live loud and proud, but I was ready to sing that way.

Valley of the Dolls

At the ripe old age of twenty-eight, my ex and I met a couple of guys who'd just graduated from college and, to my exaggerated, pearl-clutching shock, did not catch my *All About Eve* reference. They didn't even know who Bette Davis was. After hearing more about what they didn't know, we decided to host a Big Gay Movie Day to educate these children, our new friends, about the essentials—you know, the core classic films that informed the vocabulary of a good portion of gay men in the 20th century. Several times, we hosted marathon screenings of four or five films (always at least one black & white, always at least one musical) accompanied by a stream of food and drinks, from brunch and snacks raided from our pantry to delivered Chinese food somewhere around movie number four, to dinner and a pizza or two by the time the last film wrapped up. I was excited about every title we offered, but few films generated as much anticipation in me as *Valley of the Dolls*.

Valley of the Dolls is a lush production based on a very popular book that follows three women from the time they got their feet in the door of showbiz. While the dolls of the title could be a metaphor for women objectified in and by the industry, the title directly points to the tranquilizer pills that play a role in each of their lives. This movie has everything (#stefon): a stellar cast, a stunning wardrobe, and Dionne Warwick singing a moody ballad in the background. And it. Is. Awful. So awful it's fantastic. It is and will always be the highest of high camp—melodramatic acting, contrived and caricatured plots, and Susan Hayward lip syncing (poorly) while trapped in the eye of a swirling Calder-like mobile. The script is rich with over-the-top zingers that today ring anywhere from deeply offensive to the ridiculous to the ridiculously funny, from Jennifer's flippant observation—"You know how bitchy fags can be!"—to Neely, weepy and stumbling drunk in an alley, calling out for all the people who abandoned her. She stretches out heavy pauses between each name with a series of very visible revelations on her face—"Mel? God? Neely?...NEEEEEEEEELY O'HARAAAAAAAAAAAA!" And then there's the best conversation wrap in history as Jennifer shouts into the phone, "Mother, I know I don't have any talent. And I know all I have is a body. And I *am* doing my bust exercises. Goodbye, Mother."

The best—no, most outstanding—parts of the movie are two musical numbers, each an idealized glimpse into the worlds they're, well, sort of, portraying. We see rehearsals backstage at a Broadway theater that belong in a production of *Summer Stock*—it's as accurate in depicting a Broadway production as *CSI* is in demonstrating crime-solving and DNA technology. We see the swinging nightclubs of the '60s built in expansive sets—a far cry from the tight and tightly packed and smoke-filled clubs of the time. We see a telethon...actually I have no idea how accurate the telethon scene is, but it's the telethon that gives Patty Duke's Neely her big break and the movie its first great—er, outstanding—moment. Duke takes the stage before a tally board to sing "It's Impossible" in an orange turtleneck, a gray skirt, and two gold chains that liberally swing across (and frequently and awkwardly frame) her breasts. Instead of standing still or doing any sort of real choreography, Duke takes the middle road with enthusiasm and jerks and frets like she taught Elaine Benes how to dance.

The second outstanding moment comes from the out-of-town opening of a big Broadway star's new show. Susan Hayward, as Helen Lawson (based on Ethel Merman) sings (well, lip syncs over Margaret Whiting's voice) "I'll Plant My Own Tree" in a glittering white gown and the strangest wig you've ever seen while dodging the translucent panels of an enormous Calder-esque mobile. Choreography isn't really the word for it. Occasionally she takes a few steps forward like a bridesmaid who hit the bar before the ceremony, and just as the song comes to its climax, she spins around and throws her arm in the air like a four-year-old who just—sort of—completed a cartwheel. The moment of moments, though, comes with the final lines of the song.

"I'll plant," her right arm rises, "my own tree…" Her left arm rises, but it doesn't float quite as high (shoulder injury, perhaps?) so she turns it into a little swipe along her cheek. "My own tree…" She leans forward with Up-With-People enthusiasm."…and I'll make it grow…" With the long, final note, both arms rise dramatically, palms down, hitting an "I surrender!" posture with the end of the note, and then—here's the magical moment—her gaze drifts up all dreamy, but the rest of her leans back one more notch like a mannequin that's been bumped.

I'm not sure any of the youths we tried to educate came to love *Valley of the Dolls* as much as I do, but that wasn't really the point. The movie gave us something to laugh at, and it linked our joy to the joy of gay men who, for decades, escaped to the melodrama and the extravagance of the *Valley*. The Boston Gay Men's Chorus sang a medley from the movie, and with the final notes, we, 150 singers on risers, let our right arms drift up, let our left arms drift up (not quite as far), and then both arms up for a hold and a slight bend to the left. Best choralography ever. The best part of performing the number wasn't our near-perfect imitation of Hayward, but how much everyone laughed when the move was introduced to us, the giggles every time we practiced it, the special joy when our audience laughed knowingly, clearly aware of the reference. Even the ones who hadn't seen the movie or didn't have Neely O'Hara quotes at the ready at all times understood that it was an iconic—and iconically laughable—moment. And it was our duty as performers to make sure the next generation could laugh along, too.

A Boy's Own Story &
The Beautiful Room Is Empty

"What if I could write about my life exactly as it was?
What if I could show it in all its density and tedium and
its concealed passion, never divined or expressed?"

from *A Boy's Own Story*

During my junior year in college, I took a course called "Gender and Sexuality in Film and Literature." I wasn't sure what to expect because the course's description was vague, but the general objective to understand how gender and sexuality were portrayed in the second half of the 20th century was enough to draw me in, mostly because the words "gender" and "sexuality" didn't appear anywhere else in the catalogue. Or on campus. Or in our day-to-day conversations.

However, these were words and ideas I was raging to explore. It was a critical juncture for me—after hitting pause on any step toward coming out during high school (since it started with being tossed up against a wall and called *faggot*), I was preparing to tell my parents. Over the first two years of college, I told friends and a couple of my siblings, and I'd started to venture to queer spaces in the vicinity of campus. I started to explore at home, too. During my summers back in Chicago, evening gigs as a tour guide gave me an excuse to stay downtown and hang out in whatever bars in the gayborhood I could slip into with my fake ID. I started to build my persona as a gay man, but beyond sneaking into bars and knowing my musical theater standards, I didn't know what that would require.

From the moment she walked in, I was in awe of our professor. She was tall, lean, in a slim black suit with a long, narrow skirt with a slit high enough to reveal tall boots. Striking red hair was cut at a severe bob, framing her face like a centurion's helmet. One earring dangled in her right ear, but a series of little hoops and studs in her cartilage, from the lobe to her ear's peak, ornamented her left. Her skin was pale, her eyes narrow but occasionally flashing bright blue eyes. Her posture rarely varied—either lecturing with a book in one hand, her other hand akimbo, her weight shifted to one leg, or walking slowly across the front or around the room with her arms crossed, her shoulders rolled forward as her head slowly nodded. Her overbite slightly muffled an English accent, but whether because of her deliberate diction or her personal intensity, I heard every word. She never identified as queer in any way. At the time I accepted it as part of the norm of Catholic communities, our own version of "don't ask, don't tell," but now I recognize: she didn't have to. She said words like *gay* and *lesbian* and *AIDS* and *sex* without hesitation or shame, and without titillation or derogation. She was everything I wanted to be. Well, maybe not *everything*, but, looking around the room, I knew I wasn't alone. I seriously considered dying my hair iron-red to show my devotion.

Everything we read, everything we watched was new to me. Sometimes I felt outrage (why didn't they tell me this before?), sometimes I felt smug (I can't wait to drop this in conversation and sound super smart). Surprisingly, though, I didn't see myself in many of the films, stories, and books we engaged. That was a lesson in diversity itself, that our stories are not the same, but when I started reading Edmund White's *The Beautiful Room Is Empty*, I felt my story come into closer view. The second of a loosely connected and often autobiographical trilogy, the novel follows its nameless narrator from prep school in Chicago to the Stonewall riots. Focusing on the narrator, it's about his journey to resolve the conflict he experienced as a homosexual in a fiercely heteronormative world, but I was enthralled by the depiction of the world gay men navigated in the '50s and '60s—stumbling into corners and pockets of joy and hedonism while living in a world that would toss homosexuals, Jews, and communists on a pyre. Or worse, a world that wouldn't even acknowledge our existence.

The Beautiful Room ends with the narrator feeling hopeful, giddy—alive!—after seeing the queens fight back against an unjust raid for the first time. It was an above-the-fold, headline-worthy event that didn't get a mention in the next day's press. Finally, they had the courage to kick down the closet's door—in a chorus line, no less—but when they emerged, there was no one there to see them. I remember weeping as I closed the book for the first time, seeing my greatest fear reflected back to me. What was worse, I wondered, being hated or being unseen?

Over time, I gleaned a couple of insights from White's narratives that continue to inform how I see the world and know myself. First, Stonewall marked a significant shift for gay men—or at least for White gay men. Progress for lesbian, bi, and trans people and for queer folx of color continues to lag behind. Life before was in the shadows, and the closet was both a prison that trapped them and a fortress that protected whatever real living they could assemble. While life after, outside the closet, brought the vulnerability and scrutiny that comes with exposure, it also led to increasingly secured rights and dependable protections. I lived an easier life than White's narrator, and my students and niblings are living easier lives than I did, and this wouldn't have been possible without increasing visibility.

Second, these books showed me that, while the phrase we use for claiming our identity is pithy and sometimes useful, it's not really about "coming out." Age by age, experience by experience, and without any model or exemplar to follow, as White described it, there was no single moment that he understood who he was, whom he desired, and whom he desired to be, no single moment when he stepped into the light and was seen from all angles. He evolved. He made choices. He constructed himself, and he chose his family. And besides, "coming out" suggests that there's a closet to come out of and justifies the idea that some people should stick with the hangers. It took me a while (about twenty years) to really understand what this meant for my life. As broader visibility has led to better understanding of sexual identity, kids now have exemplars to learn how to name themselves, how to share their authentic and integrated selves, how to ask questions, how to be vulnerable, how to be loved.

The first time I claimed my sexual identity with my parents, the first time I said "I'm gay" to them, happened the following summer, just a few months after I read White's novels. A few weeks later, my mom, who was finally able to talk to me without bursting into tears, and I were watching TV when a rerun of *Ellen* came on. Either one of us would've changed the channel if we knew exactly which episode was coming, but by the time we realized it, making a move for the remote would've betrayed the critical criterion of our detente: avoidance. So there we were, each pretending to watch with detachment and hoping the power would go out before Ellen arrived at the airport. Yep, it was "The Puppy Episode," the one when Ellen finally says loud and clear—and unwittingly into the microphone of an airport gate lounge—"I'm gay." My eyes were fixed on the screen, my throat tight, and without looking I knew Mom was frozen, too, similarly fixed on the screen. Here we were, finally communicating again after weeks of silence and tears, and we found ourselves stuck in a conversation we'd both been hoping to avoid. The room was suddenly very hot, and my mind raced, wondering what she was thinking, replaying what I'd said, what she'd said, what I'd forgotten to say, what I refused to say. Ellen got closer to the microphone, and the anticipation from the studio audience oozed from the screen. She leaned in. "I'm gay."

Out of the corner of my eye, I saw Mom's lips purse and the corners of her mouth rise. And then she looked at me and chuckled. That's when I knew that I hadn't "come out," that I wasn't drifting, exposed, and vulnerable. Instead, I found myself in a new space, a beautiful room that my mom and I could build and explore together.

Paris Is Burning

The camera pans from head to toe. We get a glimpse of a sharp black bob and heavy bangs, three strands of oversized pearls, and a white fur stole as it reveals an elegant, breezy suit. Satin-gloved hands reach down to lift an Italian greyhound with a matching pearl collar.

Junior LaBeija is at the side of the dancefloor-runway in a blue sweater and a dark cap turned backwards, but all you really notice is his eyes, his inimitable expression. He shouts, "O-P-U-L-E-N-C-E: Opulence!"

He turns his hat around, like it's helping him see better. He leans forward slightly as his right hand rises to his hip. Strings of lights blinking inconsistently are dangling in the background, a dozen people in the frame are chatting or watching other corners of the dancefloor.

"You own everything."

He looks back to the table and readjusts to lean forward.

"Everything is yours."

His left hand rises to pat his cheek like a powder puff.

It's an essential moment in *Paris Is Burning*, the 1990 documentary by Jennie Livingston that, shot over the course of seven years, captures Ballroom culture in the '80s. While rap, hip hop, and breakdancing were springing a few miles away in the Bronx and starting their ascendence in pop culture, queer people of color in Harlem created, developed, and perfected art forms that remained on the margins but are suddenly dominant in pop culture today. Realness. Reading. Voguing. Madonna might've introduced the rest of the world to the Ballroom, and the *RuPaul's Drag Race* franchise might be its most ubiquitous descendant, but it was the legends, or more specifically the "Legendary Children" of that era who innovated and planted the seeds that feed us today. The vision of Pepper LaBeija. The movement of Paris Dupree and Willi Ninja. The wit of Freddie Pendavis, Venus Xtravaganza, and Dorian Corey. The sheer style and beauty of Pepper LaBeija and Octavia St. Laurent. It wasn't just entertainment or art or expression—it was identity construction, and these were the moments that continue to shape how the rest of us see and navigate the world.

She stands tall, regal, executive. She's cold and aloof, and her little greyhound is the reminder that she's human, that she can show affection, though probably after business hours. I knew that woman—I saw that woman every day as a kid, the woman who is a swirl of power and leisure and grace, who didn't need to be reminded that she owns everything, that everything is hers—except that in my lush suburb that was a cisgender White woman and the one on film was, well, not.

This was, for me, a formative introduction to drag. I mean, I knew what drag *was*, or at least generally consisted of—boys dressing as girls. *Paris Is Burning* exploded that notion, giving me a front-row seat to the construction of identity and prompting a long journey to understand why, as a definition, "boys dressing as girls" is incomplete and reductive. I was twenty, White (though for too long I clung to "Irish&German"), cisgender (though I didn't know that word till my late twenties and how to use it until my thirties), raised in an affluent suburban life (though it took me a while to understand privilege), educated (though riddled with impostor syndrome), and Catholic (and mostly surrounded by other Catholics in most of my experiences). There's no reason I should have ever been introduced to the Harlem Balls...but one significant reason prompted me to enroll in a course on gender and sexuality in film and literature in college: I'm gay. That's not enough to claim any understanding or ownership of the experience, but it was a starting point.

Paris Is Burning took me to the streets of New York City and into the private spaces of old queens and youths, of the mothers and members of the legendary houses of the Ballroom. Watching it nurtured a seed that was planted in me years before, a desire to get as far away from the suburbs as possible. But most importantly, it instilled in me a deeper understanding of identity. I was raised to be an essentialist (I *am* this, therefore I *do* that. I am White, cis, male, affluent, Catholic; I should pursue things that other White, cis, male, affluent Catholics do, like live in suburbs and find a job that lets me wear a range of suits and ties), but the artists of the Ballroom, the marginalized among the marginalized, perfected the art of constructing identity. Their ability to create and assume a persona through styling, language, and movement blurred the line between performance and realness (there's really no better word for it) and mocked the privileged whose power is reinforced by image and status.

Pulling back the curtain on identity and being able to see its transience, its illusoriness, opened a door for me—I didn't have to fall in step with the identity handed to me. I could construct my own. For that insight, for that revelation and wonderful unburdening, I've been grateful to the people featured in *Paris Is Burning* and for its ongoing, even increasing relevance, and each time I watch it, I want to channel the spirit of Junior LaBeija, uplift everyone I see on a similar journey, and let them know, "Everything is yours."

Auntie Mame

As Patrick's first party winds down, he sees Vera Charles, the best friend of his aunt and new guardian, being carried up the stairs.

> Patrick: Is the English lady sick, Auntie Mame?
> Mame: Oh, she's not English, darling, she's from Pittsburgh.
> Patrick: She sounded English.
> Mame: Well, when you're from Pittsburgh, you have to do something.

Patrick arrived a few hours earlier, orphaned by distant parents and accompanied by an Irish housekeeper, and he was dropped in the deep end of his new life, in the middle of a raging, bootleg-fueled party in the last days of the roaring '20s. Patrick and his new guardian click quickly, but, instead of fitting into conventional molds of parenthood, Mame aims to show Patrick the world and how to be fully alive. "Life is a banquet," she proclaims, "and most poor suckers are starving to death."

Mame Dennis is the fictionalized version of the real-life Patrick Dennis' aunt, the guardian, guru, and glamazon who defied any convention that constricted her efforts to live, live, and live. She's the guardian that many gay boys dreamed of having (or being), someone who opened the window to see beyond the trappings of their lives. There's much to say about *Auntie Mame*, the film that earned six Academy Award nominations based on the play that earned four Tony nominations based on the beloved book, but three things about the movie have stood out to me since I first saw the film as a kid.

First, the production itself. Had it been produced a few years later, *Auntie Mame* might've felt a bit more modern or at least less like a Broadway play transported directly to a movie lot, but it's not a distraction for me. Instead, I'm hooked by the script (a nearly perfect lesson in storytelling and witty repartee), the style (oh, the style!), and the performances, especially the master class on nuance, timing, and wordless storytelling that Rosalind Russell delivers. Mame's personal style is a clever device in the film—her constantly renovated home echoes her changing clothing and hair color and marks both the passage of time and Mame's personal evolution. And those outfits! Why Russell's wardrobe throughout the film hasn't made it to the runway of *RuPaul's Drag Race*, I can't explain. Style and storytelling come into special focus when Mame returns to New York after months retracing the paths that she and her late husband trod. Ready to inhabit a new role, that of the glamorous, grieving widow, Mame is introduced to an attractive Irish poet who, shall we say, stirs her creative juices. When he lobs a compliment her way, Mame shifts gears, slowly struts across the room, and sheds the layers of her widow's garb to reveal a sleek, elegant dress. At the very last moment, she turns to reveal her back, completely exposed by the cut of the dress and confirming that Mame is, indeed, ready to reenter the world. It's one of those moments that makes a viewer sigh with the lament, *they don't make 'em like they used to.*

Second, Mame's family. Mame and Patrick are the last ones left in their biological family, but she gives her young nephew (and all of us watching) a lesson in "chosen families." We meet Mame, Ito, Patrick, and Nora as caricatures, as comic types that would've been familiar to audiences—the oddity of the eccentric spinster, the comedy of broken English and subservience of the Japanese butler, the helpless orphan, the prudish and gossipy Irish housekeeper—but Beekman Place proves a crucible where they can shed those trappings and, seeing each other as their fullest and best selves, make a home together. A few weeks before Christmas 1929, with the bills piling up, Mame loses her job at Macy's and returns home to find that Patrick hocked his chemistry set to buy her a bracelet of "almost diamonds" and that Ito and Nora have scraped together their savings to pay off the grocer and butcher bills. There are ample warm-and-fuzzy moments between Mame and Patrick through the film, but the tenderest one comes with Mame's response to her little family's extraordinary generosity. Eyes about to well, she pauses and says, "You are both so dear to me." When Beauregard Jackson Pickett Burnside arrives to save the day, he doesn't whisk Mame away. So enamored by Mame, he doesn't pay any mind to the eclectic composition of the group; he just asks to join their family for the night.

But not everyone would be welcome in Mame's family, which leads me to the third thing that has always stood out to me: the Upsons. We meet Gloria Upson and her parents, caricatures of Connecticut snobs, another familiar mid-century stereotype of the ambitious newly-moneyed who pride themselves in collecting colonial kitsch, mingling with "top drawer" people, and maintaining "restricted" (read: Jew-free) neighborhoods. Despite his upbringing, Patrick is lured into the world that the Upsons provide. The exaggerations of the Upsons, so diametrically opposed to Mame in every way, provide comic relief but, instead of finding warmth and connection, peeling back the layers of stereotype only reveals the prejudices that fuel their ambition and that make for a shallow and ultimately uninteresting life. If life is a banquet, the Upsons stagnate among the appetizers. Mame was a fish out of water at Upsons Downs, their colonially appointed home in Connecticut, but, in the climactic scene, Mame invites the Upsons to Beekman Place—not necessarily to tell Patrick who he is, but to illuminate the contrast between his worlds and remind him who he *isn't*.

In so many ways, I've always related to Patrick, and the snobbery that he oozes as a young adult is painful to watch. The white-washed world of affluent suburbs, life among the Aryans of Darien, has its lure to be sure, but it's a life that brought out Patrick's worst. Mame calls him on it after meeting Gloria and the world manifest in her. "Should she know," Mame says clearly and directly to Patrick in response to his desire to hide the world that raised him, "that I think you've turned into one of the most beastly, bourgeois, babbity little snobs on the eastern seaboard? Or will you be able to make that quite clear without any help from me?"

It isn't just the facts of their lives that opens Patrick's eyes and cuts the lure that ensnared him. A copy of Mame's autobiography arrives, the result of a project that Patrick contrived to keep Mame afloat after Beau died. Having once given Mame a path out of mourning, the book transports Patrick back to the company of the people who shaped him, the people he still holds close, the people who love him and are loved by him and who live well outside the boundaries of the Upsons' restricted world. I've always interpreted this twist as a spotlight on the transformative power of storytelling, but it's also a cautionary tale about the importance of telling one's own story—and a warning to tell my own, especially before someone tries to tell it for me.

Madonna

If we've met, you likely know two things about me: I'm the youngest of a sprawling family, and I have a master's degree in no small part because of my obsession with Madonna. If you stuck around for any further conversation, you probably got a lecture from me deconstructing the "Like a Prayer" video. You see, in my final year of Divinity School, I finally, freely identified as a Madonnawannabe, an identity I'd hidden since sixth-grade me caught a glimpse of "Open Your Heart" on a local channel's afternoon music video hour. For my independent research as part of a course that explored the intersections of eroticism and mysticism in various cultures, I turned to the intersection of religion and pop culture, and there was no better exemplar than Madonna Louise Ciccone, whose then-fresh *Ray of Light* album brought electronica and spirituality to the dance floor and the mainstream. Twenty-eight pages and about 142 citations later, I was a step closer to my degree and three miles deeper into a lifelong obsession.

While I respect the fanatics who pore over every detail of her personal history and, thanks to social media, maintain a steady engagement with her daily life, it's not Madonna Louise Ciccone that I'm interested in. Instead, I'm interested in "Madonna," the output of the entire production team that has pursued Ciccone's vision and that, through monumental success in the music industry and constantly evolving personae and styles, has made a measurable impact on American and global culture. Over time,

I transposed my research into a workshop for colleagues and, eventually, into a multi-week symposium that explores four threads throughout her oeuvre: Madonna as social commentator, cultural parasite, reinventor, and catalyst of postmodernism.

As a social commentator, through her music, performances, and interviews, she has fiercely advocated for queer people and integrated their experiences and stories into her art. From "Vogue" and "Secret" to "Dark Ballet," she brought the Harlem Ballroom and trans people of color to the mainstream. Through videos like "Express Yourself," "Human Nature," and "What It Feels Like for a Girl," she barreled through the blockades that limited women in the music industry and offered a not-so-subtle critique of the patriarchy, and in videos like "Batuka," she gave a microphone (and a stage and camera) to women whose stories had been sidelined for generations. With increasing intensity, she has addressed gun violence and more generally the violence that is so endemic to our culture in "American Life," "Ghosttown," and her devastating and poignant response to the 2016 mass shooting at Pulse Nightclub, "God Control."

Talking about Madonna as a cultural parasite is a little trickier. Over time, she has received a fair amount of criticism for mining marginalized groups and appropriating their styles, practices, and message. But I also notice that, over time, she increasingly removes herself from the spotlight when bringing another group to the mainstream, making her look more like a "mutualist" than a "parasite." In a revision of "La Isla Bonita," she partnered with the Gypsy Punk group Gogol Bordello to mash up the song with "Pala tute" and performed it at the 2007 Live Earth concert. Sure, she starts front and center, but then she starts singing in Romani and then hands the stage over to Eugene & Serge. In "Dark Ballet," she plays a supporting role, barely on screen, as the camera focuses on Mykki Blanco's Joan of Arc. In "Batuka," she is absorbed into a group of Cabo Verdean women and blends her pop with their percussion and call-and-response singing. The impact: the voiceless are given a voice, the unseen a stage, the marginalized a platform.

She's frequently called the "reinventor"—with each album and tour, each era, she adopts a new persona and style, but I think of her less as a *reinventor* and more of a *revealer*. She doesn't take on an image crafted by someone else; instead, she peels back a layer and lets something else out. While it presents differently, giving her a different language or starting point for communication, each persona is deeply rooted in her core. When she turned sixty, Wesley Morris cited her as the first great "identity artist," which struck me as particularly profound: she introduced the world to the concept of identity and intersectionality not through esoteric academic dialogue but through pop culture. She modeled for the rest of us—particularly those of us who needed the permission to construct identities distinct from, even in opposition to, the ones we inherited—how to change, and change, and change, and still remain oneself. "Bedtime Story" wanders through surrealist art and archetypes, but instead of telling us all to accept the notion that each of us has a single, essential type, as Jung believed, she demonstrates that all those types, all those surrealities exist within each of us. We are not condemned to conform to the type that others want us to be.

Finally, from her first performance at the Danceteria to the adventures of her most recent persona, Madame X, and her monumental Celebration Tour, Madonna has demonstrated four key characteristics of "postmodernism," simultaneously effecting and reflecting a change in our culture: rejection of modernism; deconstruction, and systemic and structural critique; pluralism, and multiplicity of voices and sources of authority; and juxtaposition and intersection. "Open Your Heart" and "Express Yourself" might've been her first videos to explicitly react to modernism, but it's The Confessions Tour in 2006 that thoroughly manifests it. In a single set of "Live to Tell," "Forbidden Love," and "Isaac," we see Madonna on a giant, disco-mirrored crucifix; we hear heart-rending stories of abuse and isolation from her dancers; we see a number rising on screen, the number of children in Africa orphaned by AIDS; we read excerpts from Jesus' parable of the Sheep and the Goats; we watch pairs of male dancers, branded with Jewish and Muslim symbols, delivering supremely precise arm-choreography; we watch a woman in a burqa dance with such passion she explodes the cage she's trapped in; we hear a shofar and the voice of a Yemeni Jew. It's impossible to take it all in, and I've been processing this moment since I saw the concert in 2006. That's the point, isn't it? We focus on what we *can* or *need to* focus on, we apply it to our own lived experiences, and whatever happens next is up to us. We can take action to change the world, or passively allow others to change it for us.

All of these threads converged in The Celebration Tour. Fans and critics expected a retrospective victory lap, but instead of just revisiting her greatest hits (which would've been satisfying enough) Madonna reframed them. Ever a maximalist, Madonna didn't just create an experience that narrated her history. It also gave her fans a deep insight into how she moved the needle in popular culture over the previous forty years. A tour like this risks radical narcissism, but while looking inward, she also looked outward. With each song, with each phase of her life and career, and even with her political and social messaging, she invoked the memories of people who inspired and influenced her—and who continue to do so. The fingerprints of her parents, Keith Haring, Michael Jackson, and Martha Graham are all over the show, several of her children joined her on stage in poignant and impressive moments, and she highlighted—even recreated—moments in the club and Ballroom scenes of NYC in the late '70s and early '80s. Instead of lionizing her contributions to culture, the concert asked her audience to look around, to remember the shoulders we stood on, the uplifting and adversarial relationships that shaped us, and the future that we can build.

The Song of Songs

Oh, if you were my brother
Nursed at my mother's breast,

I'd kiss you in the streets
And never suffer scorn.

I'd bring you to my mother's home
(My mother teaches me)

And give you wine and nectar
From my pomegranates.

O for his arms around me,
Beneath me and above!

O women of the city,
Swear by the wild field doe

Not to wake or rouse us
Till we fulfill our love.

Marcia Falk, *The Song of Songs: A New Translation
and Interpretation*

I was not introduced to the *Song of Songs* in Catholic school. I mean, I knew it was there, but, beyond the occasional excerpts at weddings, we didn't spend much time with it. Maybe it wasn't a priority because it's one of two books in the Christian canon that doesn't even mention God, but when I stumbled across its pages in high school, I was struck by the bold sexuality of the Song. I realized quickly that the absence of the Song from our curriculum had more to do with our own (collective) discomfort with sexuality, one of the unfortunate stereotypical hallmarks of Catholic culture. Even saturated in the flowery language of the King James or other conventional translations, the language of desire is loud and clear throughout the Song. Because of the absence of God in the text and its overt sexuality, "official" interpretations projected the Song as the vestige of an ancient wedding ritual or as a metaphor describing the relationships between God and Israel (for Jews) or between Christ and the Church (for Christians).

As a teenager, I did teenager things, like listening to songs for hours, attempting to learn the lyrics by rote, alternately wallowing in the pity of sad songs and ecstatically dancing with the happy ones. I spent a lot of time with the *Song of Songs*, too. At one point, I thought the Song would be the inspiration for my first great musical composition, a choral setting of the Song. That never happened, mostly because I'm not a composer, but phrases like "Let him kiss me with the kisses of his mouth" and "How delicious is your love, more delicious than wine!" sang in my head. I knew the text lived in a world of gender norms—I knew that the voices of the Song were a man and a woman...but those voices also gave me language for desire that, as a closeted teenager in the era before *Will & Grace* and *Ellen*, I wasn't learning anywhere else, and descriptions of intimacy in the text that didn't highlight a woman's anatomy (which is a fair amount of the total text) were seared into my mind, giving my teenage self two important insights: First, this is relevant. Like, oh my god, scripture actually reflects life. Who knew? And second, sex isn't just part of life—it's at the core of our experience. It's included, quite explicitly, in scripture. #mindblown

I connected with Marcia Falk in college when she guest-lectured in one of my courses. After much research and reflection, she put aside interpretations of the Song that treated it as pure metaphor; she even set aside the notion that it was a single work composed by one hand. Falk approached it with a poet's sensibility and uncovered the music and sentiment of the original Hebrew text, typically lost in literal translations of the Song. She also approached it with a feminist sensibility and suggested that the Song could include canonical texts composed by women. Falk asserted that the Song itself is an anthology of love poems. While some editing over time probably sought to cohere disparate voices and make the text adaptable for ritual use, distinction between poems remains. Falk identified thirty-one. What stayed with me the most, though, was her insight that reinforced my own instincts, that the poems were not metaphorical, that they reflected sexuality as an essential and important component of the experience of being human.

When I started to teach scripture, Falk's insights guided me to find ways to introduce sacred text not as distant and ancient or as a series of prescriptions for living. I wanted students to see it as living and evolving and responsive; I hoped students would see that the intersection of scripture with life is, at the very least, an interesting juxtaposition. The Song was, I thought, a perfect text to introduce the problem of translation, and the history of its interpretation was fodder for exploring how our context both enables and limits our understanding and application of a text. What I didn't anticipate, though, was how shocking the Song would be to my students. I later tweaked my scriptural interpretation unit to explore issues of translation with the first line of Genesis and to consider divergent interpretations with the Akedah. *Then* we moved to the Song and focused on the intersection of sacred text and life; in this case, we talked about sex and sexuality as central to the human experience, so central it made it into the Bible. If this resonated with any of my students, I thought, I've done my job.

When I read this poem in particular today, I'm struck by the juxtaposition of love and fear, a juxtaposition anyone who has been "in the closet" might relate to. If you were my brother, the speaker laments, we could be affectionate, intimate, and authentic. The speaker hints at suffering public scorn, but she finds safety at home, protected by her mother and by the women of the city. She finds safety with her lover's arms around, beneath, and above her, and the love they share is not metaphorical or cerebral or agapic—it is physical and passionate. She offers the wine and nectar from her pomegranates...the Song is not subtle. Falk's translation of the text beautifully excavates the passion that was buried beneath the florid King James translation and filtered by our collective and individual shame for so long.

I'm reminded that these were among the words that first led me to understanding and owning my sexual identity, long before pop culture and therapy found me there. Finding my own life reflected in and energized from an ancient poem is affirming, and while there's no mention of God or ultimate concern, these words also invite me back to the world of the text, to the world of mystery and revelation and transformation.

Designing Women

From 1986 to 1993, Linda Bloodworth-Thomason channeled righteous rage into Julia Sugarbaker. People give Dixie Carter the credit for her delivery, but the fury was all Bloodworth-Thomason's. *Designing Women* provided a portrait of the South that I'd never seen from the suburbs of the Midwest—the show intentionally leaned into stereotypes about Southerners and about professional women—and for tween-me, it was exotic in all the best ways. Glamorous women running an interior design business in shoulder pads—such shoulder pads!—it was everything. Like other shows that echoed Norman Lear's legacy of mining real-life for comedy and insight, warts and all, *Designing Women* engaged some of the biggest social battles of the era, and Julia Sugarbaker became an unlikely superhero. She didn't show up in a cape and armed with some fantastic weapon or extraterrestrial strength; instead, she showed up to the scene in a helmet of stiff hair with battle-ready high heels and shoulder pads. Her superpower, a secret weapon wielded to protect the vulnerable, the righteous, and the marginalized, was her tongue, which was capable of cutting all the villainous Marjories, Ray Dons, Imogenes, and Phyllises of the world down to size, or at least down to our common humanity. Who wouldn't want Mrs. Sugarbaker in their corner?

My friend Adnan and I visited Palm Springs several years ago, and we found a gay bar that peppered clips from TV shows and movies among music videos. Video bars, a staple of the modern gay scene and the grandchild of the sing-along piano bar, constitute a vital resource for disseminating queer culture. Like the memes that fill social media, they capture moments worth celebrating, deconstructing, or satirizing, moments that inform popular consciousness and teach us when to laugh, but when it comes to queer culture, piano and video bars also introduce legends and legendary moments of the past to the children. Stumbling into one of these spaces can be disorienting for some—and a lifesaving delight for others.

Within minutes of getting a drink, Julia was on the screen, slowly moving toward Marjorie in one of her earliest and greatest take-downs. Julia overheard a few young pageant queens mocking her baby sister, Suzanne, a former Miss Georgia, for gaining weight and touting her talents as a baton twirler, and she took it as an opportunity to educate Marjorie on what she missed.

> You probably didn't know that Suzanne was the only contestant in Georgia pageant history to sweep every category except congeniality, and that is not something the women in my family aspire to anyway. Or that when she walked down the runway in her swimsuit, five contestants quit on the spot. Or that when she emerged from the isolation booth to answer the question, "What would you do to prevent war?" she spoke so eloquently of patriotism, battlefields, and diamond tiaras, grown men wept.

By this point, every man in the bar recited along in a variety of affected Southern accents, each of us marking the name *Marjorie* à la Julia, with exaggerated emphasis and smiling disdain.

> And you probably didn't know, *Marjorie*, that Suzanne was not just any Miss Georgia, she was *the* Miss Georgia. She didn't twirl just a baton, *that baton was on fire*. And when she threw that baton into the air, it flew higher, further, faster than any baton has ever flown before, hitting a transformer and showering the darkened arena with sparks! And when it fi-

nally did come down, *Marjorie*, my sister *caught* that baton, and 12,000 people jumped to their feet for sixteen and one-half minutes of uninterrupted thunderous ovation, as flames illuminated her tear-stained face! And that, *Marjorie*—just so you will know and your children will someday know—is the night that the lights went out in Georgia!

Adnan, the only one in the bar who wasn't reciting along with everyone, was completely overwhelmed. What could make a bar full of men stop in the tracks to recite an eighties-era TV monologue with devotion often reserved for the Preamble of the Constitution?

Over the course of the series, Julia challenged prejudices about Southerners. She challenged archaic notions about womanhood, autonomy, and professional life. She challenged assumptions about relationships, marriage, and divorce, about parenthood and civic engagement. She highlighted sexism in health care. She offered a more complex portrait of identities of faith and demonstrated that one could be both liberal and religious. She even gave a lecture resulting in the message, "We don't care!" to Donald Trump (that we all should've heeded more closely).

In the '80s, queer folx were making gains in visibility, social acceptance, and legal protections, but that visibility made them more vulnerable. Their gains were treated by some as dilutions or subtractions of dominant groups' pieces of the American pie. But civil rights—and the dignity of living—aren't pie. It's not a limited amount to be portioned and rationed or hoarded by a few. The AIDS epidemic fueled both obvious and latent prejudices against gay men toward a fury woven with fundamentalist Christian rhetoric and centuries-old myths. While complicated in its origin, the message from those corners was clear: queer people aren't "us," and "they" deserve to die. Despite this, Julia Sugarbaker had our backs.

The scene that stays with me today, from an episode I can't watch without weeping, introduces Tony Goldwyn in a guest role as a client, a gay man diagnosed with AIDS who hires the Sugarbaker team to design his funeral. When his path crosses with Imogene, an old friend and longtime client of the Sugarbakers, Imogene embodies the animus against queer people and lays into Tony and the Women with a familiar manipulation of scripture and circumstances to justify her hatred. Goldwyn's character and the Women respond with facts, but Imogene says clearly and plainly what too many people believed, what too many people still believe: "[AIDS] has one thing goin' for it: it's killing all the right people." That's the match to the fuse that Julia needed, that transformed her into the hero who handily escorts Imogene out of their lives and reminds her that "If God was giving out sexually transmitted diseases to people as a punishment for sinning, then you would be at the free clinic *all the time*. And so would the rest of us."

I was eleven when the episode aired, just starting to develop an understanding of myself and of sexuality. Like most queer kids, I didn't have a guide to navigate the changes and construction of identity that happen with adolescence like my peers had. I didn't have people like me in my world (that I knew of). I only knew that I was different, and the world was telling me that my difference would kill me, and it would be all my fault. Thank God I had Julia to stand up to bullies, at least the fictional ones. Thank God we all did, and the best way we can express our gratitude is with reverent and enthusiastic recitation of Julia's most sacred words.

Indigo Girls

When I was in high school, I visited my brother Joe and his family in rural New Jersey for a long weekend. It's called the Garden State for a reason—parts of the state retain stretches of beautiful farmland and countryside, dotted with houses that date back to colonial times (or at least foundations and hearths that do)—but it's not the most exciting part of the world for a teenager. Joe arranged a day in NYC to walk around Manhattan a bit, give me a taste of city life, and see a show. The next night, we were back in his quiet living room, in his quiet stretch of farmland, in a very quiet part of the world, and he asked me a series of get-to-know-you questions, picking my brain for interests, tidbits that might point to a personality underneath all the acne and awkwardness. "What music do you listen to?" Without thinking, and without activating my *don't-let-anyone-know-you're-gay* shields, I blurted out, "The Indigo Girls." He paused, furrowed his brow in the way that my family members furrow our brows when we're detecting something. "That's sort of a… niche band, isn't it?"

He didn't say it with judgment—more with curiosity, as if to say, "Did you just confirm what I've always suspected, what we *all* suspected?" When I did start to share this part of my life with siblings, the majority responded with a distinct lack of surprise, which made me wonder, why didn't anyone say anything? Or worse, why didn't anyone care? It would've been very counter to my family's culture for anyone to speak up like that, to ask probing personal questions, or really to say anything explicit about sex or, you know, how to live. And besides, if any of them had broached the topic with twelve-year-old me who was lonely as fuck (but nobody asked and I never told), or fifteen-year-old me who was conflicted as fuck (but nobody asked and I never told), or seventeen-year-old me who was angry as fuck (but... you see where this is going), I probably would've responded with embarrassment and deference, if not denial.

"That's sort of a...niche band, isn't it?" There I was, sitting on a slightly comfortable loveseat in a quiet corner of his home, wondering, *Is this when it happens?* Was Joe about to squeeze some truth out of me? Would he volley euphemisms and hints and wait for me to name it? As the youngest sibling, I was trained in the art of deference, so all I could do was wait until someone asked. And when he didn't ask, I was aware that this would be one more mystery, one more aspect of my life that my family might've recognized but wouldn't or couldn't embrace. Over time, I leaned on my siblings' experiences and wisdom for all sorts of things—their music and movie tastes introduced me to both pop culture standards and how to appreciate satire and when to laugh at irony; their own ebbs and flows showed me how to navigate Mom's moods and manipulate Dad's generosity, how to sneak into the house after the curfew, and how to throw a party without getting caught (lesson #1: don't leave a trash bag of beer cans by the kitchen window); a subtle competition underlying all our interaction taught me how to read a room, how to identify the ways I could succeed, and how to avoid any chance of failure (and the litany of jokes and jabs that would follow)—but now, suddenly, I had to figure it out on my own.

"That's sort of a...niche band, isn't it?" Indigo Girls constituted a substantial amount of my high school soundtrack. I went to an all-boys high school, my girlfriends and most of my friends who were girls went to an all-girls high school, and it was the '90s. *Say Anything* didn't lie: at every party, there was at least one girl with a guitar, ready with an angry song to sing. Seriously, wherever and whenever we gathered in any sized group, a guitar would emerge, and at least two parts of harmony would float over the strums from the Indigo Girls' songbook.

As far as I knew, none of these girls was gay (or, at least they weren't openly so at the time), but grunge was in. Except for uniform hours at school and a few fancy occasions, we all adopted the mild androgyny of Birkenstocks, plaid shirts, baggy sweaters, and baggier jeans. You know, just like the Indigo Girls. Actually, I don't know if they ever wore Birks—they probably rocked boots—but when they recruited me as a backup singer in my fantasy, we all had matching sandals. Nobody could accuse anybody of dressing like a dyke or dressing like a fag. Indigo Girls made dressing like a dyke cool. This was my niche, my little corner of the world where everyone loved a duo of lesbians rocking it, where I didn't let anyone else know what was going on, and where I was listening very closely for clues about what would come next.

"Closer to Fine" was an anthem for me in those days. When we sang it, I smiled a little brighter than everyone around me because I was singing something that made me stand tall, that fueled me with pride and filled me with hope, and I wasn't singing it alone (even if I was the only one who knew what the song was really about). My path followed strangely closely to the journey that the Girls sang about. The questions I started asking about my identity, my desires, my limitations led me to questions about the nature of people and things, about what people mean and what people say, about the experiences that really transform people and communities. Some kids escape their burdens and their cages by imagining someplace else and going there in the safety of their dreams; I escaped by thinking deeply, thinking broadly, constantly asking myself who I was, where I was, where I would be next so that by the time I was fully myself, I'd have the tough questions out of the way. In other words, so I could start clean slated, so that the hardest to learn would be the least complicated, so that I'd be even closer to fine (see what I did there?).

Camp

There are iconic songs. And then there are *iconic songs*. Let me set the scene: you see, Effie had the strongest voice in the group (the other two were supposed to sing backup), but she was pushed to the back row because Deena was prettier, more moldable, thinner. The relationship among the Dreams frays, they scold Effie for being late, being hard to work with, being inconsistent, and then Curtis, their manager and Effie's lover, cuts her out of the group right there in the dressing room before a big show. She turns to the girls she'd sung with since they were kids, appealing to their loyalty, but they respond succinctly and harshly, "You were our trouble...and now we're telling you, it's all over."

They're singing this exchange, and the music underneath is rapid, like a panicked heartbeat. And then Effie tells us, "I'm not going." A single note repeats like a clock-chime, marking the start of *that song*, and Effie begins an epic plea to be loved, to be respected, to be kept. Effie thrashes and soars as each of the people she counted on walks out of her life. The music under her is stark, letting her voice own every last corner of the theater. She starts in a forte, with wide-mouthed, wider-eyed notes, and somehow builds in volume and stature. I heard once that, in the original production, audience members were on their feet applauding and stomping by the time she holds the impossibly long and breathless note eliding two verses, only half-way through the song. She climbs to the last bars, "You're gonna love..." (she stretches and wrings the syllable for every last morsel)...and then the moment that secured Jennifer Holliday a Tony Award and launched her into the stratosphere of Broadway divas comes. She finishes "love," nearly collapsing, wringing oxygen from every cell of her body, and she takes in the deepest, fastest, most piercing breath, and belts "me," on a single, clear note that lasts for eleven seconds.

Dreamgirls dominated Broadway for four years, a master-piece from the mind of Michael Bennett that won six Tonys. The movie that followed many years later launched another Jennifer into the stratosphere and earned her an Oscar. The play is great. The movie is great. But ask a homosexual about *Dreamgirls*, and there's only one moment that matters: Jennifer Holliday's desperate gasp before her last note. It's revered. It's imitated in gay bars (and showers) around the world. It's sacred. So let's be clear: you don't fuck with Effie's song.

Flash forward to Cambridge, 2003. A group of twenty-some-thing homosexuals files into a movie theater. They watch a much-anticipated indie flick about a musical theater summer camp. They laugh, they cry. When one of the Black campers complains about the dominance of White-centered plays and colorblind casting that put kids of color into White roles, his little brother dressed as the rebbe of Anatevka at his side, the director stages *Dreamgirls*, but the small number of Black campers means that, well, a White girl plays Effie. It was a ridiculous and hilarious plot twist in an already brilliant and wickedly funny movie. But then that clarion note sounds, and the White girl started singing, and the homosexuals froze—the whole row of them, captive, each thinking, "Is she gonna do it? Oh God...*is* she gonna do it?" And then she did it. It was the clutch of pearls heard round the world.

I relish recounting musicals—I always have. I adored Angela Lansbury and Bernadette Peters for their musical roles well before I learned algebra. I could sing three Sondheim librettos by the time I started high school, and though I shudder to admit it now, three by Lloyd Webber, too. I was a theater kid, and in my small, Catholic school, I was the only one. I auditioned for *Bugsy*

Malone in the local community children's theater, the first in my eight-year career of illustrious roles like Sidekick in *Li'l Abner*, Father Rabbit in *The Wind and the Willows*, and (drumroll please) the Wiz in, well, *The Wiz*. I was a founding member and officer of my high school's chapter of the International Thespian Society and looked forward (perhaps a bit too much) to the annual high school theater festival downstate. Sure, we got to see a lot of plays and go to a lot of workshops—I giddily learned the choreography to "One" from Michael Bennett's *other* masterpiece—but the anticipation wasn't rooted in a desire for developing my skills. I was going to be around a lot of other people like me. People who knew the difference between *Funny Girl* and *Funny Lady*. People who understood why Stephen Sondheim was a national treasure. People who didn't really care if I slipped and let out a lispy "s" or crossed my legs or blushed when a cute boy walked by.

Our little drama club—er, excuse me, Thespian society— was a safe space inside my enormous all-boys high school. At the annual theater festival, I heard about summer camps that focused on theater and music, and despite my passionate cries (I asked awkwardly three times), my parents wouldn't send me. When *Camp* premiered, I had my chance to see what I'd missed, but when we saw an eleven-year-old kid say to the sports counselor on the bus, "We have sports?" and then turn to join a singalong of "Losing My Mind" from *Follies*, I knew I was witnessing the summer camp of my high school dreams.

Camp opens with a dream sequence, a fantasy performance, with the cast of campers singing backup to Sacha Allen's warm and vibrant rendition of "How Shall I See You Through My Tears." The camera splices vignettes of a few of the main characters at home, in the worlds they're eager to escape, including Michael who, rejected from his prom because he showed up in drag, falls victim to a gay bashing. As a group of boys is punching and kicking him, his eyes drift to a happy place, back at camp, surrounded by the other misfits who, at least once a year, gave him space to be himself. I'm not sure I stopped crying during that first screening, from the moment Michael looked beyond his bullies to the final credits, mostly because I couldn't stop thinking, "What if...what if I'd gone to a camp like that? What if I'd been more insistent, more clear? What if...what would be different?"

I imagined myself at that camp, on stage with those characters. I saw myself in the trash cans doing Beckett, in the background of "Turkey Lurkey Time," just offstage, appalled, as Anna Kendrick's Fritzi wreaks her revenge on the queen bee and takes over "The Ladies Who Lunch." But more importantly, I saw myself bunking with other boys who didn't care that I was the one with a portrait of Stephen Sondheim on the wall, in rehearsals laughing at my foibles in tap dancing without worrying that I looked too fey, waking up early and donning drag to surprise Michael for his birthday. I'm still sappy and wistful when I watch *Camp*, but I don't mourn the path-not-taken anymore. I'm heartened that other kids *did* have that experience, that the students I've taught grew up in a world where life at Camp Ovation is, if not the norm, acknowledged as a legit way to be a kid and to tap into talents that form a lifelong foundation for joy.

The film culminates in the biggest production of the camp season, the benefit, and at the last moment the camp counselors recruit Tiffany Taylor's Jenna. Because her father wanted Jenna to lose weight, the movie begins with her jaw wired shut, but the counselors snip the wires and unleash the voice we've been waiting for. Jenna, front and center and suddenly unsilenced, sings the song I wish I could've sung as a teenager, the song I wish I could've believed as a teenager. "Here's where I stand," she sang, "Here's who I am. Love me, but don't tell me who I have to be." She sang to her father, but, like a diva, like Ethel and Lena and Judy and Diana and Liza and Madonna before her, she sang for every kid on that stage. She sang for every kid who wanted to be on that stage. She sang for every one of us who filled the theater that night in 2003.

Noël Coward &
Paul Lynde

"It is discouraging how many people are shocked
by honesty and how few by deceit."

Noël Coward

I once heard a story from a lounge singer about Noël Coward. A famous playwright at the time—playwrights floated at the height of celebrity in those days—he was being interviewed by a group of reporters. One asked, "Mr. Coward, is it true that you are a practicing homosexual?"

It's a shitty question for a reporter to ask. Well before the dominance of shock journalism, the question was a trap. You see, in the UK, sodomy was punishable by death until 1861 (when the penalty was softened to ten years in prison), and the so-called Blackmailers' Charter in 1885 made any homosexual act illegal, with or without witnesses. A discovered love letter was often enough to prosecute. The Wolfenden Report of 1957, officially titled "The Report of the Departmental Committee on Homosexual Offences and Prostitution," debunked the idea that homosexuality was a disease or mental illness, but it took a decade for the UK to legalize same-sex acts (only partially, at that). While much of the developed world was moving forward with recognizing the rights of queer people, the Iron Lady (whose name I dare not speak) pushed through Section 28, banning any "promotion" of homosexuality. That translated to teachers letting their students be bullied and harassed because intervening would be construed as such promotion. It wasn't repealed until 2003. Along the way, countless queer people suffered legal and social persecution with inhumane punishments and devastating consequences. Oscar Wilde, the master of 19th century wit, was imprisoned; Alan Turing, whose mathematical genius famously won the war and laid the foundation for later innovations like, oh let's see, the internet, was chemically castrated.

So to ask a public figure, "are you a practicing homosexual?" is to invite a confession. How did Coward respond? True to the mastery of language and timing that drive his scripts, he responded, "Practicing? Darling, I'm perfect."

I've never been able to confirm the story, but it's believable because of other, better-documented anecdotes. He quipped that he'd love to sing "There Are Faeries in the Bottom of My Garden," a popular song at the time, "but I don't dare. It might come out 'There Are Faeries in the Garden of My Bottom.'" He noted that "homosexuality is becoming as normal as blueberry pie," though his logic for the observation was wildly sexist. But most profoundly to me, he wrote "Mad About the Boy." Ostensibly written for a woman's voice, the singer pines for a star of the silver screen, but when I heard a recording of Coward singing it himself, I knew it came from deep within him. It's a song of unrequited love—charming, when you think it's about a movie star whose celebrity keeps love from becoming a reality, but heartbreaking if you hear a man who longs for another man.

Mad about the boy
It's pretty funny but I'm mad about the boy
He has a gay appeal that makes me feel
There may be something sad about the boy

Walking down the street
His eyes look out at me from people that I meet
I can't believe it's true but when I'm blue
In some strange way I'm glad about the boy

I'm hardly sentimental
Love isn't so sublime
I have to pay my rental
And I can't afford to waste much time

If I could employ
A little magic that would finally destroy
This dream that pains me and enchains me
But I can't because I'm mad about the boy

A few decades later and across the Atlantic, another perfect homosexual's star rose. Paul Lynde debuted on Broadway with Eartha Kitt and performed with Carol Burnett in the early days of television. After starring as Harry MacAfee in *Bye Bye Birdie* on Broadway and in the film adaptation, he was among the most recognizable actors of his generation and occupied the center space on *Hollywood Squares* for years. The situation for queer people in the US wasn't any rosier than for folx in the UK, and social stigma translated into lost housing, employment, and autonomy. Despite this, one zinger at a time, Lynde made America laugh with plainly gay humor.

Marshall: According to Billy Graham, is immorality contagious?
Lynde: I know he was down with it for about a month.

Marshall: You get a headache right after romance. According
to Dr. Thotusen, is there anything wrong with you?
Lynde: No, but I need a softer headboard.

Marshall: During the War of 1812, Captain Oliver Perry made
    the famous statement, "We have met the enemy and…"
    What?
Lynde: They are cute.

Marshall: According to legend, who looks better, a pixie or
    a fairy?
Lynde, in a deeper voice: Well, looks aren't everything!

As a kid, I got glimpses of Lynde's tenure in the center square through reruns, but I really met him as Uncle Arthur, Samantha's prankster warlock uncle and Endora's agitating brother on *Bewitched*. Though the show tried to give him a girlfriend in one episode, Uncle Arthur was undoubtedly gay, and his sister, Endora, was the first drag queen I adored. Unlike most of the men I saw on TV or in the movies, Lynde, with effete manners and flowy, vocal-fried parlance, wasn't overtly masculine or tough. And unlike most of the men on TV or in the movies who shared those traits, Lynde wasn't the butt of anyone's jokes. He wasn't funny because he appealed to crude stereotypes—he was funny because he delivered witty and cutting insights from a distinctly queer point of view.

Marshall: According to the old song, what's breaking up that
    old gang of mine?
Lynde: Anita Bryant.

Coward and Lynde each embodied a particular type: the witty homosexual. It's a type that has been reduced to insulting tropes like the sissy or the gay best friend in rom-coms, but it has also soared in characters like Jack McFarland on *Will & Grace* and the Sassy Gay Friend. Like Coward and Lynde before them, they make the jokes on their own terms and reveal depth, experience, and edge, but unlike Coward and Lynde, Jack and the SGF exist in a popular culture in which queer characters are given flattering portraits rooted in lived experience. In the worlds that Coward and Lynde navigated, comical, clownish, grotesque depictions reinforced notions that queer people were either dangerous or expendable, just as Anita Bryant would've had us believe. Even as a kid watching reruns, I knew that Lynde's humor was a form of deflection, a form of defense, but it was only as a grown man that I recognized his humor as more than a shield from the harshest currents of social norms. It also decimated others' desire to reduce him to type.

Yaz & Erasure

In the summer of 1991, my parents and I participated in the Ulster Project, in which an American town would host teenagers from Northern Ireland. The group—half Catholic, half Protestant—spent the month touring the city and doing lots and lots of ice breakers, all intended to build bridges and dismantle the barriers to peace in the region. The experience sledgehammered open my worldview. On one level, I couldn't unlearn the things I'd absorbed about the conflict in Northern Ireland, the stories I'd heard about fear and violence and despondence, the legacy of hate. On another level, I made deep and resonant connections with people who grew up half a world away. I suddenly had friends from Europe, which, in my head, upped my cool factor considerably. We spent hours giggling at the different phrases we used for this or that, outlining how we understood words and experiences differently, and comparing our customs. And one new friend, Roisin, introduced me to Erasure.

At a time when grunge was dominant, when our local soundtrack was filled with dissatisfied-with-the-world tracks from Nirvana and REM, Roisin opened a door to a dancefloor with driving rhythms, catchy hooks, and creative synth. Vince Clarke and Andy Bell made compelling and brilliant pop music, but, more importantly for me, they introduced me to queer art and culture. "A Little Respect" became a glamorous anthem in a world of un-showered, plaid-clad angst. When I got my driver's license a year and a half later, three tapes were on steady rotation when I drove: Madonna's *The Immaculate Collection*, Mandy Patinkin's *Dress Casual*, and Erasure's *Wild!*

Once I had my license and could get myself wherever I needed to be, I found myself running a lot of errands to bookstores. "They didn't have it in stock," I'd tell my mother when she asked about the success of my ventures. That may have been true, but I never made it to the info desk to ask. Upon entering a Borders or Barnes & Noble, I'd detour to the magazines, giant walls covered with the month's editions of every serial you could imagine, sometimes from all around the world. I'd casually flip through magazines focused on the news, drift into gossip and pop culture, make my way through design and spend too much time obsessing over *Architectural Digest*, and feign surprise when I landed in front of all the gay rags. "Oh," I'd show on my face, "where'd all this come from?" I'd subtly slip a copy of *The Advocate* onto my stack (and slip one or two others with photos of beautiful men underneath it) before moving away from the racks. Once I was in a spot to safely and discreetly peruse them, I'd always be surprised at the number of guys lingering around this section of magazines. We never acknowledged each other except the occasional, muffled "excuse me" or "sorry" when we accidentally and horrifyingly bumped into each other or found ourselves blocking someone's exit, but each of us had a copy of *The Advocate* covering the rest of his collection.

One afternoon, I was practicing this little dance at the Borders in Boystown, and once I'd gotten my fill of gay info and imagery and returned the magazines to their places, I walked through the CD aisles and stumbled across *Upstairs at Eric's*. The album was the debut for Yaz, a collaboration between Vince (of Erasure) and Allison Moyet. Between the connection to Erasure and the surrealist image on the cover, I was convinced, so I put the CD on top of the two very-not-gay magazines I'd snagged for purchase and headed to the register.

The cashier was in his twenties, friendly, and quickly detected my story. He didn't say much, but the look that accompanied his "Did you find everything OK?" said it all. He saw me; he saw me at the magazine rack; he saw me smiling and blushing while flipping through the rags; he saw lots of boys like me; he was a boy like me. He rang up one magazine, then a second, and then, picking up the CD, said, "*Upstairs at Eric's*. I love this album. Have you listened to it?" I blushed, took a slow breath, and eked out, "Not yet." He held the CD to his chest, his shoulders rolled forward a bit, and his eyes closed as he said, "'Midnight.'" His eyes clenched for a moment, like a wince, followed by a little sigh. "Such a good song." He returned the CD to the pile and continued with the transaction, but my eyes were locked on his. He gave me a smile and said, "Have a nice day." I mumbled some form of *thanks* and heard him as I walked away, "You're going to enjoy the album."

I replayed the interaction approximately 693 times on the drive home.

By the time I was home, made it to my room, got the layer of plastic off, got the sticky strip along the edge off, and got the CD into my Discman, I was shaking, slightly but steadily. I hit play. The music bounced and bounded, expanded and contracted. Bright synth and midi sounds contrasted Allison's smoky voice. As she approached the end of the first verse—*Can't stop now, don't you know*—I flopped down on my bed—*I ain't ever gonna let you go*—I closed my eyes—*Don't go!* Remembering the way the cashier looked at me, *saw* me, I let the music wash over me and waited for "Midnight" and a chance to shiver and sigh the way he did just thinking about the song.

The fourth track is experimental, layers of voices, nonsensical phrases, occasional swells of chords and echoes of laughter. And with one last burst of laughter, the track drifts off and is replaced by Allison's voice. *Midnight, it's raining outside, he must be soaking wet…* She sings of heartbreak, of regret for making mistakes that drove her lover into the rain. She pleads for his return and makes the pain of the moment seem epic and eternal. *In all of this, I tell you, I have learnt*—I felt my face contort, the first warning of an ugly cry arriving—*playing with fire gets you burnt, and I'm still burning.* By the time the track finished, I was weeping. I didn't have any heartbreak to cry about, but I feared that I never would. And until that moment, I never had the words to explain my fear, my sense of isolation, my desires, my hopes. I wanted so badly to have an experience that rocked me, to love and be loved in a way that fueled and exhausted me, even when the world denied me the language and tools to find it and told me in small and big ways that it never would, never could, never should happen.

Borders is defunct. CDs are dead. That stupid sticker along the edge of CD cases is, mercifully, a thing of the past. Kids don't have to meander the aisles to find something that looks interesting or wait for word-of-mouth to make it to their ears. They stumble into songs and artists via streaming services whose algorithms and listening patterns generate remarkably precise recommendations. It's a mark of progress—instead of surreptitiously lurking in stores to find music that speaks to them, they can search and find thousands of acts, from the undiscovered to the divas, but an algorithm isn't a friend who is eager to share a slice of the world you haven't seen yet, nor is it fanatical about the shock and sparkle of synth-pop. An algorithm couldn't sense my isolation, couldn't demonstrate the emotional impact of a single song through a sigh, couldn't know me as well as that stranger at the register, couldn't give me a dose of confidence that, someday, I'd know burning and consuming love.

The Women &
All About Eve

There's a moment in *All About Eve* that everybody knows. Celeste Holms' Karen Richards smells a looming outburst and calls out Bette Davis' Margo Channing. "We know you. We've seen you like this before," she says directly. "Is it over or is it just beginning?" Margo, in an off-the-shoulder brown silk dress with a sable trim and a diamond brooch over her heart, holds a Gibson martini and lit cigarette in her right hand and a skewered onion in her left. As the pianist plays a bright, bouncy version of "Thou Swell," she downs the drink in one gulp (her third or fourth already), drops the onion back in the glass before passing it off to the lover who has kindled her jealousy, and sashays to the step. Cigarette still perched between her fingers, she turns, pauses, and announces, "Fasten your seatbelt. It's going to be a *bumpy* night."

It's an interesting, but misleading, moment. Yes, it's a great example of wit, movement, and timing—no one has surpassed Bette Davis' mastery at this intersection, just as no one has surpassed Davis' skill in making her cigarettes supporting players—but it's not the greatest moment in the film. It's not even the greatest moment in *that part of the movie*. It follows a cat-and-mouse chase around the living room before the party starts, with an increasingly jealous Margo and Gary Merrill's Bill Sampson, her recently-returned-from-Hollywood but might-be-crushing-on-Margo's-young-assistant partner, a chase that is a masterwork of writing, choreography with tchotchkes, and steadily building tension. It precedes Margo's soused stupor on the piano bench while she insists the pianist repeat "Liebestraum" ad nauseum and—my favorite moment in the party sequence—drunkenly confronts Anne Baxter's Eve in front of her friends and frenemies. George Sander's Addison DeWitt responds, capturing the sequence perfectly, "You're maudlin and full of self-pity. You're magnificent."

I kind of hate that "Fasten your seatbelts" is the moment people choose to celebrate in *All About Eve*. They could instead point instead to Margo's rant in the empty theater while locking horns with Hugh Marlowe's Lloyd Richards. "All playwrights should be dead for three hundred years," Margo hurls. Lloyd retorts, "It's about time the piano realized it has not written the concerto!"

Or Bill and Margo on the empty stage, swinging from virulent to tender, and Davis demonstrating why she was the best at integrating Martha Graham's technique into her acting.

Or Margo and Karen keeping warm in the out-of-gas car and letting their hair down, and Margo switching off the radio when "Liebestraum" played, sneering, "I detest cheap sentiment."

Or Eve blackmailing Karen in the ladies lounge at the Cub Room. "You'd do all that just for a part in the play," Karen wonders, mystified at Eve's cunning. "I'd do much more," she responds, "for a part that good."

Or Addison's skillfully-timed revelation of Eve's past that puts Eve under Addison's control, prompting Eve to rush to the door to throw Addison out. "You're too short for that gesture," he quips. "Besides, it went out with Mrs. Fiske." And then, wrecked, weeping on her bed, and thinking herself unable to go on stage that night, Eve strains to lift up her head and say, "I couldn't. Not...possibly," before Addison instructs her to give the performance of a lifetime.

Or every time Thelma Ritter's Birdie gives a knowing

look—that alone probably secured an Academy Award nomination for her.

The biggest problem with the "seatbelts" moment is that, isolated, it presents Margo as a brat, as an irrational, if glamorous, drunk preparing to stir up the wasp nest. Sure, that's *one* dimension of Margo, but it's largely an outgrowth of her particular situation, being a woman living in a world that forced a choice between love and success. The film is less about women displacing each other and more about navigating unchallenged, heavily gendered norms that don't let women choose how to be in the world.

In Hollywood, it has always been a rarity when women are able to tell women's stories, but *All About Eve*, not necessarily a beacon of feminism, was adapted from a short story by Mary Orr. About a decade earlier, on the other side of World War II (in fact, it was released the day the Nazis invaded Poland), *The Women* distinguished itself from other films of the day—and other films since—with an all-female cast. It doesn't quite pass the Bechdel Test since the whole plot orbits their relationships with men, but the screenplay was adapted by Anita Loos and Jane Murfin from Clare Booth Luce's play. *The Women* often gets dismissed as a frivolous and melodramatic portrait of upper-class women. It's true—some of the acting is over the top. The final image of Nora Shearer's Mary walking, arms outstretched before her, toward the camera to reunite with her husband is hard to separate from Charles Busch's Angela Arden. But buried under the brilliant barbs that the characters toss at each other like spears is a meditation on women's friendships (and frenemy-ships).

I was introduced to *The Women* by The Gays. A small group watched the movie on a VHS tape in someone's apartment, and, between moments of mesmerization by *every* outfit on screen, I laughed. Sometimes, I laughed at the movie; other times, I laughed at my friends who, half a second before Rosalind Russell or Joan Crawford did on screen, recited their lines like re-vered scripture.

"There is a name for you, ladies, but it isn't used in high so-ciety... outside of a kennel."

I've always delighted in gay men's ability to integrate the greatest wit and repartee into daily conversation (I mean, I've become that man!), but that alone is not why these films sur-vive and get passed on to new generations of queer viewers. It's a bit of our history—gay men could relate to the daily struggles reflected in *The Women* and *All About Eve*; they understood what it meant to navigate a world without being able to make one's own choices. They also understood that members of an already marginalized group could turn on each other. I saw parallels to the viciousness of *The Women* and the manipulation of *Eve* among gay men in Boston. It wasn't a friendly community when I arrived in the summer of 1998.

Before online networks and smartphone apps afforded easier outlets to connect with other people, finding friends included a regular game of "will these people talk to me?" in bars. Even among other gay men, I was in search of a safe place, and I found it among guys who shared my disproportionate commitment to classic films and standard musicals. Beside the piano in Club Café or in front of the screens at Luxor, I found people who could quote them better than I, but I also found people who were as manipulative and disloyal as Eve, as catty and unselfaware as Ro-salind Russell's Sylvia. Luckily, I got to know the playbook (you know, the scripts) and learned to sniff out the Eves and Sylvias, the ones who feed on drama and schadenfreude, and search out the Karens and Birdies, the best companions for Mary and Margo on the road to becoming their best selves.

ManRay

"Daring to be different was worth it"
Shawn Driscoll, author of *We Are But Your Children*

I arrived in Cambridge on a Tuesday. I was twenty-one, start-ing grad school. No furniture, no TV, no internet, no mobile phone. *I'm from before mobile phones, can you imagine? How did I ever find, remember, or accomplish anything?* Just a trunkful of clothes, a PC, and the delirium of living on my own for the first time, of a kid let loose in the Wonka factory. Arriving mid-day, I was able to empty my car, search out hardware and grocery stores to grab the essentials my mother outlined before I left Chicago, and create something like a bed from layered blankets and towels. It got dark. I got tired. I slept on my improvised mattress. I woke up at sunrise with two spider bites on my face and one on my hand and a particular urgency for installing win-dow treatments. I took a shower and hoped that I wouldn't stink of the plastic liner all day, and I set out to start a new chapter. First stop: coffee.

I left my little map behind, deciding to bravely wander my new neighborhood, and walked to the end of my little side street. Turning right would bring me to Central Square, but I decided to turn left and wandered past a couple of blocks of painted ladies and three-flats to the impossible intersection of five streets at varying angles that form Inman Square. I was doubly confused: where's the "square," and how do I get across to the corner shop from which the smell of fresh coffee was wafting? I arrived at the door of the shop, which was propped open but blocked by a chair—it was still five minutes to opening. Jackie quickly introduced herself and asked me to hang out till she got the rest of the place open, and during my five-minute wait I found her likeness in the mural of the neighborhood painted on the side of the building. Jackie was the first butch lesbian I'd ever met. I was simultaneously delighted and terrified, but it felt a good omen for life in Cambridge if Jackie was my first new friend in the neighborhood.

I sipped on my coffee, served in a glass mug, and pecked at a scone from the counter while I flipped through a copy of *Bay Windows*, Boston's go-to gay paper which was stacked near the register. I might've noticed a story or two, but I was foraging for essential information: where was the closest gay bar? A map showed two within a quick walk from my apartment (huzzah!) and a whole cluster in Boston's South End. *My future stomping grounds*, I thought. Wednesday and Thursday filled up with all the things you do when you move someplace—find the post office, update this and that, find that or this, go here and there— and by sundown on Thursday, my body's schedule still disrupted by my cross-half-the-country drive and lack of curtains, I was overwhelmed, exhausted, and thrilled. *Friday*, I thought, *Friday is the night to go out*.

Cute. Dark jeans, a blue T-shirt (it's not New York, so color is OK, right?), my long hair enjoying a very good hair day. *No glasses*. I wouldn't need them; I was staying in the neighborhood, and my eyes weren't that bad. I brushed my teeth one more time, stepped out the door, turned right at the end of my little side street, and glided through Central Square on my way to ManRay. A few people stood in line, in all black. *Damn. Should've worn black*. A bouncer checked my ID, and I got a particular not-gay vibe from him and the two people who'd entered ahead of me. I stopped at the window and paid a cover, then entered. A room to the left, a dance floor to the right, another dance floor straight ahead just past...*that bar.*

I started toward the bar, conscious of being the "new kid" and tunnel-visioned on my destination. I ordered a drink, took a sip, and finally looked up. On a stage across the dance floor, I saw a whip. On another stage, a sling. *I should've worn my glasses.* I looked around at people for the first time and noticed everyone not just in black but wearing all sorts of variations on leather, rope, and latex. *I think I'm here on the wrong night.* Not wanting to look like a prudish asshat, I stood by the bar, enjoyed the music, looked around to take in the crowd, finished my drink, and then feigned an excuse to leave abruptly (though I wasn't talking to anyone who might need an explanation).

On the way out, I picked up a copy of *Bay Windows* from a stack by the door and decided to read information about the club more closely. ManRay had a rotation of themes: Goth, Gay, New Wave, Alternative...quite literally, something for everybody (and every *body*). I'd inadvertently arrived on Fetish Night but vowed to return the next night, and from that night I was at ManRay just about every Saturday and Thursday for three years.

I arrived particularly early one Saturday night and found myself among about a dozen other gawkers, sipping our drinks and fixated on a lone figure on the dance floor. He was tall and wore a long black turtleneck that extended to his ass and was cinched by a belt over black leggings. He wore a broad-brimmed hat, a caricature of a fedora, and danced expansively, expressively, *mostly* moving with the rhythm of the music but *really* moving with some internal beat. He wore oversized sunglasses, Jackie O-style, and didn't seem to notice anyone around him. It got closer to ten and people started trickling onto the dance floor, limiting but not halting his movement. When the first beats of a Whitney remix dropped, a wave of young gay men surged onto the dance floor, and I watched the lone dancer, now unable to keep his sweeping gestures flowing, take a breath and exit.

He was there every week. He didn't talk to anyone, no one approached him. Once, I saw a tall guy in a suit and tan overcoat, carrying a large paper shopping bag, exiting the club. *Strange*, I thought. *Who comes here in a suit?* A few weeks later, I saw the suit arrive. *I wonder...* He went down to the bathrooms and emerged in his turtleneck and belt, the brim of his hat clearing a path to the dance floor for him. He owned every corner of the dance floor until some song invited the surge, which prompted him to slip down to the bathrooms, switch drag, and disappear from the club.

When ManRay closed in 2005, I grieved. The building was sold, demolished, and replaced with an apartment tower. It wasn't the loss of a club that hit me, though it did seem to foretell the end of queer enclaves in Boston. It was the loss of *that* club, of that particular intersection of people, styles, and experiences. That intersection served as a safe space for people to hear and see things they'd never encountered before, they'd never encounter elsewhere; to experiment with new ways of being, of dressing, of connecting with others; to dance with whatever level of skill and whatever degree of abandon.

I found my core group of people at ManRay—if we couldn't find each other elsewhere, we knew we'd see each other on Thursday. Once, in the middle of a hurricane, we found each other at ManRay and laughed off the wimps who let a little rain keep them from going out. I kissed my share of frogs and princes on the dance floor and in private corners of the lounge. I met people from all over the world. It was a touchstone, a reminder and recharge to resist the monotony and conformity that the world desired for us. I never had the courage, but I knew that if I wanted to wear an ensemble of black, from my fedora to my toes, and take over the dance floor, I could have, and folx would've watched me from the side wondering what fantasy fueled me in that moment.

Boston Gay Men's Chorus

We gathered in a large conference room off the lobby of our hotel. We'd just arrived in Berlin and were told to report for an update on our itinerary and a "security briefing."

Security briefing?

The Boston Gay Men's Chorus journeyed to Europe in the summer of 2005 to sing in Germany, Poland, and the Czech Republic. In Berlin, we'd march in the Christopher Street Day parade and perform on the bandstand in the center of the Tiergarten with hundreds of thousands of people watching and sharing the stage with the mayor of Berlin (and his very distracting husband). We'd also give a concert before busing to Wroclaw, where we'd do the first openly gay performance in Poland in the only concert hall in the country that would host us, and then whisk off to Prague for one final concert in the Rudolfinum.

Our total group—singers, staff, spouses, tour leaders—was over 100 people, and we packed ourselves tightly into our meeting room, all feeling a mix of jet lag, travel fatigue, and excitement. A group of right-wing, anti-gay activists had been trying to stop the concert in Poland from happening, we learned. Our promoter in Wroclaw, a successful entrepreneur and owner of a few queer establishments, had been arrested without clear cause. Staff at the venue and people from a local LGBT rights organization would be screening ticket holders at the door to admit only the people they knew to be safe, including regular subscribers and concert goers, folx in the local queer community, and groups of supporters traveling from Krakow and Warsaw for the concert.

A few years earlier, in his welcoming remarks at our first concerts after the 9/11 attacks, the executive director of the chorus quoted Leonard Bernstein, saying, "This will be our reply to violence: to make music more intensely, more beautifully, more devotedly than ever before." That was the moment that I embraced the reality that art is political, that art wasn't an escape from the world but a tool to respond to and shape it. In the 1980s, in the early days of the Chorus, just walking out on stage as a group of openly gay men who weren't apologizing for being alive, who were navigating a ravaging epidemic with little outside support, who embodied a message of "This is us, now let us sing" was an act of political demonstration—I marched with the Chorus in Boston's annual Pride parade with that notion in mind. Singing with the chorus helped me to see that Pride wasn't just a party; it was our chance to own the streets we walked, to be seen as we wanted to be seen, to tell our story as we would tell it. By the time I joined the chorus in 1999, we didn't encounter the resistance and vitriol that the earliest members experienced. We sang to a diverse audience and relied on generous corporate sponsorships—indicators of safety and impact—but there, in a crowded meeting room in Berlin and wondering what we were walking into in Wroclaw, I got my first taste of the consequences of political art.

Though our hotel in Wroclaw was a few blocks from the concert hall, we traveled in our coach buses surrounded by police vehicles. We walked through a column of armed, uniformed police from the bus to the stage door, which was at once titillating and deeply terrifying. At our warmup, we met the promoter who'd been mysteriously arrested and just as mysteriously released that morning. He didn't know us, and he'd have every right to be bitter, to be angry, to be frustrated by this busload of American gays who were stirring trouble that *he* got arrested for, but he was only kind, humble, enthusiastic about our presence, grateful that we were there, and excited to give us a party after the concert.

From the dressing room a few stories up, we could hear a group of protestors gathering. They were chanting, yelling, waving posterboard signs. It took a bit for us to discern what they were saying and what was on the posters: the repeated refrain of "No butt-fucking!" was accompanied by the crude depiction of stick figures engaged in, well, butt-fucking, under a big red circle-and-slash. A counter-protest emerged as a few voices who started shouting louder (and less crudely) suddenly matched the volume of "No butt-fucking!" and then overwhelmed it when a busload of supporters arrived. *Who are these people?* I thought. Not the protestors—our apparent supporters. *Why would they show up just to deal with...this? And for us?"*

We got a standing ovation for just walking onto the stage. In our opening number, we heard a commotion in the foyer and a slam against a wall. All eyes were fixed on Reuben, our director, who flashed back a look of "yes, that's happening, but just keep singing." I don't think we ever performed better, with as much heart, or with as much devotion to our music and to our audience. We finished with an encore, and then another encore, and when half the group was already in the dressing room taking off our soaked-from-sweat tuxes, they called us back onto the stage in whatever state of dress we could muster. They kept applauding and cheering, and we did a third encore, a repeat of "Down by the Riverside," the most rousing number from the concert.

Reuben once told me that he didn't want to take the chorus to fluffy destinations like other groups who toured safer (read: gay-friendlier) spots in Europe and the Americas. He wanted to make a difference, and since the trip to Poland the chorus has traveled to Turkey, Israel, and to South Africa, each a journey designed to bring excellent performance with a message, "This is us, now let us sing." I muttered out something like, "Cool!" with an image of traipsing the world with the chorus forming in my mind, but I wish I had been quicker in my response to Reuben. I should've said, "But haven't we already made a difference?"

When my friend Mario and I joined the chorus, each of us a post-college transplant to Boston, we expected new social connections and a chance to keep singing and get gussied up in a tux once in a while, but my expectations shifted at the end of our first rehearsal. It was tradition to bring all the new chorus members to the front of the room and to sing them a lullaby. Mario and I stood close together, scanning the room and aware that we were being scanned, but it wasn't the kind of scanning that happened in a bar or even just walking down the street. I watched groups of guys cluster together, some swinging their arms around each other, some holding hands. Reuben explained that this was the group's way of welcoming new members, and with the opening notes of "Everything Possible," I felt a warm blanket surrounding me, the embrace of a new, chosen family.

We sang together. We partied together. We flirted, we gossiped. Sometimes, we frustrated each other, and other times, we watched in awe as our chorus brothers stepped up to the mic for a solo or tumbled and leaped in the dance corps. We stood, shoulder to shoulder, with reverence for the history we entered on the stages of Symphony Hall in Boston, of Carnegie Hall in New York, of the Rudolfinum. We stayed out too late after rehearsal on Wednesday nights, avoiding whatever or whomever was at home and needing to stretch out more time with each other. When Pride came around, only a few members volunteered in advance to make the float, but everyone arrived at the last minute to march. We supported each other through grief and upheaval. We sang in support of equal marriage. And a week before the national holiday, we gathered for Chorus Thanksgiving in small groups in members' homes. Sometimes, it was cliques and close friends; sometimes it was people who had no place else to go. One year, while serving myself more potatoes, I asked a guy about his plans for Thanksgiving. He looked at me like I didn't hear him answer the first five times. "This." He either didn't have a (nuclear) family to join, or he didn't want to be with them. It was clear: this was all the family (and turkey) he needed.

Each season, during the first rehearsal with new members, I'd feel anticipation swelling in me. Rehearsal would come to an end, Reuben would invite newbies to the front, and I'd read the confusion in their faces. They'd gather awkwardly in front of the piano, Reuben would say a few words, and I'd move closer to or throw my arm around the friends I always sat next to. This would be the most important concert of the season, the one to welcome our new brothers into the fold, the one to reinforce our ties to each other.

This was our annual reminder that the chorus wasn't *just* about music—it was about making a space where people could be safe, could be brave, could be who they are and be celebrated for all that they are. This was our chance to tell new members for the first time and to remind ourselves, "This is us, now let's sing."

Marlene Dietrich

At the 2003 MTV Video Music Awards, Madonna recreated her debut at the show nearly twenty years earlier and added a twist to her performance of "Like a Virgin." The number opens with Britney Spears starting the song, pushing back a veil as she descended a giant cake in a Madonna-like wedding dress, and then welcoming a second, veiled singer for the next verse—Christina Aguilera unveiled herself, though her voice was a dead giveaway. Two of the dominant pop stars of the era, two celebrities whose relationships and public foibles were the stuff of gossip magazines and the pre-Twitter internet, they paused with the music, looked to the top of the cake, and welcomed Madonna, in full tuxedo, as she descended and sang her then-new satirical single "Hollywood." The trio came to the front of the stage, and, over a musical bridge and the din of an audience that exploded with shocked and titillated cheers, Madonna turned to Britney to give her a full-mouthed, lingering kiss, and then to Christina to do the same before the song moved on. Watching on TV, you would've barely had the chance to see Madonna kiss Christina—after settling on Madonna and Britney, the producers cut to Justin Timberlake (Britney's recent ex), only to catch a self-conscious and steely reaction. It was, one more time for the Material Girl, a surprising and controversial performance...

...but not for the reason you might assume. The twist that Madge added *wasn't* a macking sesh with two other women. The twist was invoking one glorious scene from *Morocco* as homage to Marlene Dietrich's impact on culture. Dietrich plays a cabaret singer, Gary Cooper a French Legionnaire, and they...actually, the rest of the film doesn't matter. Suffice it to say: people fall in love, there are complications, there is pride, yadda yadda. The scene that everyone remembers is in the cabaret. Dietrich emerges in a full tuxedo, top hat and tails to boot. Her left hand hangs casually from a jacket pocket, her right fidgets with a cigarette. The camera cuts to Gary Cooper in the crowd, handsome, dusty, lusty, and bewildered. Dietrich saunters over to a table, pauses to leer at a beautiful woman, and plucks the flower that is set in her hair. She stares at the seated woman, sniffs the just-snatched flower and shifts it to her other hand, allowing her to bend down, lift the woman's chin, and give her a full kiss on the mouth. She stands and tips her hat to the woman, and the restaurant explodes with laughter and applause, a mix of delight and disgust, before Dietrich wanders off, still inhaling the flower's scent. Gary Cooper leaps to his feet with applause, and Dietrich tosses the flower to him before she tips her hat to the crowd and saunters back off stage.

This was before the Hays Code, when Hollywood agreed to censor itself to retain autonomy over an increasingly influential industry and appease meddling legislators. It was an era of bold storytelling and artistic experimentation, and artists like Dietrich moved between the media of film, recorded music, and cabaret with little difference in terms of their free expression. Still, such a scene featuring two women and a stylized sexual pounce was boundary-pushing. Most audience members, like the audience and producers of the 2003 VMAs, were probably shocked and delighted at the cheek of it and more focused on how it shaped the romance between the protagonists, but can you imagine how queer moviegoers might've reacted? Marlene in a man's suit, openly and without reprimand or consequence, kissing another woman to the cheers and applause of an audience of strangers.

Dietrich's career blossomed in the cabaret scene of the German 1920s. She starred in silent films and some of the earliest German talking pictures and performed on stage and in films into her seventies. Throughout her life, she was aggressively unconventional, unwilling to bend to norms that didn't suit her. She relished the drag balls in Berlin and was openly bisexual and unashamed of her variety of lovers—her relationships ranged from Gary Cooper and Mercedes de Acosta to Edith Piaf and JFK. Somehow, her memory has faded among some, but celebrities and commoners alike should look to her as the grandparent of androgynous style. David Bowie, Annie Lennox, Pete Burns, Tilda Swinton, and Harry Styles all walked a path first cleared by Dietrich.

Dietrich's singing voice was iconic and remains hard to imitate, though that doesn't stop gay men from trying when "Falling In Love Again" plays at a piano bar. It's Dietrich's signature song, and if you've heard it once, you can summon the lilt of her voice as her thickly-accented English sighs out, "I can't help it" at the end of every verse. It's a fitting signature, in part because the song seems part of her breath, and in part because the lyrics tell us all we need to know about Dietrich. In most cases, I trust a translator to convey the meaning of a lyric and to make it relevant in another language, but in this case, the English lyrics don't do Marlene justice. They're passive and apologetic—"Falling in love again/ Never wanted to/ What am I to do?/ I can't help it/ Love's always been my game/ Play it how I may, I was made that way, I can't help it"—but the original isn't so apologetic. A more literal translation reads like an anthem, a self-possessed declaration, a bold assertion claiming the singer's place in the world.

I am from head to toe
Attuned to love
Because this is my world.
And nothing else.
This is what I should do,
My nature,
I can only love
And nothing else.

Ellen DeGeneres

"Thank you, Ellen, for giving me
a shot at a good life."

Kate McKinnon

At the 77th Golden Globe Awards, Kate McKinnon introduced Ellen DeGeneres, the second recipient of the Carol
Burnett Award. The moment brought together three generations of genius comedians who share a common thread that
McKinnon articulated beautifully: "a desire to bring everyone
together by laughing about the things that we have in common" and "a way to be funny that is grounded in an expression of joy." These could've been taglines describing every
season of *The Carol Burnett Show*, Bob Mackie wardrobe and
all, and they applied equally well to Ellen's legacy through her
standup, sitcom, and talk show (before the ugly truth of a toxic work environment came to the surface), and to McKinnon's
own burgeoning contributions through *The Big Gay Sketch
Show* and a decade on *Saturday Night Live*. Each of them has
avoided mopping laughs from crassness, lewdness, insults,
or derogation in favor of magnifying the silliness of our lives
and giving us the mirror and the motive to laugh at ourselves.
McKinnon delivered a particularly poignant reflection on the
impact DeGeneres had. As a young, queer person starting to
figure things out, seeing Ellen on TV gave her "a sense of self,"
but that gift came at a cost to DeGeneres. "She risked her en-

tire life, and her entire career, in order to tell the truth, and she suffered greatly for it. Of course, attitudes change, but only because brave people like Ellen jump into the fire to make them change."

Media like television and film are powerful, so powerful that control over it means the direct control of how people see the world. If you were not the focus or the target of the people calling the shots, you were invisible. That's common to the experiences of many groups, but it's especially true for queer people. Visibility on screen was important because we weren't being seen off it. If we were seen, we'd be legitimate; we'd be real. People would get a glimpse into our lives and recognize that, underneath it all, we're human and deserving of the same rights and responsibilities as everyone else. To a younger version of me, any glimpse or hint or even mention of queerness was a morsel, and, in an era in which most narratives about queer people that made it to the big screen connected them to grisly or villainous ends, visibility *not* connected to tragedy made me feel like everything I felt and knew was valid.

I started watching her sitcom before it was rebranded from *These Friends of Mine*. Most folx remember *Ellen* for its build up to "The Puppy Episode" and its aftermath, for being a pioneer in depicting queer people on their own terms, but from the start of the show to the end, even and especially through the coming-out story arc, the show was fundamentally about a group of friends. Most episodes prompted Lucy & Ethel-like entanglements for Ellen and Joely Fisher's Paige or *Three's Company*-like misunderstandings for Spencer or Audrey or Joe to stumble into. The show dropped funny and relatable characters into classic sitcom formulas, but, unlike other shows of the era that revolved around a love-interest or introduced a baby when they ran out of believable plotlines, it kept viewers' focus on that group of friends. They had relationships; they didn't have relationships. They struggled; they needled each other; they showed up for each other. When Ellen (the character) came out, each of her friends reacted differently—*that* was the most important aspect of the whole arc, the depiction of diverse reactions to learned truths. Everybody doesn't respond the same—some are supportive, some *too* supportive, some uncomfortable or angry—but that didn't keep them from sticking together and helping one of their own navigate the storm.

Ellen was important to me not just because I resonated with DeGeneres' humor or because of its synchronous timing with my own coming out. It showed me what to expect from my friends, what was too much, what wasn't enough. DeGeneres' character mimicked the things she experienced in real life—the things we *all* experienced, the things that kept so many in the closet. You've heard the horror stories, right? People share their sexual identities and family members abuse, try to "convert," or disown them. Friends reject them and leave them socially, and often physically, vulnerable. Not too long ago, homosexuality was classified as a mental illness, and losing employment and housing was a real risk.

For the first three years of high school, I was suicidal. I didn't want to harm myself—but I just didn't want to be *here*. I wasn't quite drowning, but I was barely treading water in a sea of depression, anxiety, and loneliness. People who learn this about me are often shocked—a colleague once said to me that she just couldn't reconcile the easy-to-laugh, easier-to-smile, and always-friendly-and-mannered Bill with the child I described. "Neither could I," I tried to explain. "That was part of the problem." People knew and liked—loved, really—the talented young man who was built like a beanpole and rarely said "no" to any request. I was engaged in my classes and constantly involved in a theater production. I had friends and a relatively full social life. I never wanted for anything, and most of my siblings were kind to me and, if not really interested in my life, didn't find me a bother. I went on retreats and found myself comfortable and energized in silent prayer, liturgies, and reflecting with friends about the big questions on our minds.

But when I found myself alone—when the house was empty, when I was in the shower, when I was riding my bike through the empty paths of the forest preserve near home—I wept. My whole body clenched and convulsed as tears flowed and the skin on my neck and face got blotchy. I'd look in the mirror, disgusted by the disfigurement that comes with the "ugly cry" and sink a little deeper. I only acted on my darkest thoughts a few times, and each was a classic "cry for help." I never succeeded in damaging myself physically, but the fact that *no one* heard my cry shattered the little self-confidence I had. During my junior year, with my darkest days behind me, I shared the story of my attempts with a couple of friends who did the right thing. They listened. Then they told my guidance counselor at school, who promptly showed up at the door of my Algebra class to take me to her office where I'd find my dad, who was, betrayed by his face, puzzled but oddly calm.

He took me for a drive through the forest preserve, and we parked in front of one of the long lagoons where we watched a few people fishing and others paddling by on a kayak. "Your counselor tells me that you're struggling." I kept looking at the water, hoping for more kayaks or fishers or ducks to appear and give me something to hold my gaze. "You know, when I was about your age, I tried to hurt myself a few times." *He what?* We might've talked for a while, or we might've sat in silence—I really don't remember. I was lost, trying to assemble the puzzle of my father's life, suddenly aware of *why* he never told stories about growing up. *If he felt like I do, no wonder he didn't want to talk about it. Or maybe he didn't know how.* On the way home, he told me that the counselor provided a few recommendations for therapists, and I agreed to meet one the next day.

I met with this therapist once a week for the next year and a half, my last session a couple of months before I left for college.

I liked him. He was serious but unstuffy, and I felt safe to talk about the isolation I felt among my peers and my siblings while growing up and about the impact that my family's dynamics and my parents' drinking had on me. We talked about the darkest times, and he helped me make space to heal from, or at least cope with, the anxiety and depression that would overtake me. After a few months, I was ready to start talking about sexuality, but despite my attempts to tack in that direction, he never took the bait. Instead, we kept talking about my siblings, about the kids I grew up with, about my parents. Among my family, at school, among friends, and even in my therapist's office, nobody offered me the language I needed, and nobody asked me the questions I wanted so badly to answer. This still surprises me—I'd declared my devotion to Bernadette Peters and Angela Lansbury by the time I was twelve, I was consumed in doing community and school plays, I even did a pretty good impression of Ethel Merman, and not a *single* person thought I might be gay. Or, rather, if they did suspect, not a single person threw me the lifesaver by asking the right question. Without the help of my therapist, I discovered my deepest, most terrifying fear: that I'd never be known, that I'd never be worth knowing.

Ellen's barriers emerged in sessions with a therapist played by Oprah Winfrey in the weeks leading up to "The Puppy Episode." Ellen fears that being gay excludes her from having a normal life, to which Dr. Oprah, smelling internalized heterosexism, responds, "And what is a 'normal' life, Ellen?" She cites the American dream—a house, a picket fence, a dog and a cat, and "someone to love, someone who loves me, someone I can build a life with. I just want to be happy."

Explaining how this feels to her therapist, Ellen jokes that being gay is "not exactly an accepted thing. You never see a cake that says 'Good for you! You're gay!' Except maybe in West Hollywood." But even when those fears are allayed, even when friends and family embrace the change, even when laws are instituted to protect from unfair discrimination, we still have the biggest hurdle of all: internalized hatred and attachment to the life that straight, cisgender people are promised, a life filled with love and prosperity, a life of being known and loved, a life, we're taught to believe, that we forsake with the words "I'm gay."

In the episodes that followed, *Ellen* poignantly explored her parents' reactions with scenes that echoed the experiences of countless queer viewers. One particular scene between Ellen and her dad was a beacon—as her dad tries to wriggle out of talking about Ellen's identity, he argues, "Well you weren't gay yesterday," sparking a laugh from the studio audience. But when he continues, the audience is quiet, almost stunned. "Your brother Stevie had exactly the same childhood and he turned out perfectly normal." Taking a beat to let "normal" reverberate, Ellen responds, "I *am* normal, Dad." She directly negates him when he suggests that she won't have a family, and, finally, the source of his fears emerges: "I don't know any gay people."

She responded, "Yes, you do. You know me."

My parents reacted in similar ways—like to a death, they reacted to my news with deep sadness for the life I wouldn't be able to live. What *Ellen* tried to articulate for the audience is that yes, there is a death—of an illusion, of a false construction, of a fantasy. Ellen's and my parents had to let go of gendered expectations like so many other parents do, expectations that are projected the moment a child is born. They had to let go of an image that was so clear in their minds and so oppressive in mine. They had to let go of an ideal that I was supposed to pursue so they could embrace the child they created. The side effect of this wasn't just family harmony—it's a reorientation of what we expected from each other. We were able to maintain a relationship because instead of grasping at a person I'd never be, they met me where I was, and we walked forward together. Other relationships didn't survive—friends drifted, and a few family members turned cold shoulders to me. It was painful to lose those relationships, to see people refuse to grab my hand and walk the road together, but so many more kept walking with me.

For many of DeGeneres' fans, her coming out was a shock, perhaps because they suffered from a lack of gaydar or because they had *hoped* that they'd never have to reconcile their image of the celeb with an unfamiliar sexual identity…but I think those viewers were mostly shocked because of the novelty. Like her sitcom dad, they thought they didn't know anyone who was gay. But for queer folx, it was thrilling. Finally, we were part of the conversation. Finally, we were visible. Finally, we were normal. Finally, three decades after Stonewall, we had a shot at a good life. And for me, it instilled an idea that I'd eventually believe: that I was worth knowing.

In 2020, DeGeneres was moved to the "cancel" column along with the flurry of celebrities whose actions, inactions, or ignorance led to hostile workplaces and accusations of harassment. Like others who are publicly or privately wrested from their platforms or positions of trust, she was publicly reprimanded, her flaws were exposed, and she closed the door on another chapter of her career. Now that we take certain things—things like visibility, power, and privilege—for granted, I hope that LGBTQ folx stay at Ellen's side—not with blind praise or ignorance of her faults, but with memory of her shepherding us through one massively impactful transformation. For DeGeneres—really, for every queer groundbreaker—I hope we can let go of the illusion and embrace the person with awareness that, flaws and all, she still has an important story to tell.

"You keep hearing the question, is America ready?" In a 1997 interview with *Entertainment Tonight,* DeGeneres responded to the question she was getting from every direction—Why? Why now? Why you? "Nobody is ever ready," she continued. "You can't just wait for America to be ready for things, and that's how we effect change."

musicals

I'm five. I'm with my enormous family in the enormous Arie Crown Theater, and we're seeing the touring production of *Joseph and the Amazing Technicolor Dreamcoat*. It's colorful, every song is different, and it dawns on me that *I'm* Joseph, the little brother that gets picked on and left behind. When his brothers debate leaving him in a well or selling him to a passing group of nomads, I think about the times I was trapped in a toy chest or dangled over a laundry chute to amuse older siblings. When Joseph is at his lowest and loneliest, the chorus cheers him on, "Go, go, go, Joe!"

I'm seven, sitting on an aisle in the same theater for the touring production of *Cats*. Throughout the show, the performers leave the stage to interact with audience members and demonstrate their most convincing feline traits. Jenny Any Dots is on her hands and knees in the aisle, inviting me to scratch her neck. Mr. Mistoffelees lays his head in my lap and purrs. I've had a complicated relationship with cats ever since.

I'm thirteen. My dad and several of my siblings head west for a rafting trip. My mom takes me to New York City, giving herself (and me by extension) a theater weekend for her birthday. We did all the things that were "classic New York" in my mom's imagination—we had dinner in the Oak Room at the Plaza, had a drink (well, I had a soda and she had a drink) surrounded by the caricatures at Bemelmans in the Carlyle, and saw four shows in three days. *Dancing at Lughnasa* tapped into my mom's deeply revered Irish roots. *Lost in Yonkers* introduced me to the magic of Neil Simon's writing and Mercedes Ruehl's acting. *Crazy for You* featured the actor who played Kirk in *Dear John* and the actress who voiced Ariel in *The Little Mermaid* in a song-and-dance spectacular of Gershwin tunes and a contrived love story. But it was *Will Rogers Follies*, Tommy Tune's fantabulous, Ziegfeld-style tribute to the humorist, that flicked a switch in me. I marveled at a stage full of dozens of chorus girls and four chorus boys who told the story of Will and Betty Rogers. Through Coleman, Comden and Green's score and Tune's effervescent choreography, the production embodied (and bedazzled) Rogers' unique wit and commentary. Dee Hoty's voice soared with joy and melancholy, making me think, "I want to do that." The chorus boys danced and sang and danced some more. They were dazzling to me, making me think, "I want to do that."

Throughout my childhood, other boys memorized and rattled off statistics for baseball and football players with Rainman-like intensity and precision. They tossed out figures and terms like everyone just understood what an RBI or what a "line of scrimmage" was. About 90 percent of the time, I was picked last when teams divided in gym class or recess, at least in part because I looked at them with a panicked blank when they mentioned positions and strategies. When I was up to bat, boys in the outfield moved closer to the plates—the ultimate straight-boy shade, the unspoken consensus that I posed no threat, that I'd be an easy out. They watched action movies and loved when people got beaten up or objects exploded. I was the kid struggling to hold back tears during a Halloween sleepover when the hosting parents thought it was OK for a bunch of third-graders to watch a horror flick. Those boys didn't seem to have any feelings, or at least they weren't occupied with theirs or distracted by the constant navigation of people and expectations and rules that weren't instinctive to me and didn't seem to be written down anywhere.

By the time my body started to change, ahead of most of my classmates' biological timelines, I was already isolated, an easy target for teasing. Any crack in my voice or quirk while moving was an invitation to highlight my sudden growth spurts and suddenly low voice. Changing into the uniform shorts and T-shirt for gym class was the most terrifying part of my day. I'd taken to wearing two pairs of underwear—a pair of briefs under loose boxer shorts, intended to hide the parts of me that were suddenly and radically different from others'—but that backfired when another boy spotted my doubling effort and launched a new line of assault from my classmates.

When I started doing plays in our local children's community theater, I suddenly didn't have to navigate the traps that had been laid for me in school. All the bits that I'd been collecting, that had been swirling in my head with nowhere to land, finally had a place to go. Tony Award winners, who played which iconic role, who played it better, how to tell Rodgers and Hammerstein apart from Rodgers and Hart or to identify a Sondheim or Kander and Ebb tune in the first couple of bars, why Bernadette Peters was one of the best of her generation and why Angela Lansbury was the best of any generation—I could share these things with people who actually understood, who actually wanted to hear it, who actually had more and better details on hand to add to my burgeoning encyclopedia of otherwise useless musical theater trivia.

It's cruel, isn't it, to torture kids who are just looking for themselves? While other boys saw themselves in the strengths and prowess of star athletes or superheroes, I looked to musicals. It bothers me when people reduce musicals to silliness or contrivance. "People don't just burst into song on the street," someone told me once, his final argument on the worthlessness of the genre, but this was a person who was keenly interested in the *Dark Knight Trilogy*, who saw only hyperbole and impossibility in musicals but wisdom and commentary in the fantasy of a comic book hero. They're different paths of magical realism, aren't they? Whether the devices are choreography and a witty libretto or CGI and a battle of magics, the common denominator is storytelling through condensed or distilled abstractions of human experience. Some look to fantasy and sci-fi to make sense of it; I look to Sondheim.

"They're so cheesy," someone else complained. I responded, "You haven't seen Sondheim, have you?" Through *Into the Woods*, Sondheim excavated the dark sides of fairy tales that Disney buried long ago and investigated the complications of desire. Many see in it a metaphor for the AIDS crisis of the 1980s. *Follies* peels back the layers of convention and, one gut-punching song at a time, reveals the raw consequences of making the wrong choices in life. *A Little Night Music* is itself a journey of blossoming identities, with each character getting closer to his or her most authentic self, one waltz at a time.

I had the soundtrack of *Company* memorized by the time I was sixteen, and it gave me a roadmap for adulthood. Bobby, deeply lonely and more deeply resistant to being loved, is surrounded by his married friends. What looks like a comedy about relationships actually explores how hard it is to identify what you want (not what you're supposed to want) and how hard it is to be yourself (not just what everyone else wants you to be). In the final number of the show, Bobby names what's so scary about love and marriage—being stuck with someone who holds you too close, hurts you too deep, needs you too much, and puts you through hell. But then he breaks through, finally recognizing that's exactly what he needs. "Somebody need me too much," he sings. "Make me alive," he pleads. The song's lyrics served as a kind of mantra for me, and, for when I finally felt integrated, closer to my authentic self, Sondheim gave me language for what would come next.

nuns

"I choose not to collaborate in my own oppression
by restricting a basic human right. To me this is
a matter of conscience."

Sr. Jeannine Gramick, SSND

Like my siblings before me, I attended our local Catholic
school from junior kindergarten through eighth grade. Part
of my family's parish, the school was primarily staffed by Sinsini-
wa Dominicans, an order of women religious based in southwest
Wisconsin. Photos from the parish's early days showed dozens
of women in wimples and habits that looked like stylized and
oversized widow's peaks filling the front pews of the church. By
the time I was a student, though, we only had two or three Sin-
sinawas at the school, and the fanciful dress of the pre-Vatican
II convent was replaced by simple skirts, blouses, cardigans, and
sensible shoes.

Sister Vivian was our campus minister. In third and fourth
grades, she'd walk small groups of us out of our classroom and
down to her office where we'd plop down on the bean bags on
the floor, and she'd teach us the greatest hits of the Guitar Mass
era. A small projector cast slides of the lyrics with images of
trees and rivers, little glimpses of God's vast creation well beyond our suburban lawns. During Advent, we learned "Joy to
the World," and Sister Vivian was visibly moved at the thought
of heaven and nature singing. During Lent, we learned "Eagles'

Wings" from lyrics floating over a photo of a bald eagle soaring over a forest. It's a song I'd hear over and over, mostly as an altar boy working funerals. Almost every time, I'd wish it was Sister Vivian on guitar instead of the pipe organ underneath the song—the organ just made the song more depressing, while Sister Vivian would be practically levitating from joy while strumming its chords.

Sister Mark didn't work at the school, but she'd visit our house with a trunk-load of cinnamon bread and rolls from their bakery at The Mound (their convent in Wisconsin). Apparently the sisters were concerned that the family with ten kids wasn't getting enough to eat. To this day, I experience specific cravings for cinnamon bread from The Mound. Once, I asked her what the OP at the end of her name meant. "Order of Preachers, Billy," she said earnestly. I'm ashamed to admit that I didn't see the irony until I was in grad school—both Dominican men and women punctuate their names with OP, but the Catholic Church officially restricts "preaching" to men.

Sister Mary Agnes was the school's librarian. She was tiny, with thick-lensed glasses. She had short, curly hair and a little hump at the top of her spine, pushing her neck and head slightly forward. Every class in the school would spend time with her in the library to learn the Dewey Decimal System and other fundamentals of library life. She'd award us with gold-star stickers and public praise when we'd submitted short summaries of books from the library, just enough incentive to get us to read. During recess or lunch, I'd pop down to the library to visit or help to sort books because ten minutes in the basement library with Sister Mary Agnes was definitely more fun for me than navigating the playground. Unlike other teachers who'd encouraged me to go back to recess or wondered why I was there, Sister Mary Agnes always smiled at my arrival and had something for me to do. I'd watch her interact with another group of students or parent-volunteers. I never saw her look at a class list or keep notes with her, but she called every student by name, she knew what everyone was or should've been reading, and she remembered with gentle reminders whose books were overdue. It's like she devoted her whole life to us.

Unlike most of my classmates, I got to see nuns outside of school, too. My dad's aunt was a Daughter of Charity. Family photos capture her in a dramatic *Flying Nun*-wimple in the pre-Vatican II days, but she was a pharmacist, working in the Daughters of Charity health-care ministries until she retired. She was passionate about her family history and eager to connect with distant cousins until she discovered they were Protestant. My mom's sister is a Benedictine, and, after a career as an educator, she was elected prioress of her community. She'd always join us for holidays or events with another nun in tow, giving me a referent for the old joke about nuns traveling in pairs. We'd visit her at the monastery for various events, or just to visit, and I marveled at the community of women who shared their lives, their work, and their prayers with each other. They were my first example of a chosen family.

So, you see, when people talk about nuns, I have a definite and empathetic perspective. There are people who had terrible experiences with nuns who were teachers or other authority figures—the stereotype of the nun rapping a child's knuckles with a ruler is rooted in some reality—but I'd guess that those women would've been brutal teachers or authoritarians in or out of a habit. In grad school, I started watching movies about nuns to get a sense of how American culture has treated them as people and as a type, which was a depressing and puzzling exercise. I'd guess that the writers and directors of 90 percent of films that depict nuns have never met a nun and fewer still have intersected with the community life of women religious. Sure, *The Nun's Story*, centered on Audrey Hepburn's Oscar-nominated depiction of Sister Luke, injected a precise (if idealized) depiction of life behind the convent walls into popular consciousness, and *Dead Man Walking* presented Susan Sarandon's Sister Helen Prejean with sensitivity to the life of women religious engaged in social justice ministries. But most movies about nuns conform to the old Hollywood habit (pun intended) of depicting women as virgins, whores, and/or psychos. We see the ethereally angelic and naive (like Ingrid Bergman's Sister Mary Benedict in *The Bells of St. Mary's* and Kathy Najimi's Sister Mary Patrick in *Sister Act*). We joke about the fetishization of nuns in porn or the use of the habit as a laughable contrast for a slutty woman (see Whoopi Goldberg in *Sister Act*). We relish vindication against the gruesomely abusive nuns in *The Magdalene Sisters* and the stripping of the ego of Anne Bancroft's corrupt Mother Miriam Ruth in *Agnes of God*. It shouldn't be a surprise that the popular understanding of who nuns are is skewed.

I'd rather see a movie about Sister Simone Campbell, SSS, who has been engaged in social justice work through political action. Or about the Sisters of Loreto who invest in companies with questionable ethical practices so they can show up at board meetings and agitate for change. Or about Maureen Fiedler, SL, who brought her ministry of facilitating interfaith dialogue to NPR. Or about my aunt, Judith Murphy, OSB, who co-founded an innovative educational experiment that launched the network of Cristo Rey schools to give underserved communities access to a solid education and career paths. Or about Mamie Jenkins, RSCJ, whose charisma animated her teaching and innovative music therapy.

I'd rather see a movie about Sister Jeannine Gramick, SSND, who cofounded New Ways Ministry to make a safe space for LGBTQ Catholics and, despite being censured by the Vatican and forced out of her original religious community, continues to attend to the needs, rights, and dignity of queer people. Or about the avalanche of support for blessing same-sex unions in the Church from communities of women religious.

Nuns have been formative for me not just as a Catholic person but as a gay man. The few times I've said that to people, I've gotten puzzled reactions. I struggled to articulate then how they helped me look past the walls of school or the boundaries of the burbs, how they made me feel safe as a kid, how they modeled a family rooted in commitment, not coincidence, how they projected clarity about social justice, peace, and what it meant to walk the walk. I didn't think to cite the ways that I learned to navigate and defy stereotypes from them, or that I learned to show love by delivering a trunk-load of food. But when people ask me, as they often do, "How can you still identify as Catholic?" the answer is always easy: the nuns.

The Front Runner

Vince, Billy and two girls were right in the middle of the floor, and the other couples were stopping and watching. The two girls were doing a rather abandoned heterosexual version of the Flop. Vince and Billy were not. They were doing the gay boogie. And they were doing it as I had seen it done only in films and at parties in New York.

The gay who is a good dancer can turn even the fox trot into an uninhibited celebration of male sexuality. Billy and Vince were doing the boogie about six feet from their partners, not looking at them or at each other. They were dancing like blacks. They were loose, cool, with all the foot-stomping and finger-snapping that goes with it. Their shoulders and torsos barely moved. All the action was in the hip-jerking, the crotch-gyrating, the buttock-twitching and the thigh-weaving.

Vince was aware of the crowd, grandstanding a little. But Billy was a shade more restrained, inner-directed, as if he were dancing to that fantasy-lover that every gay sees in his mind...

I looked around. Judging by the students' faces, they had never seen anything quite like this before. A few started clapping to the beat, and pretty soon the whole room was clapping and stomping. I could hardly hear myself think. I watched a little nervously. On occasion, I had seen this dance progress to pants falling, the dancer dexterously flipping his goodies around and finally jerking off magnificently. I couldn't believe these two would do that, especially Billy. If they did, they would be off the team tomorrow.

Patricia Nell Warren, *The Front Runner*

At the beginning of *The Front Runner*, Patricia Nell Warren's 1974 novel, Harlan Brown briskly narrates the years he struggled and suffered through life as a closeted athlete, Marine, and husband, and describes how he scraped and hustled to stay alive and build a life as an openly (if barely-so) gay man, how he was given a chance to coach again by a progressive-minded college president, and how all of that prepared him to fall in love with Billy Sives. Throughout the rest of the novel, we see Harlan help Billy grow as an elite runner ready to take a medal at the Olympics, and we see Billy help Harlan grow, after decades of inner conflict and social isolation, as a person who is at peace in his own skin.

I hate reading. OK, "hate" is a strong word… I don't enjoy the technical exercise of reading. It's hard for me—I move slowly through the text and struggle to maintain interest, especially if it's dense or requires the reader to retain multiple abstractions or statistics. Don't get me wrong—I love the experience of having read, of storytelling and artistic expression. The introduction of books on tape (and then CD, and then streaming through my phone) changed things dramatically for me, giving me the option of leaning into my stronger (or at least more confident) auditory capacity for comprehension and retention. When someone refers to "a real page turner," says, "I couldn't put it down!" or talks about reading an entire book in one sitting, I typically respond with a mix of awe and despair.

That said, there are three books that I have read in one sitting, each pushing late into the night because I just could not put it down to be able to detach and sleep. During my first year of high school, *The Manchurian Candidate* hooked me with a blend of political, psychological, and sexual intrigue and kept me up till five a.m. When I was 19, *Mariette in Ecstasy* was a Christmas present from my mother, and I was finished with it by Boxing Day, drawn in by its poetic and nuanced depiction of life in a cloistered convent and its weaving of the mystical and the sensual. And then, for a college course on the depiction of gender and sexuality, I read *The Front Runner*. I read a chunk of it in a coffee shop, till it closed; I read the next chunk of it in the campus townhouse I shared with five friends until they all went to bed; I drove to the local twenty-four-hour Dunkin' Donuts for another chunk; and I finished, weeping in the kitchen while I made a pot of coffee before my housemates woke up. I wept because of the plot. I wept because of the raw authenticity of the love story at the heart of the book, written well before Annie Proulx published "Brokeback Mountain." I wept with joy because of the window it opened to me, giving me a much-wanted glimpse of the lives of gay men, but when I realized that this was the first love story I'd ever encountered that I could see myself in, the first time I felt what the characters were feeling, feared what the characters feared, and was turned on by what turned the characters on, my joy mixed with surprise and resentment.

While running and elite athleticism are central to the story, that's not what I could relate to. Warren explained that the story was inspired by a competitive runner who agonized over coming out in the early 1970s, knowing it would hurt his running career. That's a fear that wasn't limited to athletes, but while other industries and contexts have seen greater openness and safety for queer people for decades, the world of sports is (to say the least) a bit behind. Billie Jean King was outed in 1981 and maintained her status as a favorite in tennis, despite having to navigate plenty of backlash. Except for outliers like Martina Navratilova, the few professional athletes of the '70s, '80s, and '90s who openly identified as queer only did so after they retired. More recently, we saw Robbie Rogers come out in 2013 and Michael Sam drafted by the NFL the next year. After years of rejection from coaches and sponsors because of his transition, Patricio Manuel became the first openly transgender boxer in the US when he stepped back into the ring in 2018, and Megan Rapinoe was never really "in" any sort of closet (unless there's one where she stores her cooler-than-anything lavender hair coloring). When Carl Nassib announced that he's gay, the first active NFL player to do so, it had the oompf of a big shrug. No drama, no carefully worded statement, no kowtowing or apologetics to appease sponsors and managers. Still, it was titillating news—even the fact that it wasn't problematic for the NFL made headlines.

I wasn't a promising athlete, but my dad was a great tennis player. Several of my brothers were swimmers, one even reaching All-American status, and my mom expected me to join the high school swim team, or some team, as they did before me. During the first week of high school, though, tryouts for the volleyball team conflicted with auditions for the fall play. My mom told me a freshman probably wouldn't get cast, so to delay any dejection that would come from that rejection, she reminded me daily that tryouts for the swim team were on Friday. She was stunned that I made the callbacks…scheduled for Friday.

As a kid, something kept me away from sports, some deep instinct, some voice whispering urgently whenever the opportunity arose, "this is not safe for you." It was one of those instincts that kids try to articulate and that adults quickly, even with a chuckle, dismiss. My mom wanted me to play sports as a social outlet, an antidote to my isolation. She tried hard to get me to join the football team in eighth grade so I wouldn't be the only boy in my class not playing. I'd never thrown a football in my life (actually, I still haven't), and I knew that the laughter and derision that would ensue after they saw me struggle with the basic mechanics of the game would cut deeper than the status quo.

Thinking about *The Front Runner* today, the relationship between Harlan and Billy strikes me as not just a generational juncture but as a metaphor for life before and after Stonewall. Harlan's fears resonate with the announcements of athletes who hid or denied themselves from teammates and the prying public, but Billy's courage oozes a little more from each subsequent generation of athletes, each facing fewer and fewer obstacles to reconciling their jobs and their lives. Would my life have been different if, as a child, I'd seen an openly gay athlete compete in the Olympics or on a professional team? Would I be healthier, more fit? Would I be less afraid of straight men? Kids are coming out earlier and earlier. Queer kids—or, at least, *more* queer kids—are playing sports now without the hurdles and hang-ups that I experienced. So, yeah, life may have been different.

But if I'd joined the volleyball or swim teams, I'd never have butchered the Stage Manager's monologues every night of *Our Town* that freshman fall, and I'd never have soloed in *Godspell* the following spring. I may have put piano-playing aside and stunted my understanding and appreciation of music. In that life-that-didn't-happen, I wouldn't have sung at Carnegie Hall or the Rudolfinum. It's not a possibility that I ponder with much regret.

The Front Runner didn't keep me reading because of its reverence for sports. But it did keep me turning the pages because I had never heard a story about gay men that wasn't thoroughly tragic. My mother's first response after I told her I was gay was, "Well, I'm concerned, because I've never known a happy homosexual." *The Happy Homosexual*, I thought, *that'd be a great name for a musical*. Harlan and Billy were more real and more potent to me than any characters I'd encountered before, and Warren didn't reduce them to one-dimensional heroes, villains, or victims. And she didn't skimp when it came to sex. Harlan and Billy presented my first encounter with gay sex. I'd never seen it—I sure hadn't had it by that point—and I'd never even heard it described. Their budding lust and care for each other was familiar, and reading Warren's depiction of the first time they fucked was the most comprehensive sexual education I'd ever had.

Another reason *The Front Runner* grabbed me and maintains a grip on me extended from my personal "what ifs." If talented celebrity-athletes came out in the '60s and '70s, along with folx in other industries and fields, would that have mitigated the burgeoning anti-gay tactics of the far right that picked on queer people (and are still picking on queer people), the hate and political pressure embodied in Anita Bryant? Would that have made a difference in the late '70s and '80s as AIDS emerged and spread, as members of Reagan's administration dismissed it, even openly laughed about it, and attitudes, like Imogene's in *Designing Women*, dominated, perpetuating the notion that AIDS was "killing all the right people"? Would there have been more stories like *The Front Runner* that depicted the lives and loves and complications of queer people without reducing them to victims or accessories? Would queer people have had more and better models to follow, guides to navigate the changes in our bodies and our desires? *These* are the possibilities that I ponder with so much regret.

There's one more reason *The Front Runner* kept me turning the pages that night. There was a "gay boogie"? A couple of days later, after I'd gotten a full, un-caffeinated night's sleep and I had the house to myself, I cranked up Madonna and, using Harlan's description of the dance floor as an instruction manual, set out to master it. After all, I learned, "the gay who is a good dancer can turn even the fox trot into an uninhibited celebration of male sexuality."

Big Eden

"There's so few nice surprises in life.
Seems to me that it'd be kind of a shame
to squander one of them, don't ya think?"
                    O'Neal Compton's Jim Soams in *Big Eden*

This is like Schitt's Creek," my husband said suddenly, "but, you know, before *Schitt's Creek*."

Arye Gross' Henry Hart is a successful artist in NYC, who returns to the small town in Montana where he grew up to care for his grandfather, George Coe's Sam, who suffered a stroke. By the time he arrives, the town's schoolteacher, Louise Fletcher's Grace Cornwall, has already developed a plan to help care for Sam—Nan Martin's Widow Thayer would make dinner nightly, and Eric Schweig's Pike Dexter, the debilitatingly anxious and shy owner of the town's general store and Henry's high school classmate, would deliver it to Sam and Henry. For a while, Pike refuses their nightly invitation to stay for a meal, but along the way, not impressed by the Widow Thayer's cooking and responding to a deep desire to make things nice for Henry, Pike starts to prepare meals inspired by gourmand magazines and cookbooks. Pike's interest in anything new catches the gaggle of men who hang around the store by surprise, and they help him to make increasingly elaborate meals and maintain the deception. Once the Widow Thayer figures it out, even she gets in on the action, joining the rag-tag group of sous-chefs in their conspiracy to make Pike happy.

I saw the film in the theater when it was released. It was an exciting time for independent films—still "low budg" relative to Big Hollywood, they were recruiting bigger names, taking better artistic and narrative tacks than the big-studio productions of the era, and spotlighting characters whose identities were usually pushed off the screen. Films like *The Incredibly True Adventure of Two Girls in Love*, *Trick*, and *Jeffrey* gave queer characters humanity and complexity, and *Boys Don't Cry* and *Paragraph 175* conveyed hard truths that most of the movie-going audience had never heard (or wanted to hear) before.

Big Eden stood out from its contemporaries. For one thing, no one utters the word "gay" or talks about "coming out." The entire conflict of the script is rooted in its characters' inability to be their fullest and best selves. It gives viewers the opportunity to see sexual identity as more than a "problem" to be resolved or a parade float to jump on. It forced me to see sexuality as connected, interdependent, integral to every other aspect of being a person. Some use sexual identity to exclude others, but *Big Eden* zeroes in on the experience of hiding behind labels, to use them as indefinitely lasting buffers from our pasts. Henry isn't able to be at peace, to be happy, until he figures this out.

After college, I opted not to return home to Chicago. I stayed on the East Coast for a long time before venturing to the West Coast. The farther I got from the lovely suburb where I grew up, the safer I felt. I planted myself in dense, urban neighborhoods that would guarantee diverse folx intersecting each other every day—"the grittier the better," I once told a realtor. I believed that it was a moral compass that was guiding me, extracting me from a world of unchallenged privilege. Like any good, overly self-righteous and confident twenty-something, I told myself that I couldn't reconcile the bubble I grew up in with the needs of the world. When my parents' health declined for the last time (my dad's stroke followed by my mom's cancer), I was back in Chicago for every long weekend, every vacation.

Those trips weren't hard because (or *just* because) of the challenges facing my parents and the sudden role reversal of the kids becoming the caregivers. They were hard because they brought to the surface all the things that really kept me at a distance, geographically and emotionally. For too long, I held on to the idea that my parents *resigned* themselves to the fact that I'm gay, that it was a concession for them, that it was a lingering disappointment. I believed that they didn't like my ex because he wasn't my wife and the mother of my children, the image they imagined I'd fulfill. It turns out, they just didn't like him. I was the one reinforcing the notion that *this* family and *my* identity were irreconcilable. It took the deaths of my parents and my sister within sixteen months for me to recognize that I was the only one responsible for integrating and balancing these different aspects of my self. If there were wounds to heal, I had let them fester. If there were questions to answer, I'd let them linger unasked. The people who wanted to walk that journey with me were the ones I'd kept at a distance.

When Henry tells Grace that he's returning to New York, she holds up a mirror that he'd refused to look in.

> "Listen, you know what they say when you get lost in the woods? If you stay put, stay in one place and don't wander, they'll find you. And I was just hoping you'd let yourself be found this time. I was hoping you'd let us find you. But you keep wandering and we can't."
>
> Louise Fletcher's Grace Cornwall

I was twenty-four when the movie came out, and this moment in the film was a comfort, giving me language to describe my deepest desire and the scars in my heart. It was also a warning shot, starkly reminding me that happiness doesn't just happen on its own. Watching the film, I was enamored of Pike and had massive hair-envy for Eric Schweidt's locks, but, even more than my indie-flick crush, I was moved by the way this little town loved him and, to paraphrase Jim Soams, wanted things to be nice for him, too. Each of the men who loiter in the general store presents a gruff, rough, and rugged exterior, but on the inside and in their actions, they are doting, gossipy, loving, and eager to perfect their cappuccino-making and culinary skills. Sure, *Big Eden* idealizes small town life, but it also demonstrates that we can at least *imagine* a world where this is believable, a world where a whole town rallies to bring out each other's best, works on behalf of each other's happiness, especially the lost and broken among them. It planted a seed in my head of what an ideal (and achievable) existence might be.

The film also showed me the impact and value of honesty and candor—not a lesson I learned growing up. For Henry, the film's "prodigal son," New York is a metaphor for the barrier he hides behind, the collection of experiences and responsibilities he thinks make up his life. Sam, like the father in the biblical parable, welcomes his grandson home and, puzzlingly, *isn't* interested in rehashing the past. He only wants Henry to be fully alive, fully himself, and honest with himself and with Sam. "Did we teach you shame?" Sam asks Henry earnestly, in what could've been a masterpiece of guilt that he instead spins into a blanket of love that Henry can't resist anymore. "Can't you see what a good job God did here? Can't you see how beautiful he made you?" Honesty isn't just about confessing the hard stuff, about naming mistakes and accepting blame. It's also about recognizing, about fully seeing and accepting the good stuff, too.

I used to dismiss plots like this as cliché. A parent is sick, a prodigal returns, every memory and feeling comes to the surface, the prodigal resolves to live better and disappoints himself and everyone around him, there's a last-minute complication, and resolution in the affirmation that he's seen and loved. But then I had sick parents, and when I returned home, all the memories and feelings from the previous forty years came to the surface. I was my best and my worst during that time, and it broke me. My grief absorbed whatever energy and resilience I had, leaving me vulnerable and paralyzed, unable to care for myself and in a job that demanded constant attention to the care of others.

I was lucky to meet my husband at my worst.

Rephrase: I was lucky that Jon wanted to meet me, even at my worst. We met through the apps and played a game of conversation tag during the window of time between my sister's death and my dad's. I kept him at a distance, but I didn't tell him that I deliberately stalled every time he suggested we finally meet and connect in person because people kept dying around me. Besides, we lived so far away from each other that it (whatever "it" was) wasn't going to happen. Those were stories I hid behind—the facts of the stories were true, but it wasn't honest. The real truth was that I didn't believe that I deserved something good.

In the end, Henry didn't walk *away* from his life in New York. He walked *toward* something new, ready to be seen, to be loved, to be found. I walked away from what I thought was my life with confidence from a seed planted in me by *Big Eden* as a young man. Despite the well of grief and anxiety I'd fallen into, recognizing that I was ready to be found opened the door to making peace with the past and healing and sealing old wounds. Through that door, my own Pike, who shows me he loves me through food, walked into my life, and for the first time, I was ready to walk toward something new with someone by my side.

Joan Crawford

I'm twenty. My friend Melissa takes me to a house party hosted by a thirty-something gay couple. Not knowing anyone but the friend who brought me along, I could politely detach from small talk and let my gaze wander through the sea of gay men and sprinkling of women sipping out of plastic cups and tiki mugs. Some clusters laugh uproariously, some are speaking quietly and covertly, some seem to know everyone while everyone else seems to know someone who knows everyone. Lots of folx are in Hawai'ian-style shirts, there are fake leis here and there, flowers behind various ears—all the effects of a beach party I'd once tagged as "tacky" were suddenly charming, ironic. Someone handed me a tiki mug filled with something far too fruity, and we descended to the basement where the movie was about to begin.

I don't remember much about the plot (something about a rich widow seduced by a toxic playboy, blah blah blah, you know the drill), but I remember two things about the viewing experience. First: Joan Crawford. Every gesture was full and dramatic, and her wardrobe was its own fashion show ranging from gowns and jewels to nightgowns and jewels to casual wear and jewels to swimwear and jewels. But best of all, she delivered punch lines and insults like she was shooting arrows from a crossbow. How does she like her coffee, he asks.

"Alone."

"I'd like to ask you to stay and have a drink, but I'm afraid you might accept."

"I wouldn't have you if you were hung with diamonds up-side down."

And best of all, in a stunning, glittering gown (and matching diamond choker and bracelet...told you, jewels...) she throws a freshly mixed martini in old what's-his-name's face. How does one forget Joan Crawford at her most...well, at her most Joan Crawford?

The second thing I remember about watching the movie is the fact that every gay man in the room (and even a few of the women) seemed to recite every peak line with her. They had her timing, they had her oompf, they had her gestures, and one even looked like he would let his drink fly into someone's face. Several peppered the screening with commentary, and though I'd never seen the movie, though I knew none of these people, though I'd never been in a place and time like that place and time, I *got* why this line was over the top, why that outfit was ridiculous, why the drink in the face was so, so perfect. This, I later understood, was my introduction to *camp*.

I started pursuing showings of campy old movies or renting them at Blockbuster (remember Blockbuster?), developing my own vocabulary of comebacks and witticisms, wondering if I, too, would someday have the pleasure of tossing a drink in a man's face. When it came to over-the-top drama, the melodramas on screen gave voice and form to things I couldn't articulate in my life, but the contrivances of their plots, the extravagance of their settings, and the stretch of their scripts made the world laughably manageable. Leading women were strong, glamorous, and deeply flawed—you want to love, hate, destroy, and crown them all at once—and Joan Crawford was the best of the best when it came to the genre.

If *Mommie Dearest* is to be believed, Crawford blurred the line between life on screen and life in the world. Her deepest fears, her soaring talent, and her rage swirled and roared and left a wake in her own life that lets a caricature of her stay alive in popular imagination. When I lived in Boston, a mashup of ABBA's "Mamma Mia" with scenes from *Mommie Dearest* started playing in gay bars, and within weeks everyone was screaming along with Faye Dunaway's Crawford. "Why can't you give me," everyone chanted at a slow pace and with restrained rage, "the *respect* that I'm entitled to? Why can't you treat me," we got louder and sillier and more dramatic, "like I would be treated by any *stranger on the street*?!"

Drinks were set down or covered, bodies shifted, and throats cleared as the bar crowd prepared to accompany Diana Scarwid's Christina with, arguably, her best line in the film.

"Because I am not....one of your....FANS!"

With the last word, the video looped Christina's full-throated, in-her-mother's-face retort, giving the bar a full ten seconds of scream-time before the video pauses on Crawford taking a piercing gasp and lunging at her daughter's throat. They tumble to the ground, the peppy opening bars of "Mamma Mia" enter, and the bar crowd keeps singing with Agnetha and Anni-Frid. It's not that *Mommie Dearest* is slapstick or that child abuse is funny. The mashup, like *Female on the Beach* or any other camp classic, worked so well because it gave a crowd of people who'd been pushed to the margins a chance to magnify the worst of humanity and laugh at it.

Ella Fitzgerald

"Hey, Billy Strayhorn, we're going to change piano players at this point. Would you come over here to the mic, please? I think it only fitting that Billy should have the responsibility of the concluding statement."

Duke Ellington casually trades seats with his longtime collaborator, Billy Strayhorn, to preface the final portion of "Portrait of Ella Fitzgerald."

"In our musical search for a total portrait of Ella Fitzgerald, we find a melodic parallel in which royal ancestry, greatness of heart, and talent beyond category are the principal components in the quest for *total jazz*."

Long before Beyoncé declared "Black is King," Billy Strayhorn pronounced that the First Lady of Song "is of royal ancestry." *Ella Fitzgerald Sings the Duke Ellington Songbook* lives among the greatest albums ever made. One of Fitzgerald's famous songbook series that cut the definitive interpretations of the standards of the first half of the 20th century, it's the only album of the series in which the composers collaborated and performed with Fitzgerald. The result captures the magic that sparked when Ellington, Strayhorn, and Fitzgerald intersected. Maybe it's respect for this kind of magic that kept other producers from trying to replicate the project—there was no other voice that could sail through Porter, Rodgers and Hart, Berlin, the Gershwins, Arlen, Kern, and Mercer, no other voice to attract the constellation of talent that Fitzgerald did in her collaborators.

While Ella taught us how to sing and how to swing, most of her life swung between people forcing her to be what she wasn't and people not letting her be what she was. She was probably abused by her stepfather before being handed off to her aunt. She was sent to an orphans' asylum and later a reform school after working as a lookout for a bordello. At seventeen, she braved amateur night at the Apollo and won, though she was denied the standard prize of a week's booking because of her appearance and unkempt hair. After Ella and three bandmates boarded a flight to Australia with first-class tickets to begin their first tour Down Under, they were forced to disembark and stranded in Honolulu until they could get another flight three days later—Black people in first class? Nuh-uh, said Pan Am. She had a weakness for bad boys and was even engaged to (some say, secretly married to) a handsome, younger Norwegian before he was imprisoned for swindling another woman who swooned for him. At the height of her popularity, Frank Sinatra off-handedly described Fitzgerald's voice as not classically strong—the accompanying compliment to her voice's effect was buried by the insult.

From a distance, it's an unfortunately common story. Billie Holliday and Aretha Franklin each emerged from painful childhoods and being used by the men in their lives. Holliday, Fitzgerald, and Franklin each broke through circumstances that should've destroyed them, or at least silenced them and pushed them to the margins, but each, impossibly, went on to imprint themselves irreversibly on American music and culture. When I was about nine, a song was playing on the radio. I don't remember which song, but the singer had entered into an extended scat sequence, something I'd never heard before. I asked, with a hint of disdain, "What's this?" My mom replied, undistracted from whatever she was doing, "Ella Fitzgerald." "I don't like it." Without looking toward me or missing a beat, she replied, "Then why are you tapping your foot?"

I didn't know anything about Ella when I started paying attention to her. I didn't know that she was isolated and alone as a kid, that she was shy and reticent, that there were people who took advantage of her and others who fiercely protected and promoted her, knowing that she and her talent deserved the spotlight. But, a few songs in, I felt like I knew her. Or maybe, like she knew me. Whatever the combination of circumstances and experiences in her life, Ella's tone and cadences uplifted the sighs and fears that lurked beneath the melodies of love songs, and her pacing emanated from a mix of hope and disappointment. When she sang a happy song, she was exuberant—Ella could shift gears, let loose, and elevate any crowd—but the switch back to melancholy was easy, a reminder that her pain and loneliness were always right there, just under the surface.

Duke Ellington said that "Sophisticated Lady" was inspired by his schoolteachers, but the lyrics (penned by collaborators) suggest the gaze of a pianist looking out on a restaurant and making up stories about people to pass the time. The singer lands on a woman who returns to the scene, lovely and lonely, looking for a love lost long ago. When Sinatra sings it, the song is full of pity and falls flat, but when Ella sings it, she peels back a few layers and seems to immerse herself into it. The song becomes part of her body, the lilt at the end of each word in the phrase "fools in love" hints at a self-deprecating laugh. She breaks for an instrumental bridge, and when she comes back with subtle variations on the melody, her "nonchalant," lightly jumping up and floating above the song, is perhaps the loveliest note ever recorded.

Billy Strayhorn was one of the few openly gay musicians of the era, and when I hear Ella sing Strayhorn's songs, it feels like Ella is singing more of Billy's story than anyone else could, more of Billy's story than any other singer tried. "Day dream, don't break my reverie," she sings, "until I find that he is day dreaming just like me." Sure, Ella sang it in a woman's voice, but the point of view, the heart that is saving itself from breaking by fantasizing what won't or can't be, is all Billy's. Likewise, Strayhorn's masterpiece "Lush Life" uniquely crystallized queer heartbreak. Ella's interpretation on the *Ellington Songbook* strips the lyrics of self-pity and melodrama that make other singers' covers goopy and corny and adds a layer of empathy. The album was cut in summer and fall 1957, the same period in which Fitzgerald's handsome swindler was convicted and sentenced to hard labor.

Billy and Ella each impossibly faced, jumped, and stumbled over hurdles that stymied others. Like the divas who followed her and who increasingly became public advocates for their queer colleagues, friends, and fans, Ella's own experiences sensitized her to Strayhorn's and those of other queer folx. She literally lent her voice to convey the real stories, the deeper feelings, fears, and desires underneath his songs. It didn't take me long to figure out that she was singing my story before it had been written. Ella's was the voice I turned to when I crushed on boys and couldn't do anything about it, when I fell for boys who didn't fall back, when my heart broke, when I was afraid I'd be alone, when I was convinced I'd be alone, when I proved myself right.

> I want something to live for
> Someone to make my life an adventurous dream
> Oh, what wouldn't I give for
> Someone who'd take my life
> And make it seem gay as they say it ought to be.
> Why can't I have love like that brought to me?

As a teenager, as a college student, as a young man, I'd find my eyes misty when Ella got to this point in Ellington and Strayhorn's "Something to Live For." Her long, stretched-out phrases, her impassioned punches and swings, her straightforward delivery of conflict at the heart of the song gave me words and form to channel my own inner-conflicts and reflect the threads that Strayhorn lifted, the components that elevated Ella above her circumstances and sustains her in the memory of people who never met her: royal ancestry, greatness of heart, and talent beyond category.

Berlin

This place has everything.

Trance, stilts, throw-up music, an albino that looks like Susan Powter, Teddy Graham people.

Twinks, gypsies, grown men in wedding dresses, a cat from a bodega, puppets in disguise.

Don't look for a bouncer—there isn't one. Instead, the door's guarded by 10 jacked homeless guys in old-fashioned bathing suits.

Ice sculptures, winos, Germfs—German Smurfs—a Teddy Ruxpin wearing mascara, an old lady wearing Kid 'N Play hair, and none other than DJ Baby Bok Choy.

Look over there—is that Mick Jagger? No! It's a fat kid on a Slip 'n Slide. His knees look like biscuits, and he's ready to party.

Ghosts, banjos, Carl Paladino, a stuck-up kitten who won't sign autographs, furkels.

Cholos, cute people, a sheepdog that looks like Bruce Vilanch, an entire room of puppets doing karate.

Split kicks, pachucos, pile after pile of expired lunchables, a Hawaiian cleaning lady who looks like Smokey Robinson.

Sand worms, geishas, rock-eaters, a seven level course in adult education. And if you want to relax, you can kick back in your very own subway sleeping bag.

This weekend, they're having a tournament of everybody's favorite trivia game, "Shaun White or Bonnie Raitt?" Look closely—the answer may surprise you.

Backpacks, sea lions, Ron Wood, a rental car filled with bottled water, my best friend Joel, plus a special appearance by evil celebrity chef Wario Batali.

Hopscotch, double dutch, Oogieloves, sling and mesh bladder
implants, the table from Charlie Rose. And this weekend,
I'll be having my college reunion there.

from Hillary Busis, "'Saturday Night Live':
All of Stefon's clubs"

The first few times I saw Bill Hader's Stefon on *SNL*, I didn't
know why I thought the character was so funny. *Are these
real places?* I wondered, *Have I been there?* I lived in NYC for
a year, just before Hader brought the character to life. When
Stefon described Booooooooof, though, the perfect spot to find
"pugs, geezers, doo-wop groups, a wise old turtle that looks
like Quincy Jones—and you'll have your own *When Harry Met
Sally* moment when you share a special kiss with Gizblow, the
coked-up gremlin," it clicked. It wasn't in New York. It was
Berlin. In Chicago.

Berlin was a nightclub that opened in Boystown in the early
1980s, before Boystown was bougie. Like other gayborhoods,
it was diverse, dense, and busy, and the bars, shops, and restaurants around Belmont, Halstead, and Clark constituted the
heart of the city's queer epicenter. When I was in high school
in the early '90s, I knew little more about the area except that
Halstead and Belmont was the intersection I needed to find, and
I'd look for excuses to run errands or follow a route through
the neighborhood. *Oh, look at that,* I'd say with surprise—to
myself—driving down Halstead, noticing the names of gay bars
and displays in shop windows.

Once, I *couldn't find parking anywhere*, I told myself, *except
that spot in front of the gay bookstore*. In truth, I convinced myself
that, if I parked in front of Unabridged Bookstore en route to
the coffee shop a block further, I'd be able to get a better look at
what's in the window. Without purposefully visiting a gay bookstore, maybe I'd get a peek inside if someone opened the door
or catch a glimpse of real, live homosexuals on their way in or

out. *I'm just getting coffee*, I narrated as I moved past the store, slowed my pace, fidgeted with the car keys in my hands, and looked forward with the discipline of a Beefeater. On the way back, the hot latte in my hand served as a useful device, making me halt to gently sip through the lid that scratched my upper lip. Tipping the cup toward me, I didn't let anything enter my mouth. I held it steady in about-to-be-sipped position. I peered over the cup, across the sidewalk with traffic behind me and piles of mostly melted snow to either side, and saw what I could see. No one came, no one went. I finally took a sip, burned the roof of my mouth, dropped the curtain, and exited left, back to the car.

During college, I was only in Chicago for summers and holidays, and my exploration of the gay scene wasn't much more courageous than my bold visit to, or near, the bookstore a couple of years before. If I got in because it was an 18+ night, or because my fake ID worked, or because the bouncer thought I was cute enough not to bother with an ID check, I'd feign confidence, make my way to the bar to order a club soda with a lime (the cheapest thing that looked like a drink that I could think of), stand in a corner or against a wall for a few minutes, down my club soda, and exit. *With every visit, I'm getting a little bit gayer*, I thought.

When I walked into Berlin for the first time, it was chilly and nearly empty (I made the mistake of arriving before ten p.m.), but before I could empty my soda and make an exit, a boy standing next to me started talking to me, asking if I knew when it got crowded. "Not till later," I lied. I mean, it was true, but I didn't know that. He smiled, said, "Thanks," and gave me a wink before he headed to the bathroom and I headed for the door. A few weeks later and at a later hour, I returned and found myself standing against the bar, looking at a Prince impersonator on the stage in the center of the club. A few weeks after that, I returned and found myself on the dance floor in what I can only describe as a feeling of "homecoming," during the monthly Ma-donnaRama party. *All Madonna. For hours,* I thought. *I'm home.*

Once I got over myself, I stopped being shocked at the people I encountered there. Though I'd tiptoed into the gay world, I looked around and found myself surrounded by queer extravagance—colors and makeup and glitter and mesh (and, on Prince night, so much lace). I danced with boys; I danced with girls; I danced with drag queens. I was offered the occasional smoke, I'd offer the occasional smoke, I'd make out with boys at the bar or outside between puffs of our Marlboro Lights. After a while, few things stood out to me at Berlin because few things shocked anymore. I wasn't scandalized by this outfit, that piercing, this language, that hair. The extravagance (here I mean it in the sense of divergence, not of consumption or elaborateness) of Berlin drowned, or at least momentarily quieted, my reticence, and there, in a packed club in a dense neighborhood, I felt safer and more alive than I had in any place, among any others before.

The club's name was homage to the Berlin of the 1920s, a period of recovery from economic, social, and national devastation of the Great War and a flu pandemic that probably originated in Texas but was first officially reported in Spain, giving a national identity to a biological phenomenon and magnifying unfounded prejudice. People who had been pushed to the margins in various ways and at various levels of repression for centuries relished newly established freedoms, and creativity refracted and exploded and filled the culture with new ideas, new politics, new aesthetic forms. Queer memory owes much to Christopher Isherwood, whose stories captured a certain slice of this dynamic period in Berlin. Though I hadn't read Isherwood by the time I started frequenting the club, I understood that the name was an overt referent to evoke another place and time, a place where queer extravagance and the blurring of the boundaries of class and gender were lionized.

Like Berlin in the '20s, the club had a dark side. I saw people get wasted. I saw a screaming match between two women turn into a fist fight on the sidewalk. I watched people disappear to the bathroom and come back with their eyes rolling. I saw a guy collapse outside the bathroom and later learned that I'd witnessed a heroin overdose for the first time, a cherry, I decided too late, I never wanted to pop. The dark side fueled the club's impact on me as much as its splendor. Beyond the feeling that I'd found my tribe, or at least the home of my spiritual ancestors, I learned and pushed my boundaries. I took ownership of my body. I dropped my expectations and expanded my hopes. I started to let the moss of the suburbs that had grown on me wither. But, like Isherwood, who said of *his* Berlin, "Even now I can't altogether believe that any of this really happened."

The Golden Girls

Picture it: Cambridge, 1998. A hopeful young gay man leaves his childhood home behind in pursuit of every kid's dream: Divinity School. He moves into an empty townhouse, and after a week of sleeping on an improvised mattress of sweatshirts, towels, and blankets with only his PC and imagination to entertain him, his things arrive. It's a mix of clothes that didn't fit in his car's trunk, boxes of books he'll never read again, old or extraneous furniture from his parents and a few siblings, and one important leftover from his college dorm room: his television.

By today's standards, it's a tiny thing, but when he received it as a birthday present from his siblings in 1994, a thirteen-inch screen with an integrated VHS player was a marvel of dorm-room technology. Luckily, his cable was installed and activated two days before, affording access to his worldnet.att.net email account and the green and blue windows of gay.com. Before he sets out to put his mattress frame together, he assembles a makeshift pedestal of not-quite-the-same-size milk crates, the height of '90s dorm chic, to lift the screen up from the ground to viewing-from-bed height. He plugs the power cord into the wall and the cable cord into the TV and flips through his new home's channels. It's just after six p.m., and an episode of *The Golden Girls* has just started on Lifetime.

Another episode follows at six-thirty, and after that, he turns off the set and pops a CD into the stereo he'd set up three days before to give him an upbeat soundtrack for an unpacking mon-tage. Two days before he left Chicago, his mother reminded him to wash his sheets before sleeping in them, one of a dozen random instructions that peppered their last few days together before her youngest, her baby, her favorite left their nest finally—and I mean *finally*—empty. It was a kind of Irish-Catholic love language that, he'd always known, replaced embarrassing displays of affection. As he finishes breaking down boxes and pulls a new set of sheets out of the dryer he halts the music and turns the TV on. It's just after eleven p.m., and another episode of *The Golden Girls* has just started.

He wakes the next morning after the first good sleep in over a week, drifts into the bathroom to brush his teeth, meanders back into his bedroom, and turns on the TV, hoping to quickly find and pick his favorite among local news stations, but the TV is still set to channel thirty-six. It's just before nine, and another episode of *The Golden Girls* is about to begin. It was the golden days of Lifetime, or as we parodied its catchphrase in those days, Lifetime: Television for Battered Women and Gay Men. Every day, two episodes of *The Golden Girls* played at nine a.m., two at six p.m., and two at eleven p.m. The hopeful young gay man saw it as a sign that, whatever happened in the unpredictable years ahead, he'd be OK because, if nothing else, he'd have three hours with the *Girls* every day.

That hopeful young gay was me. And for the next three years, the three daily constants in my life would be grad school consuming my days, the bars and clubs consuming my nights, and six episodes of *The Golden Girls* to get me through it all—two episodes with breakfast, two with dinner, and two more while I got ready for bed or zhuzhed my fauxhawk for the clubs.

The *Girls* weren't new to me. For anyone in my generation, the *Girls* have just always been there, a staple of American popular culture, and each of the four stars was already associated with iconic characters when the show began. Bea Arthur created Vera Charles in Jerry Herman's *Mame* and gave America a feminist heroine in Maude Findlay. Rue McLanahan launched from the Actors Studio and Broadway into soap operas and sitcoms, eventually playing Maude's bestie and Mama's sister on *Mama's Family*. It took longer for Estelle Getty to reach iconic status, but her turn as Mrs. Beckhoff in *Torch Song Trilogy* on stage gave her an immediate and adoring gay following. And Betty White...from her first Emmy nomination in 1951 for hosting a daily, five-hour ad-lib show and hosting and producing *Life with Elizabeth*, one of the first sitcoms on television, to the central seats on America's favorite game shows and the ever-saucy Sue Ann Nivens on *The Mary Tyler Moore Show*... well, Betty White basically invented television. The first stroke of genius in the show was pulling these four entertainment legends into one production.

I didn't know all that when the *Girls* started. My earliest memory of them was when I was nine, watching them on the TV in my parents' bedroom while my mom and I played Scrabble on the floor, leaning back against the bed. "Oh, THAT'S what made you gay," more than one friend has joked upon hearing this. Instead of seeing them as Hollywood royalty, I saw them as four funny old ladies. I'd laugh at some things, Mom would chuckle at others, and at least once an episode, she'd marvel that Getty, who played Sophia, the oldest of these old ladies, was actually younger than her TV daughter. That was a clue to me even then that *age* was the comic hook that would lure an audience into the show—it *was* ridiculous to see old folx doing the things they were doing—working, maintaining a sex life, nurturing their friendships—because that's not what old people did...on television, anyway.

Old. When the show first aired in 1985, Bea Arthur and Betty White were sixty-three, Estelle Getty was sixty-two, and Rue McClanahan was fifty-one. My mom was fifty, and Dad was fifty-three. Though strangers frequently mistook my parents for my grandparents, though much of the world laughed about it as a monumental achievement and the beginning of the end, it never occurred to me that fifty was old. My mom's closest friends, staples in our house growing up, were her age or older. When Mrs. Crump arrived, she usually had a baked treat and could only stay a few minutes because she was so busy. When Mrs. Fox arrived, it was a privilege to be able to pick out an ashtray and hope to deliver it before her already-lit cigarette could ash on the kitchen table. When Mrs. Doherty arrived, she always had an overly cute gift from this one shop in Northfield (her love language was shopping).

Mom would sit with each of her friends at the kitchen table and gossip. Well, her friends would talk, and Mom would listen with her characteristic occasional "Hmm" or "Oh, I love it" to reassure that she was listening. They never ate cheesecake, but I'd overhear complaints about their husbands, fretting about their children, laughing about old memories or new foibles. They were the same conversations Mom had on Tuesdays with her golf league (in the summer) and her bowling league (during the winter). The same she had while delivering trays of prepared food with her Meals on Wheels companions and amidst planning for fundraisers with other volunteer board members. They were women navigating middle age, and it was clear to me: the people who would get them through the transition into this stage of life wouldn't be their husbands or their children, and God knows none of them ever considered therapy. The people who would get them through would be other women.

I learned a lot from eavesdropping on those conversations, either in the backseat of the car while joining the Meals on Wheels route or not so subtly listening to kitchen-table chats from the next room. I learned to recognize coded language to talk about menopause and to recognize the pain that came with increasingly empty houses. I learned to sense anxiety that came with increasingly frequent health scares and the grief from just as frequent deaths of friends or old classmates or children.

I learned that the *second*-worst thing a child could do to his mother was to elope. The *worst*, though, was to die.

While other TV shows introduced me to relationships or settings that were new or exotic, the *Girls* reflected a familiar world. Blanche, Rose, Dorothy, and Sophia didn't strike me as extraordinary or unusual characters—they seemed like the women who would show up in Mom's kitchen or who would deliver Meals on Wheels with her, like the women in her golf league or on her bowling team. I imagine that was the point of the show—sure, the situation of four "older" women living together was unusual, but centering it around four women who reflected familiar, beloved, and accessible types was bold. It gave women "of a certain age" a chance to see themselves on screen without pity, caricature, or disdain.

It also gave queer folx a chance to see themselves on screen—not in the same way that "older" women saw themselves, but in more subtle ways. Sure, the *Girls* took big steps toward queer visibility in characters like Coco (the gay cook who only survived the pilot episode), Jean (Dorothy's lesbian friend who falls in love with Rose), Laszlo (the charismatic artist who set off none of the girls' gaydar), and a handful of character actors who gave us playful, if stereotypical, waiters, wedding planners, and label-denying image consultants. The biggest step came with Blanche's baby brother Clayton, who comes out in season four and returns with a husband-to-be in season six. The most daring step, though, came with a character we never actually saw: Dorothy's younger brother and Sophia's only son, Phil. It's pretty clear that Phil was somewhere on the queer spectrum. I suspect Phil was supposed to be trans, but, in an era when even Bea Arthur and Estelle Getty had to play Sicilian-Americans because a Jewish mother-and-daughter duo was too risky for prime time, maybe the occasional chuckle-inducing acknowledgement of cross-dressing was all the network would let them present.

But for gay folx, I don't think they saw themselves in *these* characters. I mean, did anybody *actually* think that Monte Markham could pass as a homosexual? Was Jean's crush on Rose believable? Lord, no. Instead, queer people saw their lives reflected in the girls' reactions. When Jean came for a visit, we watched Dorothy take Jean's lead on sharing her sexual orientation and Sophia's warm and unconditional acceptance…but we also saw Blanche's daft response when finding out Jean's a lesbian ("Isn't Danny Thomas one?") and Rose's paralysis in response to Jean's affection. When Clay came out to Blanche, we watched her cycle through stages of grief—from anger and denial to begrudging acceptance—and when Clay returned with Doug, "my friend, my—very special—friend," we saw Blanche, like so many in our lives, regress to denial in a way that hurts more than the first time around.

And queer folx saw how their lives, how their relationships with family and friends *could* be. The characters don't confront their prejudices perfectly—but they model empathy with the people they love. They model growth and say the things queer folx long to hear from family and friends. "I'll tell you the truth, Dorothy," Sophia says, "If one of my kids was gay, I wouldn't love him one bit less. I would wish him all the happiness in the world." Instead of panicking and pushing Jean away, Rose says, "I have to admit, I don't understand these kinds of feelings, but if I did understand, if I were, you know, like you, I think I'd be very flattered and proud that you thought of me that way." Blanche doesn't quite come *all* the way around when Clay announces his engagement, but she prioritizes love and concern for her brother over old preconceptions. "I still can't say I understand what you're doing," she confesses, "but I do intend to try to respect your decision to do it. I want you to be happy."

For me, the hardest episode to watch in the entire series also holds the biggest lesson for everyone to learn. "Ebbtide's Revenge" tells the story of Phil's funeral and of the real root of a decades-long grudge. With a fair amount of prodding, Sophia admits that her hatred of Angela, Phil's wife, was rooted in her own insecurities with Phil's cross-dressing. "The dress thing," she pleads, "why didn't she stop the dress thing?"

> Angela: He's been doing that all his life. That didn't start with me.
> Sophia: Oh, so it's my fault?
> Rose: Are you worried that people will think it's your fault?
> Sophia: Oh, it's not like having a war hero in the family.
> Rose: Angela, was he a good husband? A good provider? A good father for your children?
> Angela: Yeah.

Rose continues with an abridged but still ridiculous story from her hometown, St. Olaf.

> Rose: The point is, it was shame that kept Aunt Katrina from loving slow Ingmar. And it ruined her life. Oh, don't let that happen to you, Sophia. Let go of the shame. So what if he was different? It's OK that you loved him.
> Sophia: I did love him. He was my son. My little boy. But every time I saw him I always wondered what I did, what I said, when was the day that I did whatever I did to make him the way he was.
> Angela: What he was, Sophia, was a good man.
> Sophia: My baby is gone.

When I watch this scene, as Sophia crumbles with grief into Angela's arms, I think about the countless parents who never really knew their children, who couldn't get past the shame and social conventions that kept them from loving their children unconditionally. I think about parents of people who died from AIDS who were, at best, distant or estranged and, at worst, disowned, and whose bodies were left unclaimed because of the shame that filled their families. I think about queer viewers who saw their parents' prejudice and paralysis in Sophia and who saw their chosen family, the friends and partners who replaced the family that left them adrift, in Angela, who only saw goodness in the spouse she lost.

I hope Sophia's breakthrough prodded some of those parents to follow her example. I hope a lot of people emulated Dorothy and Rose when their queer friends shared their identities with them. I hope these episodes gave queer viewers some peace, some relief, some insight that their families' prejudices weren't their fault. I hope…well, I hope it gave those viewers hope, because as a young, gay man, it gave me hope.

CONCLUSION

so, what's next?

What is hope?

A feeling. A sense. A desire. A disposition. A thing with feathers.

Feathers? Emily Dickinson describes it as a bird perched in the soul who sings endlessly, even persistently through storms and cold.

> I've heard it in the chillest land -
> And on the strangest Sea -
> Yet - never - in Extremity,
> It asked a crumb - of me.

It's a lovely sentiment, but this is where Emily and I diverge because hope has asked plenty of me. It's dynamic and unpredictable. It can feed and starve me, drown me in optimistic confidence and leave me parched and desperate when it withdraws. Hope isn't self-evident or self-starting—it requires cultivation, constant nurturing, and inspiration. The tools and conditions to cultivate it—and the instinct to pursue it in the first place—are baked into cultural and religious traditions. The seasons and holidays, daily practices and domestic customs, specialized vocabulary and dress—they all point to some conception of hope and all the joy, satisfaction, enlightenment, salvation, or liberation (whichever the tradition aims for) that inspires it, and we grow up thinking it's inherent or naturally instinctive. But when we find ourselves outside those traditions, or when those traditions fail, punish, or exclude us, hope seems more like a fleeting fantasy, a delusion that comes with the comfort and safety of tradition. A bird? More like a dragon—an inspiring, devastating, mythical totem.

In my darkest and loneliest times, hope was ephemeral, a tease. It was easy to hope as a kid, and even easier as a teacher. Education is, after all, a fundamentally optimistic profession—it was confidence that I could contribute to my students' growth, and confidence that they *would* grow, confidence that they would engage and change the world that got me out of bed and into the office in the dark hours of the morning for so long. That confidence eroded, though, when I saw the conflict between my work and my identity. Confidence in my students didn't crumble—instead, I lost confidence in my own ability to prepare them. The more I unpacked my identity, I found myself farther and farther from the tools once at my fingertips, the tools to stoke hope and to recharge a personal sense of purpose in my students and in me. That distance didn't inspire pessimism in me—I never doubted the *possibility* of hope—but it did force me to open my eyes a little wider, to see things I wasn't able or ready (or willing) to see before. It forced me to look past the horizon, over the borders that were established for me, over, as Judy sang, the rainbow, for an authentic hope, a hope that embraced me, a hope that grew from me and from others who had been similarly adrift.

I don't know what's on the other side, but writing these essays has helped me to see, name, and relish the people, relationships, and ideas that prepared me to keep looking. When I began to write, I hoped that walking through my experiences would help me to cultivate openness and maybe even hopefulness. My goal was never to be exhaustive or expert. Instead, I sought to deconstruct how the world shaped me, reconstruct a foundation for the person I want to become, and find the fuel I need to move forward. So, what have I learned? Three insights stand out to me.

First, I've spent most of my life assuming that I had a higher purpose, that we all do. I assumed that my purpose would be realized if I was the best I could be. If I could give all I had, I will have lived a life of real meaning and value, and if I gave any less, my life will have been at best disappointing and at worst downright evil. *Catholic guilt, am I right?* That largely meant conforming to the structures and standards that were given to me. The problem was that I inherited those structures and standards without question, without realizing until recently (really with the prompt of 2020) that I'd conformed too comfortably to those structures. I overlooked the tools in my reach that could start expanding or dismantling them. I overlooked the option to reject them altogether.

One of the standards that I've (sort of) detached myself from is the pursuit of perfection. For some, it leads toward aggressive ambition and success at all costs, and I know too many people who have paid a high price in that pursuit. For me, it was the expectation that I would make it as far, as high, as influential as possible. Some people need that encouragement, particularly when others who look like them or share their experiences have been systematically disenfranchised for generations. People who look like me, though—cis, White, affluent people—are raised to believe that we're entitled to perfection, whether in the form of a Ph.D., a corner office, steadily rising income, or a model family. I'm grateful for challenging experiences in my life because they opened my eyes to that all-consuming wave of ambition and enabled me to get out of the way.

Second, I'm deeply suspicious of purists, anyone who believes they are 100 percent, unquestionably right. Straight, queer. Religious, atheist. Conservative, liberal. Among the many layers that 2020 peeled back, I saw more and more people reveal their purist stripes, and that's only exacerbated the extreme tribalism that has emerged. Purism comes with missionary zeal, too. Once someone has found *their* answer, they assume it will respond to everyone else's questions. They impose it. They assume that everyone "like" them in *some* way must be on board with them in *all* ways. Religious purists assume everyone wants to be saved. *From what?* Atheist purists assume that religious folx are intellectually deficient. Cis-hetero purists think that anyone who checks a box outside their norms is deviant, aberrant, and damned. Queer purists don't want cis-hets in their spaces. Purism doesn't allow for engagement. It doesn't spark a question of the other. It doesn't begin with wonder or curiosity. It begins with judgment and a fair amount of pride. But even as we share experiences and intersect each other, even when we're among people "like us," we forget that we all arrived with different questions and require different answers.

And finally, I am not brave. But I'm not pitiful, either. Mine is neither a success story nor a failure, but it is perhaps a story about finding satisfaction. I only really tasted happiness when I stopped striving for the next thing: the next job, the next promotion, the next city, the next home to renovate, the next boyfriend, the next... In my Introduction to Philosophy course in college, I was introduced to Aristotle's concept of *eudaimonia* in his *Nicomachean Ethics*. It's too often translated as "happiness," but that's incomplete. *Happiness* connotes joy, pleasantness, pleasure—ephemeral sensations. Aristotle pointed to something more holistic and static—being, doing, and living well—and I think of it as being alive, being *fully* alive, so much so that I can say, as Sondheim's Petra sings in "The Miller's Son," "There's a lot I'll have missed but I'll not have been dead when I die." I wouldn't want to relive the challenges that have come to me or that I've brought on myself: hiding my sexual identity until college, the complexities and complications of a big, Irish-Catholic family, pursuing a career that ultimately burned and almost buried me, the crushing losses of my parents and my sister—but I'm grateful for them because they knocked me off of tracks that dead-ended in the illusion of happiness and helped me open my eyes to how I could be, do, and live better...or at least more fully.

gratitude

I was lucky to stumble into the support of the folx at Peanut Butter Publishing and am grateful for the wisdom, guidance, and encouragement from Danielle Harvey, Ruthie Little, Amy Vaughn, and Elliott Wolf.

I'm grateful to M. Geron Gadd, Tony Kuzminski, and Shalini Vajjhala because, seeing something in me that I couldn't recognize, their enthusiasm and encouragement spurred me to start writing, and to Joel Avery, whose vision always amazes me and whose photograph graces the cover of this book.

For all they've given me, all the ways they continue to guide me, and the myriad ways they've shaped the world, I'm especially grateful to Clare Aebersold Neiweem, my piano teacher; elementary school teachers Ann Syvertsen and Philomene McGinty; my high school teachers Robert P. Austin, Michael E. Flanagan, Patrick L. Rattigan, and Faye A. Ryan; my college conductor Carole Ann Maxwell; my college professors Nancy Dallavalle, Ellen M. Umansky, Geoffrey Sanborn, and John E. Thiel; my graduate school professors Kimberley C. Patton, Jeffrey J. Kripal, Pearl Rock Kane, Sarah Daignault, Lorri Hamilton Durbin, and Tom Sobol. I'm also grateful for the ways I was bolstered, challenged, and inspired by my communities, especially Fairfield University, the Boston Gay Men's Chorus led by Reuben M. Reynolds III, the schools in which I worked, and the many close friendships that grew from those shared experiences.

Every day and on every page of these essays, three voices

constantly whisper in my ear and guide me in the right direction, and I'm grateful for the life they've given me: my husband, Jonathon, who loves me "without problems or pride"; my sister and the other half of my brain, Patty; and my mother, Sheila Murphy Hulseman.

playlist

In case you were trying to remember that song I referred to, here's the full list. Want to hear them all? Go to https://shorturl.at/SpOzt or look for the "Six to carry the casket and one to say the mass" playlist on Spotify.

ABBA, "Mamma Mia"

Alannah Myles, "Black Velvet"

A Little Night Music (Original Broadway Cast Recording), "The Miller's Son"

Andy Williams, "This Land of Mine"

Aram Khachaturian, "Toccata"

Ariana Grande, Jessie J, and Nicki Minaj, "Bang Bang"

Boston Gay Men's Chorus, "Down by the Riverside" from *Live in Poland*

Buffy Sainte-Marie, "Bury My Heart at Wounded Knee"

Camp (Original Motion Picture Soundtrack), "Here's Where I Stand"

Camp (Original Motion Picture Soundtrack), "How Shall I See You Through My Tears"

Chaka Khan, "I'm Every Woman"

Cher, "Take Me Home"

Claude Debussy, "Clair de lune"

Company: A Musical Comedy, "Being Alive"

Company: A Musical Comedy, "The Ladies Who Lunch"

Crystal Waters, "100% Pure"

Daniel Kantor, Night of Silence/Silent Night"

Demi Lovato, "Sorry Not Sorry"

Dionne Warwick, "Theme from Valley of the Dolls"

Doja Cat, "Boss Bitch"

Donna Summer, "MacArthur Park"

Dreamgirls: Original Broadway Cast Album, "And I Am Telling You I'm Not Going"

Duke Ellington, "Portrait of Ella Fitzgerald"

Ella Fitzgerald, "Lush Life"

Ella Fitzgerald, "Something to Live For"

Ella Fitzgerald, "Sophisticated Lady"

En Vogue, "My Lovin'"

Erasure, "A Little Respect"

Fiddler on the Roof (Original Broadway Cast Recording), "Tradition"

Follies: New Broadway Cast Recording, "Losing My Mind"

Original Broadway Cast of Flora, the Red Menace, "A Quiet Thing"

George Gershwin, Prelude II

Gladys Night and the Pips, "I've Got to Use My Imagination"

Gloria Gaynor, "I Will Survive"

Indigo Girls, "Bury My Heart at Wounded Knee"

Indigo Girls, "Closer to Fine"

Judy Garland & Barbra Streisand, "Happy Days/Get Happy"

Judy Garland, "Come Rain or Come Shine"

Judy Garland, "Over The Rainbow"

Judy Garland, Ethel Merman, and Barbra Streisand, "There's No Business Like Show Business"

Katy Perry, "Roar"

Katy Perry, "I Kissed A Girl"

Lady Gaga, "Edge of Glory"

Lizzo, "Good As Hell"

Madonna & Gogol Bordello, "La Isla Bonita/Pala Tute"

Madonna, "American Life"

Madonna, "Batuka"

Madonna, "Bedtime Story"

Madonna, "Dark Ballet"

Madonna, "Don't Tell Me"

Madonna, "Express Yourself"

Madonna, "Ghosttown"

Madonna, "God Control"

Madonna, "God Control"

Madonna, "Hollywood"

Madonna, "Human Nature"

Madonna, "La Isla Bonita"

Madonna, "Like a Prayer"

Madonna, "Love Profusion"

Madonna, "Music"

Madonna, "Secret"

Madonna, "Sky Fits Heaven"

Madonna, "Vogue"

Madonna, "What It Feels Like for a Girl"

Margaret Whiting, "I'll Plant My Own Tree"

Marlene Dietrich, "Falling in Love Again"

Mary Mary, "Shackles"

Michael Joncas, "On Eagle's Wings"

Mozart, "Rondo Alla Turca"

Natalie Cole, "This Will Be"

Nellie Furtado, "I'm Like a Bird"

Nicki Minaj, "Anaconda"

Nicki Minaj, "Pound the Alarm"

Noel Coward, "Mad About the Boy"

Olivia Newton John, "Physical"

Patty Duke, "It's Impossible"

Paula Abdul, "Vibeology"

Pink, "Stupid Girls"

Promises, Promises, "Turkey Lurkey Time"

Rihanna, "Shut Up and Drive"

Robyn, "Dancing On My Own"

Salt-N-Pepa & En Vogue, "Whatta Man"

Sinding, "Rustle of Spring"

Taylor Swift, "Shake It Off"

The Beatles, "When I'm Sixty-Four"

The Pointer Sisters, "Jump"

Vince Guaraldi Trio, *A Charlie Brown Christmas*

Whitney Houston, "So Emotional"

Willow Smith, "Whip My Hair"

Yaz, "Don't Stop"

Yaz, "Midnight"